CITROEN DS 19, ID 19, 1955–66 AUTOBOOK

Workshop Manual for the Citroen
DS 19, ID 19, 1955–66

by

Kenneth Ball
G I Mech E
and the
Autopress team of Technical Writers

AUTOPRESS LTD
BENNETT ROAD BRIGHTON BN2 5JG ENGLAND

ISBN 0 85147 130 7

Books by the same author:

1100 MK 1 1962–67 AUTOBOOK
1100 MK 2, 1300, AMERICA 1968–69 AUTOBOOK
1800 AUTOBOOK
AUSTIN A30, A35, A40 AUTOBOOK
AUSTIN HEALEY 100/6, 3000 1956–68 AUTOBOOK
AUSTIN MAXI 1969 AUTOBOOK
BMC AUTOBOOK THREE
BMC AUTOBOOK FOUR
FIAT 500 1957–69 AUTOBOOK
FIAT 600, 600D 1955–69 AUTOBOOK
FIAT 850 1964–69 AUTOBOOK
FORD ANGLIA PREFECT 100E AUTOBOOK
FORD CAPRI 1968–69 AUTOBOOK
FORD CONSUL, ZEPHYR, ZODIAC 1, 2 1950–62 AUTOBOOK
FORD ESCORT 1967–69 AUTOBOOK
FORD ZEPHYR, ZODIAC MK 3 1962–66 AUTOBOOK
FORD ZEPHYR V4, V6 ZODIAC 1966–69 AUTOBOOK
HILLMAN MINX 1 to 5 1956–65 AUTOBOOK
HILLMAN MINX 1965–67 AUTOBOOK
HILLMAN SUPER MINX 1, 2, 3 1961–65 AUTOBOOK
JAGUAR XK120, 140, 150 MK 7, 8, 9 1948–61 AUTOBOOK
JAGUAR 2.4, 3.4, 3.8 MK 1, 2 1955–67 AUTOBOOK
MG TA–TF 1936–55 AUTOBOOK
MGA, MGB 1955–69 AUTOBOOK
MINI 1959–70 AUTOBOOK
MINI COOPER 1961–70 AUTOBOOK
MORRIS MINOR 1952–69 AUTOBOOK
RENAULT R8, R10, 1100 1962–69 AUTOBOOK
ROVER 60–110 1953–64 AUTOBOOK
ROVER 2000 1963–69 AUTOBOOK
ROVER 3 LITRE 1958–67 AUTOBOOK
SPRITE, MIDGET AUTOBOOK
SUNBEAM RAPIER ALPINE 1959–65 AUTOBOOK
TRIUMPH TR2, TR3, TR3A 1952–62 AUTOBOOK
TRIUMPH TR4, TR4A 1961–67 AUTOBOOK
VAUXHALL VELOX CRESTA 1957–69 AUTOBOOK
VAUXHALL VICTOR 1, 2, FB 1957–64 AUTOBOOK
VAUXHALL VICTOR 101 1964–67 AUTOBOOK
VAUXHALL VICTOR FD 1600, 2000 1967–69 AUTOBOOK
VAUXHALL VIVA HA 1964–66 AUTOBOOK
VAUXHALL VIVA HB 1966–69 AUTOBOOK
VOLKSWAGEN BEETLE 1964–67 AUTOBOOK

The AUTOBOOK series of Workshop Manuals covers the majority of British and Continental motor cars. For a full list see the back of this manual.

CONTENTS

First Edition February 1971

© Autopress Limited 1971

Printed in England by
G. Beard & Son
Brighton

ACKNOWLEDGEMENT

My thanks are due to Citroen Cars Ltd. for their unstinted co-operation and also for supplying data and illustrations.

I am also grateful to a considerable number of owners who have discussed their cars at length and many of whose suggestions have been included in this manual.

Ditchling
Kenneth Ball G I Mech E
Associate Member Guild of Motoring Writers

INTRODUCTION

This do-it-yourself Workshop Manual has been specially written for the owner who wishes to maintain his car in first class condition and to carry out his own servicing and repairs. Considerable savings on garage charges can be made, and one can drive in safety and confidence knowing the work has been done properly.

Comprehensive step-by-step instructions and illustrations are given on all dismantling, overhauling and assembling operations. Certain assemblies require the use of expensive special tools, the purchase of which would be unjustified. In these cases information is included but the reader is recommended to hand the unit to the agent for attention.

Throughout the Manual hints and tips are included which will be found invaluable, and there is an easy to follow fault diagnosis at the end of each chapter.

Whilst every care has been taken to ensure correctness of information it is obviously not possible to guarantee complete freedom from errors or to accept liability arising from such errors or omissions.

Instructions may refer to the righthand or lefthand sides of the vehicle or the components. These are the same as the righthand or lefthand of an observer standing behind the car and looking forward.

CHAPTER 1

THE ENGINE

1:1 Type, features, models, capacities

Citroen DS19 cars with numerous original features, including self-adjusting hydro-pneumatic suspension and hydraulic operation of gearbox, brakes and steering, were introduced in 1955. The ID19 variant followed a year later, in which many of the hydraulic controls were eliminated and the central power system used only for the hydro-pneumatic suspension and, in later models, brakes and assisted steering. The front-wheel-drive four-cylinder in-line water-cooled engine units are similar in each type, with bore and stroke dimensions of 78 mm by 100 mm giving a capacity of 1911 cc. Compression ratios were originally 7.5:1 for the DS19 and 6.8:1 for the ID19, later increased to 8.5:1 and 7.5:1 respectively.

Typical longitudinal and transverse sectional views of the DS19 engine are shown in **FIGS 1:1** and **1:2**. The front-wheel transmission system, including gearbox, differential and drive shafts, forms a complete power unit with the engine. A flywheel and a single dry plate clutch at the front end of the three-bearing crankshaft transmit the drive to a fourspeed gearbox with synchromesh on the three upper ratios. The gearbox mainshaft from the clutch passes over the final drive pinion and differential assembly

mounted on the end of the lower or second motion shaft. Disc brakes are mounted on the inboard end of each front-wheel drive shaft and constant-velocity type outer universal joints transmit power from the drive shafts to the wheels, as shown in **FIG 1:3**.

The engine is of the overhead valve type, the valves being mounted in an aluminium cylinder head with hemispherical combustion chambers. The valves are inclined at an angle of 60 deg. to each other and operated by long and short rockers as shown in **FIG 1:6**, with the inlet valve rockers on a common shaft and the exhaust rockers on separate short shafts. The pushrods operate from tappets which are lifted from a chain-driven single camshaft on the lefthand side of the engine. Inlet ports are on one side of the engine and exhaust ports on the other side. Sparking plugs are fitted centrally in the head at the lower ends of tubes projecting through the rocker cover (see **FIG 1:5**).

The distributor and oil pump are driven through spur gears at the rear end of the camshaft. The lubricating system is of the forced feed type, oil being circulated by a gear type oil pump in the sump. Other than a wire strainer on the oil pump intake no other filter is fitted, and it is

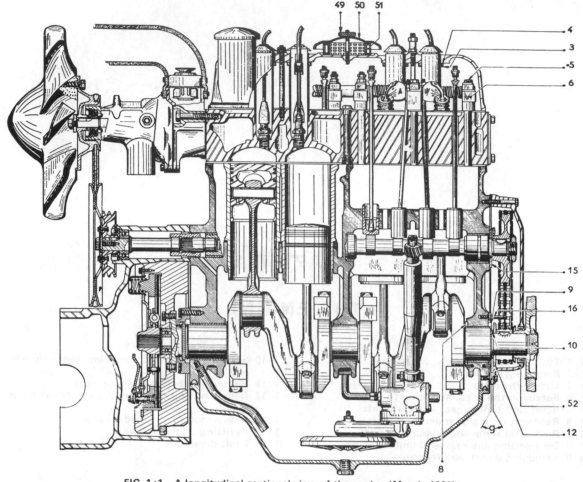

FIG 1:1   A longitudinal sectional view of the engine (March, 1961)

Key to Fig 1:1   3 Sparking plug tube cup   4 Sealing joint   5 Retaining screws, inlet rocker shaft   6 Rocker shaft rear bracket
8 Crankshaft thrust ring   9 Bearing ring   10 Adjusting shim   12 Thrust washer   15 Camshaft thrust plate   16 Timing
chain lubricator   49 Filter knurled nut   50 Filter cover   51 Filter element   52 Timing cover seal

therefore important that regular oil changes should be made at intervals of not more than 2500 miles. Cooling is by a conventional radiator and fan system, the cooling water coming into direct contact with the outer surfaces of removable cylinder barrels or wet liners in the cylinder block. An eight-bladed nylon fan is located in a cowl behind the radiator. The generator and water pump are driven from a pulley at the front end of the camshaft. Twin belts from the same camshaft pulley drive the hydraulic pressure pump providing power for the suspension system and other equipment except for clutch operation, for which before 1960 a low pressure pump was incorporated with the belt-driven water pump. In later models the pump was replaced by a belt-driven centrifugal clutch control.

1:2   Removing engine

Removal of the DS19 engine and gearbox as an assembly is undertaken as follows, referring to the Appendix for the tools mentioned and to **Chapter 2** for the sealing devices:

1 Lift the bonnet and retain it in its fully open position by the clip shown in **FIG 1:4**. Raise the front of the car and firmly support it on suitable blocks, taking special care to ensure that it will not be shaken off the supports by such jolting as is inseparable from the work being undertaken.

2 Remove the spare wheel. Referring to **Chapter 2**, release the pressure in the whole of the hydraulic system and drain the hydraulic fluid reservoir. Retain the fluid in a clean sealed container.

3 Drain the radiator and cylinder block by means of the tap situated on the righthand side of the bottom tank and removing the hexagon-headed screw located below the dipstick on the cylinder block. Retain the water containing anti-freeze.

4 Remove the crossmember supporting the spare wheel, the air deflection panel and the steering relay protection shields. Disengage the end of the bonnet catch

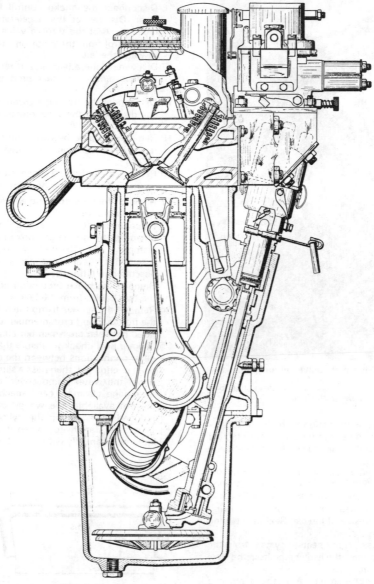

FIG 1:2   A transverse sectional view of the engine

cable and remove the two front wings by undoing the retaining nuts inside each wing and drawing the wings forward off their locating pegs. Remove the front brake cooling ducts.

5 Remove the battery and disconnect the generator wires from the regulator. Remove the coil and bracket assembly in cars produced before July 1959. Disconnect the starter cable from the terminal on the solenoid switch and remove the battery tray.

6 Disconnect the feed pipe for the high pressure pump from the outlet pipe on the hydraulic fluid reservoir and remove the fixing straps and the reservoir. Seal the apertures in the reservoir and pipes.

7 Disengage the feed pipe for the high pressure pump from the battery support. Disconnect the bonnet lock control cable from the lever on the scuttle and remove the support and cable assemblies.

8 On lefthand drive cars remove the expansion chamber by removing the fixing clips on the silencer and the manifold and detaching the fixing collar from the exhaust pipe.

9 Disconnect the earth cable from the gearbox and remove the cable harness assembly and protecting tube in cars produced before February 1957.

10 Remove the steering as follows:

(a) Mark with a spot of paint the angular and transverse

FIG 1:3   Drive shaft universal joint

Key to Fig 1:3   1 Drive shaft joint
2 Top pivot ball, showing lubrication nipples

position of the steering in relation to the bearing caps.
Mark also, opposite the slot in the end of the steering
tube, the position of the steering column in relation to
the pinion.
(b) Disconnect the steering tube from the driving pinion,
fit the stop No. 1993.T and disconnect the steering
levers from the relay spindles (see **Chapter 9**).
(c) Remove the bearing caps and take off the steering
towards the lefthand side of the car. Seal the steering
pipe assembly with a plate.
11 Disconnect the hose on the heating system from the
feed pipe and disconnect the heater pipe from the steel
tube on the righthand side.
12 Disconnect the petrol feed pipe from the pump and
disconnect the brake feed pipe from the 3-way union,
for which service agents use a spanner 2222.T.
13 Disconnect the union on the distribution block
(spanner 2219.T or 2221.T), also the union plates on
the hydraulic gear selector and on the clutch re-
engagement control in cars produced before February
1961. In later cars, disconnect the rear unions of the
pipe assembly between the centrifugal regulator and
the hydraulic gear selector. Proceed to disconnect the
feed pipe from the lefthand brake unit, also the overflow
return pipe and the feed pipe from the pressure control
valve.
14 Remove the lefthand suspension sphere, for which a
strap wrench 2223.T is available, and seal the aperture.
15 Disconnect the feed pipe and the delivery pipe from the
hydraulic gear selector.

16 Disconnect the choke control from the carburetter
lever. Disconnect the accelerator control from the
cross-piece of the throttle valve control. Disconnect
the control from the pivot on the scuttle and twist it
towards the left.
17 Disconnect the advance and retard control from the
contact breaker in cars produced before February
1961.
18 Disconnect the five-pipe assembly from the gearbox
and disconnect the speedometer cable from the gearbox.
19 Remove the pipe between the control valve and the
rear brake accumulator, situated at the front (spanner
2222.T).
20 Remove the righthand suspension sphere and seal the
aperture. Remove the heat insulation screen.
21 Remove the nuts from the engine fixing studs on the
rear side brackets.
22 Disconnect the flexible coupling (bibax) from the
driving plates on the gearbox in cars produced before
October 1961. Remove the drive shaft and pivot
assemblies in cars produced since October 1961, as
described in **Chapter 7**.
23 Remove the brake protection covers and disconnect
the two cables from the levers.
24 Remove the screws fixing the rear flexible blocks and
the front support crossmember. Do not lose the shims
fitted between crossmember and sidemembers.
25 Make a final check to ensure that no cables, pipes or
other connections between the unit and the car have
been overlooked, then pass a sling or a sheathed chain
under the water pump cover, raise the engine and
disengage it from the car. If mechanical lifting facilities
are not available, the weight of the unit should be
reduced by removing the cylinder head, manifolds,
generator, starter etc., when it should be able to be
lifted out manually with the aid of an assistant. Mount

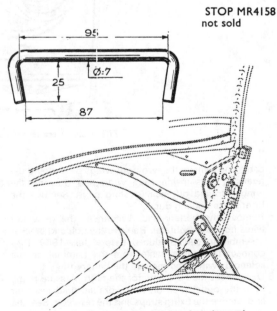

FIG 1:4   Bonnet stop (dimensions in mm)

the assembly on a stand. Pay particular attention to the pipes remaining on the car and do not damage or distort them.

In the case of the ID model, removal operations are similar except for modifications arising from the manual operation of clutch, gearbox, and steering. The following items will need to be taken into account:

1 To remove the exhaust downpipe, remove the coupling flanges on the silencer and manifold and detach the collar securing the pipe on its support.

2 To disconnect the gear selector control from the gearbox cover, first disconnect the speedometer cable from the gearbox. Then remove the gear selector cable guide and speedometer cable guide from the sidemember. Withdraw the connecting tube and release the cables on the sidemember. Disconnect the gear selector rod from the relay lever and withdraw the pipe. Disconnect the handbrake control and detach the cables from their respective levers.

3 Remove the clutch fork control rod. Release the protecting tube from its guide on the clutch casing and release the cable.

4 Disconnect the front brake feed pipe from the master cylinder and seal the pipe and master cylinder apertures in vehicles supplied before September 1961. Disconnect the high pressure outlet pipe from the pressure regulator.

5 Disconnect the contact breaker feed wires from the coil and disconnect the ignition advance control from the distributor. Disconnect the rubber return pipe to the reservoir from the pressure regulator valve, and the suspension feed pipe from the union in the distribution unit in vehicles supplied before September 1961. Disconnect the feed pipe for the front brakes from the lefthand brake unit and the control for the hydraulic brake in vehicles supplied since September 1961. Seal the pipe openings.

6 Disconnect the flexible feed pipe to the heating and demisting radiator from the steel pipe on the cylinder head.

7 Remove the fixing screws securing crossmember to sidemembers. Do not mislay either the screws or the adjusting shims between the cross and sidemembers.

1 : 3 Lifting the head

With the engine remaining in the car it will be necessary to drain the cooling system and disconnect the battery. Further operations are as follows:

1 Remove the air filter and pipe assembly. Disconnect the leads from the sparking plugs.

2 Remove the carburetter (see **Chapter 3**) and remove the screw from the plate fixing the accelerated idling pipe.

3 In later models remove the front righthand suspension sphere and remove the exhaust shield. Disconnect the rubber heater tube from the inlet manifold and the rubber feed pipe from the water pump.

4 Disconnect the clutch system pipes as follows:

(a) In cars produced before September 1960, disconnect the lower union of the feed pipe and the flexible delivery pipe from the low pressure pump. Protect the clutch from any overflow of fluid.

(b) In cars produced since September 1960, disconnect the return pipe from the centrifugal regulator. Remove the pipe assembly between the centrifugal regulator and the hydraulic gear selector and remove the seal plates. Disconnect the pipe between the righthand brake unit and the centrifugal regulator from the regulator. Plug the openings of the pipes, flanges and units. Remove the centrifugal regulator fixing nut from the tie-rod on the high pressure pump, remove the swivelling angle plate and rear reinforcement arm, and remove the centrifugal regulator. Do not lose the packing between the swivelling bearing and the thrust nut.

5 Disconnect the high pressure pump feed pipe from the reservoir and seal the opening. Disconnect the radiator tie-rod from the radiator and water pump, also the generator tie-rod and the high pressure pump tie-rod from the water pump. Unscrew the generator fixing screws.

6 Remove the water return hose, also the fan and disengage the belts from the water pump pulley. Disconnect the heater pipe from the water pump cover.

7 Disconnect the flange coupling the exhaust manifold to the expansion chamber, also the lubrication pipe from the cylinder head. In later cars remove the exhaust shield, entailing, removing the front righthand suspension sphere and disconnecting the collar securing the front exhaust pipe to the manifold.

8 In cars produced before April 1962, remove the rubber Bakelite caps from the sparking plug tubes. Remove the sparking plugs, for which a spanner 1603.T is available. Unscrew the two nuts retaining the cylinder head cover and lift it off.

9 Referring to **FIG 1 : 1**, remove the cups 3 and the rubber joints 4 from the sparking plug tubes.

10 Unscrew the inlet rocker assembly screws 5 without removing them from their brackets 6. Remove the assembly with the screws in place, in order to keep the parts in their correct positions. Then remove the exhaust rocker assemblies and brackets, noting the order of removal for refitting. The rocker pushrods can now be removed, giving each a slight twist to free it. Store them in their correct order for refitting, pushing them the right way up through numbered holes in a card.

11 Remove the cylinder head screws, slackening each a little at a time in the reverse order to that shown for tightening in **FIG 1 : 7**. Lift off the head and gasket, observing the centring dowels. If the head does not come away freely, tap it along each side with a mallet or with light hammer blows on a piece of wood. Note that if the engine is turned after the head has been lifted (e.g., for decarbonizing) the liners may come out of the cylinder bores. The liners should therefore be held in position by means of two washers, 45 mm external diameter, and 10.5 mm internal diameter, inserted between the liners 1-2 and 3-4 and fixed by a screw. Remove the exhaust manifold shield and rear plate and proceed to dismantle the components of the head as necessary for servicing.

On ID cars operations are similar, with the exception of those concerned with the hydraulic units. The retaining brackets for the front brake connection pipe must be disconnected from the water pump, also the feed hose for the heating and demisting radiator from the pipe on the cylinder head.

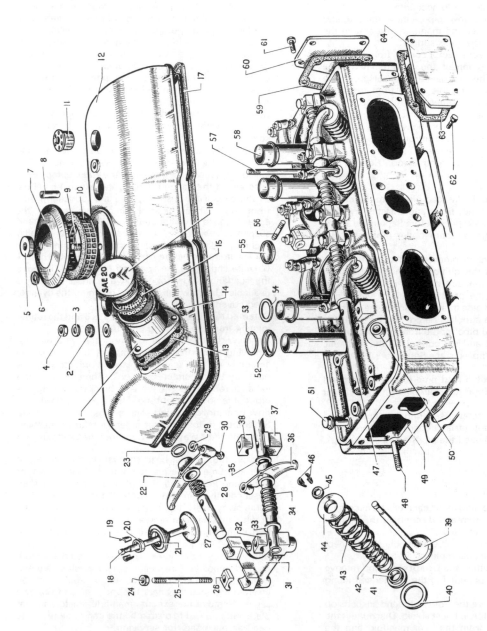

FIG 1:5   An exploded view of the cylinder head and rocker assemblies

Key to Fig 1:5   1 Oil filler   2 Joint   3 Washer   4 Nut, cylinder head cover   5 Knurled nut   6 Joint   7 Filter cover   8 Distance piece   9 Stud
10 Filter element   11 Cap, sparking plug hole   12 Cylinder head cover   13 Joint   14 Screw   15 Filter, oil filler   16 Filter cap   17 Joint, cylinder head cover   24 Nut
18 Exhaust valve   19 Split cotter, exhaust valve   20 Cup   21 Upper cup for exhaust valve spring   22 Exhaust rocker   23 Spacing washer   32 Cap
25 Stud for rocker bracket   26 Cap   27 Exhaust rocker shaft   28 Spring   29 Locknut   30 Tappet adjusting screw   31 Rocker shaft bracket   41 Cup, valve spring
33 Spacing washer   34 Spring   35 Spacing washer   36 Inlet rocker   37 Inlet rocker bracket   38 Cap   39 Inlet valve   40 Thrust washer   49 Cylinder head
42 Valve spring, inner   43 Valve spring, outer   44 Cup, upper   45 Sealing washer   46 Split cotter   47 Inlet rocker shaft   48 Stud
50 Valve guide   51 Cylinder head screw   52 Retainer for sparking plug tube sealing ring   53 Sealing ring   54 Thrust washer for sealing ring   55 Core plug
56 Stud, manifold   57 Stud, cylinder head cover   58 Sparking plug tube   59 Joint   60 Rear closing plate   61 Screw   62 Screw   63 Joint
64 Closing plate

14

1 : 4 Servicing the head, attention to valves

An exploded view of the cylinder head, cover and valve rocker assembly is shown in **FIG 1 : 5** and the assembled valve rocker mechanism in **FIG 1 : 6**. Referring to **FIG 1 : 6**, dismantle the inlet rocker shaft by removing the fixing screws 5, the caps 33, the washers 38, the springs 39 and the rocker arms 34. Drive out the plugs of the shaft 40 with a pin punch passing through the holes for the fixing screws. Carefully clean the inside of the shaft with a metal pin and make sure that the lubrication holes in the shaft are clear. Keep each rocker and its parts in a numbered container or otherwise ensure that they go back in the same locations. Valves and their parts should be kept in sequence in the same way.

Check the rocker shaft (nominal diameter 18 mm) for wear, particularly on the underside, also the rocker bores for scores and wear. Inspect the ends of the adjusting screws. If wear is uneven, renew, together with the corresponding pushrod. Similarly inspect the pushrod contact faces and check that no bending has occured. Withdraw the valve tappets, for which a special extractor tool No. 1608.T is available. Keep them in their correct order for refitting, if still serviceable, in their original bores, and examine for scores, wear or cracks.

If decarbonizing is necessary, scrape most of the carbon from the cylinder head before removing the valves, to prevent damage to the valve seats. As the head is made of aluminium the valve seats cannot be renewed without the use of special tools. Temporarily replace the cylinder head screws to avoid carbon scrapings entering the holes. If carborundum is used, extreme care must be taken to remove all traces from the valve chambers or gas passages, as even small quantities entering the engine will cause rapid wear. Remove all traces of old gasket material and finally clean the cylinder head with paraffin and petrol. Slight grinding of the surface is permissible, but the original thickness of the head must not be reduced by more than .3 mm.

Remove the valves by first compressing the valve springs, using either a suitable spring-type compressor or the special compressor 1614.T used by service agents with a support and base assembly 1616.T. Referring to **FIG 1 : 5**, free off the split cotters 19 and 46, if necessary by lightly tapping the edge of the cup 21 or 44 with a hammer. Remove the cotters, the upper spring retaining cup, the springs and the sealing ring 45 on inlet valves. A sealing ring is not fitted on exhaust valves as the action of the valve will rotate and destroy the ring. Clean the valves and the valve ports by removing carbon deposits, for which a file card will be useful. Inspect the valve seats and the seatings in the head for wear and deep pitting. Exhaust valves are liable to be burnt, when they will appear brown and discoloured. Examine the valve springs for loss of temper or fracture. Try each valve in its guide for undue side movement, indicating wear of either bore or valve stem of both. Valve seats may be refaced to the the specified angles of 120 deg. for inlet valves and 90 deg. for exhaust valves by a service agent with the necessary facilities. If necessary the valve guides may be renewed by a service agent equipped with the special tools required. New valve guides are finally reamered to a diameter of 9 mm + .015 mm —.010 mm. Each valve should then be ground in to its appropriate seat, using a light application of medium or fine grinding paste.

Thoroughly flush out the cylinder head water passages and refit the valve assemblies by reversing the sequence of removal operations. Lubricate the faces and stems of the valves, fit new valve springs if required, also a new sealing ring on the stems of inlet valves only, before fitting the split cotters.

Reassembly of the tappets, pushrods, cylinder head and rocker assemblies is in general the reverse of the removal operations. Take care that a tappet does not fall into an empty bore upside down, when its recovery would involve dismantling the engine. To refit the cylinder head, the contacting faces of head and block must be clean and dry. Remove the washers holding the cylinder head barrels and fit a new gasket, previously oiled with boiled linseed oil. In early models, place the crimping of the gasket towards the cylinder barrel. Later varnished gaskets should be fitted dry, the varnished faces towards the cylinder head. Ensure that the cylinder head dowels are in position, centre the gasket and locate the cylinder head on the dowels. Position the intermediate rocker assembly supports 41 in **FIG 1 : 6**. Oil and reassemble the rocker shaft in the reverse order of its dismantling, commencing from the front and with the lubrication holes facing downwards. Hold each assembly of a spring 39 and washer 38 with a retaining device (see **FIG 1 : 8**) to avoid damaging the shaft by tightening the washers 38 on the caps 33.

Fit the rocker assembly supports 6, inlet and exhaust, in position. Offer up the inlet rocker shaft and insert the cylinder head screws. Make sure at this stage that the pushrods are properly located in the sockets of the adjusting screws. Then fit the exhaust rockers in position, the oil holes in the shafts to be facing downwards. Put the caps 7 on the studs and tighten the nuts. Before April, 1956, shouldered exhaust rocker shafts were fitted, which should have a maximum side clearance of .3 mm adjusted by washers.

Screw up the short cylinder head screws without tightening. Then tighten all the screws in the order shown in **FIG 1 : 7**, first tightening to a torque of 21.75 lb ft and then tighten to a torque of 43.5 lb ft, which must not be exceeded. These tightening torques are very important. After travelling 300 miles and again after 1250 miles, drain the radiator, loosen the screws and retighten as already described.

Adjust the valve rocker clearances to .008 inch for the inlet valves and .010 inch for the exhaust valves. Adjust the valves of one cylinder with the piston at top dead centre, end of compression. The valves of the corresponding cylinders are then in balance, that is to say, the inlet valve is at the start of admission and the exhaust valve at the end of exhaust. Turn the engine by means of the starting handle, in DS cars after having pressed the auxiliary clutch control forward and upwards, and adjust the valves of individual cylinders as follows:

1 1st cylinder with the valves of the 4th cylinder at the point of balance.
2 3rd cylinder with the valves of the 2nd cylinder at the point of balance.
3 4th cylinder with the valves of the 1st cylinder at the point of balance.
4 2nd cylinder with the valves of the 3rd cylinder at the point of balance.

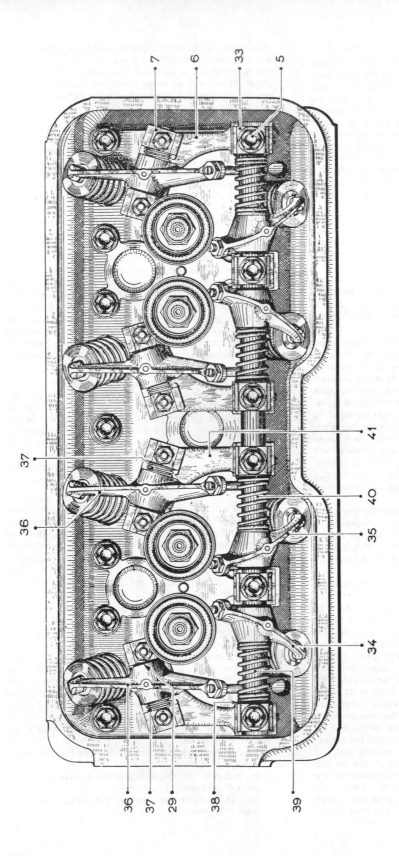

FIG 1:6 Valve rocker assembly

Key to Fig 1:6 5 Retaining screw 6 Rocker assembly support 7 Cap 29 Washer 33 Shaft retaining cap 34 Lefthand rocker 35 Righthand rocker
36 Rocker 37 Spring 38 Washer 39 Spring 40 Inlet rocker shaft 41 Intermediate supports

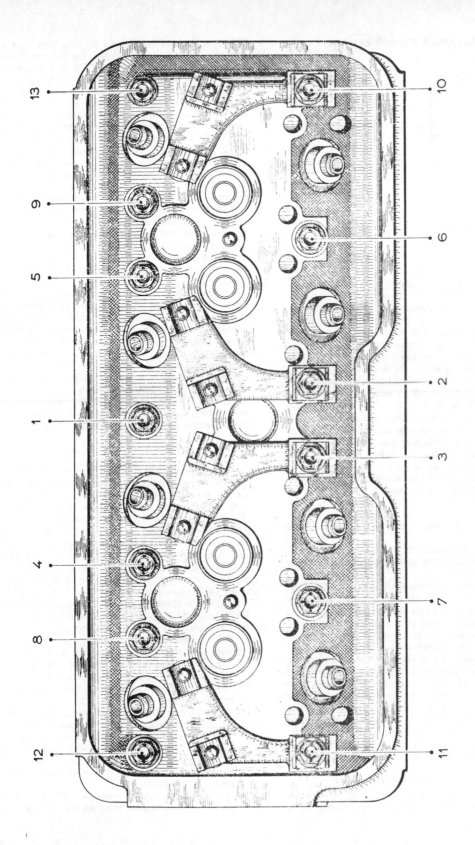

FIG 1:7   Sequence of tightening cylinder head bolts

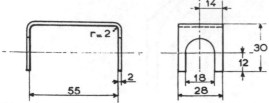

RETAINER MR 4158-20 not sold

FIG 1:8 Retainer for rocker shaft assemblies (dimensions in mm)

Locate the steel cups and the sealing joints on the sparking plug tubes and refit the cylinder head cover. Use a new gasket and attach it to the cover only with an adhesive such as Bostik. Tighten the nuts, using plain and leather washers.

Disengage the filter element (10 in FIG 1:5) by removing the knurled nut 5 and cover 7. Clean it by washing in petrol, brushing it out and blowing with compressed air. Then immerse in engine oil, allow to drain and refit. Thereafter repeat this operation every 4000 miles.

Fit the cylinder head lubricating tube, using a double leather joint when securing to the cylinder head and two fibre washers at the crankcase connection. Refit the remaining components in the reverse order of their removal, with regard given to the following details:

1 The belt or belts to be refitted on the water pump pulley are tensioned by the use of a special lever MR.4208 as described in **Chapter 2**.

2 Fit the centrifugal regulator, where provided, as follows:

(a) Put the regulator in position and fit the fixing nut. Insert the pulley adjusting nut found when dismantling between the swivelling bearing of the regulator and the thrust nut.

(b) Fit the rear support arm together with the articulating angle plate on the cylinder head.

(c) Connect the tie-rod on the high pressure pump to the regulator.

(d) Connect the rubber return pipe to the regulator and tighten the clip.

(e) Connect the pipe between the righthand brake unit and the centrifugal regulator to the regulator. Moderately tighten the unions.

(f) Fit the pipe assembly between the regulator and the hydraulic gear selector. Make sure that the three rubber protectors are fitted. Connect the flange to the centrifugal regulator and the unions to the hydraulic gear selector, inserting a seal plate between the flange and the regulator. Tighten the nut and spring washer securing the flange and moderately tighten the unions.

3 The fan retaining screws are to be tightened to a torque of 6.5 to 7.25 lb ft, which must not be exceeded.

4 On completion of the refitting operations, refill the cooling system and start the engine. Unscrew the pressure control valve bleed screw, leave the engine running for a few minutes and retighten the bleed screw. Bleed the centrifugal regulator where fitted and righthand brake unit. Check the unions for leakage.

1:5 Removing timing gear and camshaft

With the engine removed from the car as in **Section 1:2**, proceed to remove the timing cover shown at 12 in

FIG 1:9. The method differs for cars produced before January, 1961 and later models. For the former production, remove the fixing screws 10 and disengage the cover and its joint 13. In later cars it is necessary first to remove the sump, as described in **Section 1:7**. Then push the crankshaft towards the rear bearing, with the aid of a wedge between the crankcase and a crank throw. On these cars, when the timing pinion nut on the crankshaft or the nut securing the damper (23 in **FIG 1:12**, since March 1961) is unscrewed, the crankshaft can be moved laterally a distance greater than the depth of the housing for the inner bearing ring (see **FIG 1:15**). Thus the ring can fall out of its housing if the crankshaft becomes sufficiently displaced towards the front.

With the crankshaft wedged, remove the pinion nuts on camshaft and crankshaft, withdraw the wedge and turn the crankshaft until the throws are horizontal before removing the timing chain and pinion assembly. This is necessary to avoid the possiblity of a piston fouling a valve if the crankshaft is turned with the camshaft out of control.

To remove the camshaft it is necessary first to remove the sump and oil pump (see **Section 1:7**), the distributor (see **Chapter 4**), the cylinder head (see **Section 1:3**), the tappets (see **Section 1:4**) and the timing chain and pinion assembly as previously described. Remove also the fuel pump and on ID cars the retaining clip from the connecting tube for the front brakes and the HP pump on vehicles fitted with a single-cylinder pump. Seal the apertures of pump and connecting pipe. Finally remove the camshaft thrust flange 17 in **FIG 1:9** by turning down the locking tabs and removing the retaining screws. Withdraw the camshaft from the rear of the engine.

1:6 Refitting timing gear and camshaft

Before reassembling, all parts should be examined for wear and new components fitted if necessary. If the skew gear is badly worn or damaged the oil pump driving gear may also have to be renewed. Check the camshaft thrust plate and timing chain for wear. Also check the shape of the teeth on the timing wheel with those on a new timing wheel, as worn teeth will cause rapid wear of a new chain.

Referring to **FIG 1:10**, fit a sealing ring 2 if previously provided in the groove of the splined portion of the camshaft. Oil the bearing surfaces of the camshaft and guide it gently into place to avoid damaging the bearings. Fit the thrust plate 3, tighten the retaining screws to a torque of 7 lb ft and turn down the locking tabs.

Reassemble the timing chain and pinion assembly.

1 Refit the sump and oil pump (see **Section 1:7**).

2 Bring the pistons of Nos. 1 and 4 cylinders to about TDC, with care (see previous Section) if the cylinder head has not been removed for the operations on the camshaft.

3 Place the two pinions of the crankshaft and camshaft on a bench and align the reference marks on the pinions. A straightedge passing through the centres of the pinions ~ ust pass through a punch mark on a tooth of the camshaft pinion and a punch mark between two teeth of the crankshaft pinion. Then fit the chain on the two pinions.

4 Without displacing the assembly, offer up the pinions on the engine. Rotate the camshaft by means of its

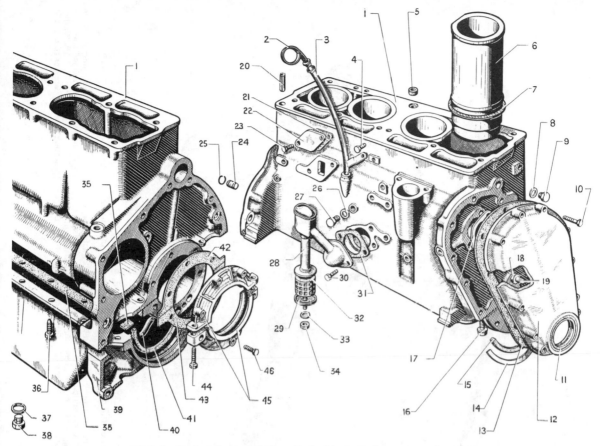

FIG 1 : 9 Exploded view of the cylinder block, timing cover and sump

Key to Fig 1 : 9   1 Cylinder block   2 Flexible dipstick   3 Dipstick tube   4 Screw   5 Dowel pin locating cylinder head
6 Cylinder barrel   7 Paper joint   8 Plug joint   9 Plug   10 Screw, timing cover   11 Sealing bush for damper (after
March 1961)   12 Timing cover   13 Joint   14 Oil seal retaining plate   15 Joint, bearing cap to timing cover   16 Bearing
cap screw   17 Thrust plate, screws and lockplates   18 Lubricator securing nut   19 Timing chain lubricator   20 Pin for
centring cylinder head   21 Joint for closing plate   22 Closing plate on cylinder block   23 Screw   24 Dowel locating
bellhousing   25 Circlip   26 Gasket for water drain plug   27 Water drain plug   28 Breather   29 Retaining cap   30 Screw
31 Joint   32 Breather filter element   33 Washer   34 Nut   35 Crankcase gasket   36 Sump screw   37 Plug joint
38 Sump drain plug   39 Sump, aluminium   40 Oil return pipe from bearing cap   41 Joint, bearing cap   42 Upper gasket,
oil baffle   43 Lower gasket, oil baffle   44 Screw   45 Oil baffle   46 Screw

pinion so that the keyways on the pinions and shafts correspond.

5 Fit the chain and pinion assembly, making sure that the keys are properly located on the camshaft and crankshaft.

6 Wedge the crankshaft as during removal operations, then tighten the camshaft nut 10 and lockwasher 9 to a torque of 110 lb ft and the similar fasteners on the crankshaft to 145 lb ft. Turn down the lockwashers on the nuts.

To fit the timing cover on cars before March, 1961, clean the jointing faces, insert a new gasket and tighten the retaining screws to a torque of 11 lb ft. Fit a brass washer under the heads of three screws which project inside the cover.

On later cars smear the oil seal with grease between the two lips and insert the seal in the bore of the timing cover with a suitable mandrel. Locate the timing cover

with a paper joint and smear the bearing surface receiving the joint, also the collar of the heads of the screws projecting on the inside of the cover, with a sealer. The makers recommend Festinol. Locate the damper where applicable, wedge the crankshaft, fit and tighten the damper nut to a torque of 163 to 180 lb ft and knock the metal of the nut collar into the groove of the crankshaft. Fit the retaining screws of the timing cover and tighten to a torque of 11 lb ft. Reassemble the remaining components in the reverse order of their removal.

1 : 7 Removing sump and oil pump

The engine and gearbox assembly having been removed from the car as described in **Section 1 : 2**, the assembly should preferably be suspended from a pulley block. Remove the plug 38 in **FIG 1 : 9** and drain the engine oil. Remove the retaining screws 36 and disengage the sump.

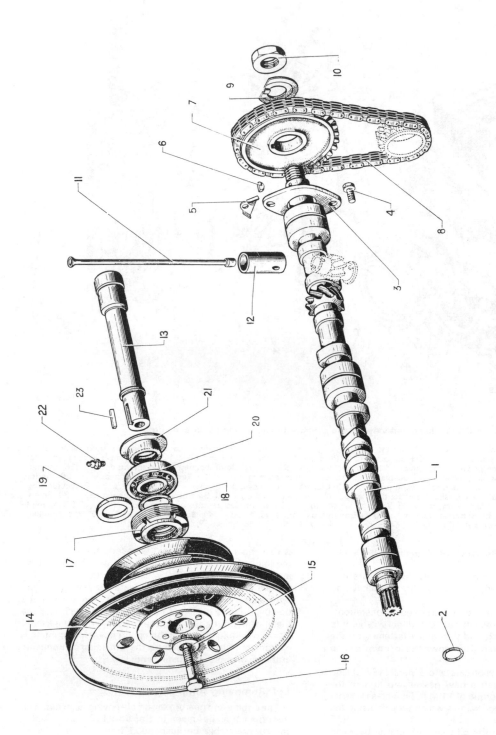

FIG 1:10 An exploded view of the camshaft, driving shaft and driving pulley

Key to Fig 1:10
1 Camshaft   2 Ring seal   3 Camshaft thrust plate   4 Screw   5 Lockwasher for screws   6 Woodruff key, camshaft pinion
7 Camshaft pinion   8 Timing chain   9 Lockwasher   10 Nut, camshaft pinion   11 Pushrod   12 Tappet   13 Driving shaft with splined end piece
14 Pulley, three or four groove (single groove on ID cars) driving water pump, generator, HP pump and centrifugal regulator where fitted   15 Washer
16 Screw securing pulley   17 Ring nut   18 Washer, pulley adjustment   19 Washer   20 Front bearing   21 Deflector (pre-1958)   22 Greaser (pre-1958)
23 Key, driving pulley

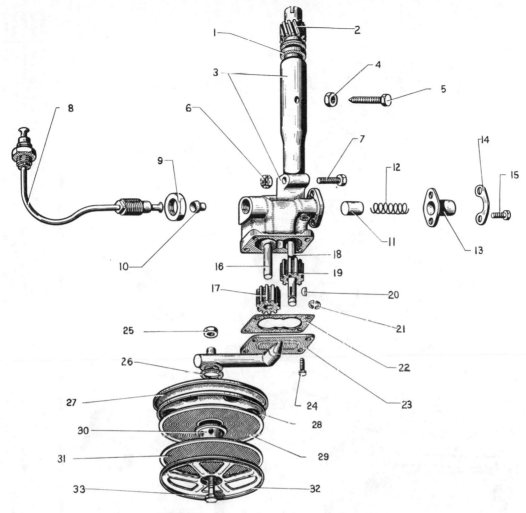

FIG 1:11 An exploded view of the oil pump

Key to Fig 1:11   1 Support tube bush   2 Oil pump and distributor driving pinion   3 Pump body with bracket
4 Locknut   5 Pointed screw securing support tube   6 Castellated nut   7 Screw, support tube to pump body
8 Oil pipe, pump to cylinder head   9 Locknut   10 Conical union   11 Piston, non-return valve   12 Spring, non-return valve
13 Housing, piston spring   14 Double lockwasher   15 Screw securing housing   16 Spindle, idler pinion   17 Idler pinion
18 Drive spindle   19 Fixed pinion   20 Woodruff key   21 Retaining cotters, fixed pinion   22 Joint, pump base
23 Pump base, supporting filters   24 Screw, pump base   25 Nut, securing filters   26 Joint washer   27 Upper housing, filters
28 Upper cover   29 Upper filter   30 Distance piece   31 Lower filter   32 Lower plate   33 Screw securing filters

Detach the cork gaskets from the front and rear bearing caps and carefully clean the grooves in the caps.

Referring to **FIG 1:11**, remove the pointed screw 5 holding the oil pump and detach the locknut 9 securing the oil pipe between the pump and the cylinder block. Withdraw the pump.

When refitting the pump, turn the crankshaft to bring the piston in No. 1 cylinder to TDC. Then engage the pump so that the driving groove is parallel to the centre line of the engine and the small side is towards the interior of the engine. Tighten the pointed screw to a torque of 11 lb ft, which must not be exceeded to avoid crushing the

tube, and tighten the locknut 4 to a torque of 22 lb ft. Locate the tapered unions in the cylinder block and the pump body and fit the oil pipe between the pump and the cylinder block. Tighten the union nuts to a torque of 43 lb ft and the locknuts to 29 lb ft.

Clean the sump before refitting, for which the use of a detergent followed by hosing out will be effective. Examine the contact faces for distortion or damage and remove all traces of jointing compound or sealer. Fit cork joints in the bearing grooves at the front and rear, smearing the ends of the joints with a good sealer. The manufacturers recommend Festinol, supplied by Societe Ripolin. Fit the

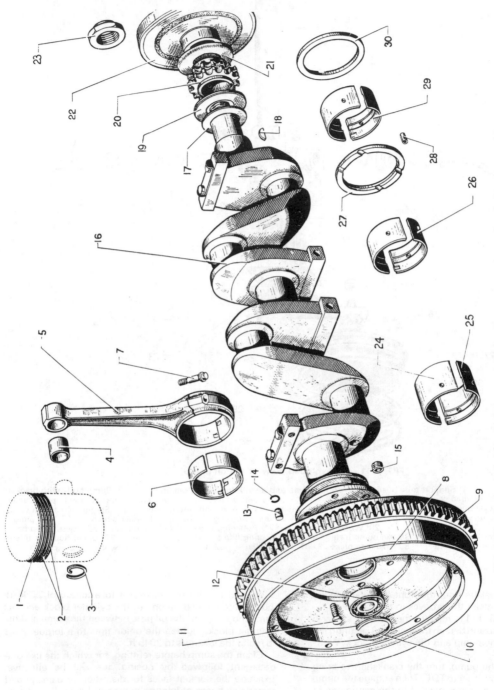

FIG 1:12 An exploded view of the crankshaft, also a connecting rod and piston assembly

Key to Fig 1:12 1 Piston rings 2 Oil scraper ring 3 Circlip 4 Small-end bush 5 Connecting rod 6 Half shell bearing 7 Screw for big-end cap 8 Flywheel 9 Starter gear ring 10 Circlip retaining rear crankshaft spigot bearing 11 Screw securing flywheel 12 Ballbearing 13 Dowel centring flywheel on crankshaft 14 Circlip 15 Cap sealing oilways on crankshaft 16 Crankshaft 17 Adjusting washer 18 Woodruff key for crankshaft pinion 19 Thrust washer 20 Crankshaft pinion 21 Oil seal washer (damper arrangment, since March, 1961) or lockplate for crankshaft nut (until March, 1961) 22 Damper 23 Damper securing nut 24 Front bearing top half 25 Front bearing bottom half 26 Centre bearing, top and bottom 27 Inner ring for rear bearing 28 Bearing ring locking pin 29 Rear bearing, top and bottom 30 Outer ring for rear bearing

22

front sealing plate of the groove in the rear bearing cap. Prepare and fit new gaskets between the sump and cylinder block, cutting each gasket level with the bearing caps with a sharp knife. Smear the bearing faces in the crankcase with thin jointing compound, diluting with alcohol if necessary. Offer up the sump and tighten the attaching screws and nuts to a torque of 12 lb ft. The longest screws are used for the front and rear bearings and no washers are fitted under the heads of the screws. Fit the drain plug using a new gasket and tighten to a torque of 21 lb ft.

1 : 8 Dismantling and reassembling oil pump

Referring to **FIG 1 : 11**, the dismantling, inspection and reassembly of the oil pump is undertaken as follows:

1 Remove the delivery pipe 8 and the conical union 10.
2 Remove the filters 29 and 31.
3 Remove the pump base 23 and the idling pinion 17.
4 Withdraw the driving pinion 2, for which service agents use an extractor 1964.T. Remove the assembly of the shaft 18 and the pinion 19, from the pump body.
5 Move the fixed pinion 19 on the shaft, release the retaining cotters 21 and take off the pinion and its key from the shaft.
6 Remove the positioning screw 7 from the tube support and remove the tube 3.
7 Drive out the spindle 16 from the idler pinion.
8 Remove the spring bearing flange 13, the spring 12, and the piston 11 from the non-return valve.
9 Remove the bush 1 from the support tube 3 with aid of a mandrel (15 mm diameter).
10 To reassemble, fit the bush 1 into the support tube 3 using a press.
11 Also with a press, fit the idler pinion 17, making sure that the pinion turns freely. Place the fixed pinion 19 in the body of the pump. With a set of feelers and a straight edge resting on the base of the pump, measure the pinion clearance, which must not exceed .05 mm. Remove the pinions.
12 Fit the support tube 3. Fit the fixed pinion 19 on the shaft with key and split cotters 21 in position. Lubricate the shafts with recommended lubricant to prevent scuffing on initial running. Insert the shaft 18 in the body of the pump. Fit the support tube locking screw, tighten the nut to 18 lb ft and fit a new splitpin.
13 Grease the entry of the bore of the driving pinion and fit on the shaft with a press. During this operation the shaft should be supported on a cylindrical block, with no force exerted on the pinions.
14 When the pinion 2 is on the spindle, an end float of .03 to .10 mm must be left. If the pinion is pressed down too far, hold the pinion in the hand and, with the aid of a copper drift and a hammer, tap on the end of the shaft until the pinion is in the correct position.
15 Fit the idler pinion 17, the paper gasket, and pump base 23, with the filter support on the outlet pipe side. Tighten the screws to 9.4 lb ft with spring washers under the heads. Lock the milled-headed screw by tapping the metal of the pump base into the slot of the screw.
16 Fit the piston 11 the spring 12 and the spring retaining flange 13. Tighten the screws with lockwashers under the heads.

17 On the intake opening fit in sequence one cork seal, the top cover, the upper filter plate, the filter (large diameter central hole), the distance piece, a second filter, and a lower plate. Tighten the screws to 9.4 lb ft and tighten the locknut.
18 With the aid of a service agent possessing the necessary test equipment the pump pressure may be checked if required under specified conditions of temperature and speed of operation.

1 : 9 Removing clutch and flywheel

With the engine and gearbox assembly removed from the car, the gearbox must first be disconnected from the engine as follows:

1 Remove the bracket for the expansion chamber where fitted. Do not mislay the distance piece for the lefthand fixing plate.
2 Disconnect the flexible pipes from the water pump cover and the steel tube. Remove the tie-rod from the radiator and remove the radiator.
3 Remove the generator tie-rod and the generator.
4 Remove the screw from the plate fixing the pump-regulator connecting pipe on the gearbox and disconnect the pipe from the pressure control valve. Remove the pressure control valve and its bracket from the crossmember.
5 Remove the lower nuts from the tie-rods supporting the brake units. Remove the fixing screws from the crossmember on the support arms of the box and disengage the crossmember.
6 Remove the brake unit as follows:
(a) Remove the adjusting nuts, disengage the sheath stops and remove the connecting cable from the righthand side.
(b) Remove the fixing screws of the rear supports of the brake unit.
(c) Disconnect the feed pipes from the brake units and disconnect the accelerated idling feed pipe from the lefthand brake unit.
(d) Remove the brake unit. If necessary remove the protection cover and remove one brake shoe.
7 Remove the centrifugal regulator in cars produced since July 1960 as follows:
(a) Disconnect the rear tie-rod on the cylinder head from the regulator.
(b) Disconnect the tie-rod between the regulator and high pressure pump and disengage the swivel angle plate.
(c) Disconnect the pipe assembly flange between the centrifugal regulator and hydraulic gear selector and remove the seal plate.
(d) Remove the pipe between the righthand brake unit and the centrifugal regulator.
(e) Remove the articulating spindle nut from the centrifugal regulator and remove the regulator.
8 Remove the high pressure pump as follows:
(a) Disconnect the high pressure pump tie-rod.
(b) For cars before October, 1968, remove the high pressure pump fixing spindle nut and remove the pipe assembly connecting the pump to the pressure regulator. Remove the high pressure pump fixing spindle and the pump.
(c) For later cars, remove the high pressure pump fixing spindle. Remove the pump assembly and pipe connecting the pump to the pressure regulator.

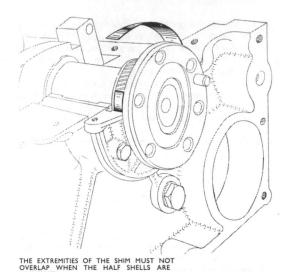

THE EXTREMITIES OF THE SHIM MUST NOT
OVERLAP WHEN THE HALF SHELLS ARE
ASSEMBLED.

FIG 1:13 Fitting shim strip for crankshaft assembly

9 Remove the driving pulley fixing screw. Remove the pulley, the key and the adjusting washers. Disenage the driving belts.
10 Unlock the locknuts and loosen the fixing screw from the bendix housing.
11 Remove the feed pipe from the clutch cylinder. Disconnect the control rod from the clutch fork and remove the clutch cylinder.
12 Support the gearbox with lifting tackle in order to avoid damaging the clutch shaft or the clutch disc when the gearbox is disconnected from the engine.
13 Remove the screws fixing the clutch bellhousing and disengage the gearbox. The gearbox must not be moved about by rolling it with the brake discs on the ground. Either fit dummy discs 350 mm diameter or use a rubber mat on the floor.
14 Before removing the clutch from the flywheel, mark the clutch housing and flywheel relationship. Unscrew the clutch retaining nuts and remove the clutch assembly and disc (or friction plate) from the flywheel. Slacken the nuts gradually by diagonal selection until the spring pressure is released.
15 Detach the retaining bolts securing the flywheel and whilst supporting it tap it off the crankshaft flange evenly, using a copper or lead hammer.

Examine the friction face of the flywheel for scores or cracks. Scores can be removed by machining within specified limits. Examine the ballbearing in the flywheel bore (12 in **FIG 1:12**) for roughness or wear and renew if necessary. The condition of the ring gear should also be examined. If replacement is necessary it is advisable to use the special facilities and experience at the disposal of a service workshop.

1:10 Splitting big-ends, removing rods, pistons and cylinder liners

Access to the connecting rod big-end assemblies and removal of connecting rods, pistons and cylinder barrels requires the removal of the cylinder head, sump and oil pump as described in previous Sections.

Details of the pistons, connecting rods, crankshaft and flywheel are shown in **FIG 1:12**. Before separating the big-ends, mark each connecting rod and its bearing cap with the cylinder number, the No. 1 cylinder being nearest to the radiator, so that they can be refitted in their original positions. Do not use a file or a punch. Unscrew the cap bolts (7 in **FIG 1:12**) and remove the caps and bearings 6 from each rod. If to be used again, keep the bearings along with their respective rods and caps. It is also important to mark the cylinder barrels before removal so that they can be refitted in the same relative positions to the pistons as they were before dismantling. Withdraw the piston and connecting rod assemblies either separately or together with the barrels and gaskets. For the latter, remove any retaining devices and lift the barrels (6 in **FIG 1:9**) out of their housings in the cylinder block. If difficult to move, gentle leverage may be initially applied by two screwdrivers diametrically opposed. Check the bores for distortion. Ovality, measured by a dial gauge, must not exceed .03 mm except in the part 20 mm from the bottom, where .05 mm is admissible.

1:11 Pistons, rings and gudgeon pins

Before separating a piston from its connecting rod the piston rings should be removed, using a ring expander. Then, for gudgeon pins turning in the connecting rod bushes, remove the gudgeon pin circlips. Heat the pistons in an oil bath or an oven to approximately 60°C, when the gudgeon pins can be pushed out and the piston separated from the connecting rod. Keep the gudgeon pins in order so that they can be returned to their respective pistons. The removal and refitting of gudgeon pins which are tight in the connecting rods without bushes entails the use of a special fixture and a press and should be undertaken by a service agent with the necessary equipment. The small-end bushes are not normally renewable and are supplied complete with new connecting rods. Note that on engines before June, 1957, it is necessary to renew the four connecting rods at the same time (thickness in centre of body 19 mm). In later engines the connecting rods are interchangeable and one connecting rod only can be renewed (thickness in centre of body 22 mm). The half shell bearings for connecting rods (6 in **FIG 1:12**) are renewable and available with diameters of 48 mm and 47.5 mm.

New pistons and gudgeon pins are not supplied separately. Complete new sets are available each of four cylinder barrels with pistons, rings, gudgeon pins and joints, for flat top pistons until March, 1961 and convex pistons, damper assembly, since March, 1961.

When fitting the pistons on the connecting rods, note that certain pistons are marked at the top with an arrow and the word 'Front' and the direction of fitting must be observed. The smaller diameter of the gudgeon pin has a marking on the end and the larger bore is marked on the boss. Fit a new circlip for the gudgeon pin in the unmarked side of the boss. Heat the pistons as previously described, coat the gudgeon pins with oil and insert them by hand. It is essential that they are not interchanged as they are weighed and paired with their respective pistons. Fit the other circlip, using a new one and making sure that both are seating properly.

Prepare the cylinder barrels or liners for insertion by wire-brushing the exteriors to remove any scale deposits.

Avoid damaging the bearing surfaces, which must, however, be perfectly clean. If new piston rings are to be used, after the liners have had some service, the internal oil glaze must be removed. Make sure that the liners seat squarely in the cylinder block. Offer up a joint on the liner, the straight edge on the joint being parallel to the flat on the liner and the reinforcement towards the liner. Work the joint onto the liner. Service agents work it on by hand as far as the first shoulder on the liner and then complete the fitting by using a flat punched plate MR.4134. Finally fit the liners in their housings in the cylinder block.

It is advisable to fit new piston rings, but first remove any carbon or other deposits from the ring grooves. Oil the pistons, expand the rings by hand or piston ring pliers and place the first and third ring gaps at 180 deg., diametrically opposite the gaps in the second and fourth rings, or at 120 deg. intervals on pistons with three rings in early models. For insertion of the pistons, ring clips No. 1656.T of a width to cover all the rings are available.

To refit the connecting rods, first remove the crankpin oil plugs and thoroughly clean the crankpin bores and the oilways in the journals. Make sure that the connecting rod lubricating holes in the crankpins are clean. Finally clean with petrol and refit the plugs, tightening them to a torque of 29 lb ft. This torque is essential to prevent the plugs unscrewing when the engine is running. Lubricate the liners, pistons and rings with engine oil and install the piston and connecting rod assemblies in their respective bores. Check the clearance of the bearings on the crankpins as described for the main bearings in **Section 1:12**, which should not exceed .06 mm. Also measure the diameters of the bearings, which should be 48.01 —.01 to —.02 mm.

Oil the bearing faces and fit the half bearings in the rod and the cap. Ensure that the lugs engage in the grooves and that the reference marks made when dismantling coincide if the existing bearings are being refitted. Fit the rods on the crankshaft as shown in **FIG 1:2**, taking care not to reverse the position of a cap on a rod. Note that the bearings are slightly narrower than the cap and the big-end of the connecting rod. The cap is likewise narrower than the big-end. Tighten the retaining screws to a torque of 36 lb ft, which must be strictly observed.

1:12 Removing and refitting crankshaft and main bearings

Removal and overhaul of the crankshaft assembly is assumed to be undertaken subsequent to the removal of piston and connecting rod assemblies as already described. In addition the timing cover, timing chain and timing pinions have also to be dismantled. If then more convenient, however, the crankshaft together with connecting rods and piston assemblies can be withdrawn as a unit. Procedure is as follows:

1 Referring to **FIG 1:9** remove the assembly screws 44 from the crankshaft oil baffle 45.
2 Unscrew the retaining screws and remove the main bearing caps, making sure that the direction of assembly is clearly marked.
3 As the centre and rear half bearings are of the same dimensions, mark them with a spot of paint so that they will not be reversed when reassembling if they are to be re-used.

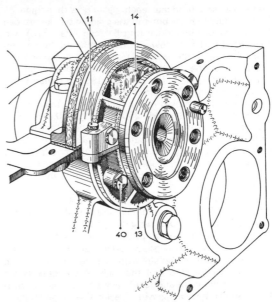

FIG 1:14 Assembling crankshaft bearings

Key to Fig 1:14   11 Oil baffle bolt
13 Top half-bearing   14 Lower half-bearing   40 Retaining bolt

4 Remove the crankshaft, the crankshaft bearing thrust ring and the upper section of the crankshaft oil seal. Referring to **FIG 1:12**, remove the damper 22 where fitted and the oil seal washer or lockplate 21.

Examine the condition of the journals and main bearings. The crankshaft may be checked for alignment by supporting it between centres and taking indicator readings on the main journals.

The main bearing housing bores should be checked by assembling the caps to the crankcase without the bearings to ensure that the bearing caps have not been filed. If so, it is not possible to fit the standard crankshaft/connecting rod assemblies. It is then necessary to renew the cylinder block or to rebore the cylinder block bearings, for which the assistance of a service agent with the necessary equipment should be obtained.

Check the crankshaft to bearing clearance but do not use steel feeler strip, otherwise the bearing surface will be damaged. Clearances can be checked by using a piece of Plastigage strip across the centre of the journal, assembling the cap and half bearing and tightening to the specified torque. The bearing and journal must be free from oil, in which Plastigage is soluble. The flattened Plastigage when removed and measured at its widest point will give the clearance in thousands of an inch in relation to the scale provided with the material. Clearances on crankshaft bearings should not exceed .06 mm. The diameters of the bearings, measured with a micrometer should be 54 —.015 mm or 53.5 —.015 mm. Half bearing shells are available with bores of 54 and 53.5 mm.

To refit the crankshaft, referring to **FIG 1:14**, fit the top half bearing 13 on the cylinder block and the lower half bearing 14 on the bearing cap. Insert the retaining screws 40, with no washers under the heads and without tightening them. Assemble the main bearings in the crankcase and lubricate each bearing with engine oil, first ensuring that the bores in the cylinder block are clean. Locate the bearing thrust ring 61 (see **FIG 1 : 15**) with the chamfered face towards the machined face of the crankshaft and the washer retaining slot towards the bearing cap. The thrust ring thickness differs for vehicles supplied before and after January, 1961, a dimension of 4 mm applying to the earlier models and 2.3 mm to the later models as shown in the table later in this Section.

Prepare a shim steel strip 200 mm long x 10 mm wide x .10 mm thick. Insert the strip around the oil thrower as shown in **FIG 1 : 13** and locate the crankshaft in its bearings. Fit the bearing cap and tighten the two assembly screws 11 of the half shells. Tighten the bearing cap screws to 72 lb ft. Do not turn the crankshaft when centring the half shells.

Tighten the half shell fixing screws 40 alternately to a torque of 9.5 lb ft. Then remove the half shell assembly screws 11 and the bearing cap. Lift the crankshaft and remove the shim steel strip. Smear the mating faces of the half shells with a good sealer. Locate the bearing caps in position complete with bearings. Fit the sump gaskets, making sure that the ends of the gaskets are well under the front and rear bearing caps (see **Section 1 : 7**). Smear these areas with a sealer, then fit and tighten the bearing cap screws to a torque of 72 lb ft. Relocate and tighten the half shell assembly screws 11.

Adjustment of the end float of the crankshaft is made according to design features at different stages of production necessitating different thicknesses of the bearing thrust rings and thrust washers. These are indicated in the following table, A, B and C referring to vehicles supplied before January 1961 and D to later vehicles.

Type	Width of rear bearing of crankcase mm	Width of rear crankpin mm	Thickness of bearing thrust ring mm	Thickness of thrust washer mm
A	35.99	44.1	4.0	5.0
B	35.99	42.3	2.3	6.7
C	37.70	44.1	4.0	5.0
D	37.70	42.3	2.3	6.7

Referring to **FIG 1 : 15**, the bearing thrust rings in the table are indicated at 62 and the thrust washers at 65. The projection of the pin 64 must be not more than 1.5 mm. In the case of C and D, keep the crankshaft pressed towards the rear to prevent the inner bearing ring 61 coming out of its recess in the crankcase (see **Section 1 : 5**). Referring now to **FIG 1 : 1**, fit a bearing ring 9 with the groove engaged on the retaining pin, a .05 mm adjusting shim 10, the thrust washer 12, the crankshaft pinion provisionally without the key and tighten the nut. Measure the clearance (g) between the bearing ring 9 and the thrust washer 12, which must be adjusted by shims available from service agents to .03 to .09 mm for vehicles supplied before March 1961 and .03 to .06 mm for later vehicles. Remove the pinion.

1 : 13 Reassembling stripped engine

Before reassembling a completely dismantled engine the cylinder block and all components should be thoroughly cleaned and all oilways checked to ensure that they are clear. Gaskets and oil seals should be renewed as required, carefully cleaning the joint faces free from old gasket material and jointing compound. All bearing surfaces and moving parts should be lightly oiled before assembly.

Much of the work of reassembling a stripped engine has already been described in previous Sections, where it has been convenient to include it with other details concerning particular assemblies. In sequence of operations, the refitting of the crankshaft has been described in **Section 1 : 12**, which is followed by refitting the flywheel on the crankshaft flange. Carefully clean the mating surfaces and locate the flywheel on its centring dowel 13 in **FIG 1 : 12**. Insert the attaching screws and tighten to a torque of 36 lb ft. Couple the clutch to the flywheel, ensuring that the bearing faces are clean, and using a mandrel No. 1712.T or a primary shaft to centre the disc. The mandrel should slide evenly to indicate a good centring of the disc. Tighten the retaining screws to a torque of 14 to 16 lb ft and using new spring washers. Remove the mandrel.

Refitting of the piston and connecting rod assemblies is described in **Section 1 : 11**, the sump and oil pump in **Section 1 : 7**, the camshaft and timing gear in **Section 1 : 6** and the valve tappets, pushrods, valves, rocker shaft assembly and cylinder head in **Section 1 : 4**. To connect the gearbox to the engine, first make sure that the dowel pins together with their circlips are in position in the crankcase. **The gearbox should be resting on a trolley or similar arrangement,** for which the service practice is to use a specially designed support fixture 1799.T. Offer up the gearbox and ensure that it is in alignment with the engine. Engage the splines of the mainshaft in the splines of the clutch disc by turning the mainshaft with the starting handle relay, also turning the driving pulley to facilitate the introduction of the splines on the end piece of the camshaft (13 in **FIG 1 : 10**). Tighten the screws securing the clutch bellhousing. Fit the clutch cylinder, connect the control rod to the fork and fit the belts on the high pressure pump in DS cars. Fit the feed pipe and connect to the clutch cylinder. Refit the component assemblies removed in the course of detaching the cylinder head as described in **Sections 1 : 3** and **1 : 4**.

1 : 14 Refitting engine in car

Operations in general for installing the engine and gearbox assembly are as follows. For more detailed instructions on refitting individual items reference should be made to later Chapters covering the assemblies concerned.

1 Check the adjustment of the rear flexible blocks. Before October, 1962, the distance between the face of the nut receiving the engine support arm and the bearing face of the flexible block on the body support should be 98 mm. On later cars, for flexible blocks with the body painted green, the dimension should be 94 mm.

2 Lift the assembly and place it into position. Tighten the nuts of the studs securing the engine on the rear flexible mountings.

3 Refit the front crossmember of the engine/gearbox assembly. Replace the shims, found when dismantling, between the crossmember and the sidemember, in order that the dimension between the brake disc and the sidemember on the lefthand side is greater by 70 ± 2 mm than the same dimension on the righthand

side. Use the total number of shims found when dismantling. If necessary, vary the number of shims between crossmember and sidemembers but keep the total number of shims constant. A shim removed from one side must be replaced on the other.

4 Couple up the flexible coupling (bibax) to the driving plates on the gearbox (before October, 1961). Fit the transmission and pivot assemblies in later cars. Connect the brake control cable to the lever and adjust the connecting cable.

5 Locate the brake coverplates in position and connect the speedometer cable to the gearbox.

6 Refit the ignition advance and retard control to the plate on the contact breaker (before February, 1961). Locate the advance control centrally, counting the number of notches. Put the plate on the contact breaker midway between the two stops.

7 Connect the union plates to the hydraulic gear selector and to the clutch corrector. Insert the seal plate (before July, 1960). Connect the unions of the pipe assembly between the centrifugal regulator and the hydraulic gear selector in later cars.

8 Fit the accelerator control to the carburetter. Connect and adjust the choke control.

9 Connect (a) the feed pipe and the outlet pipe from the hydraulic gear selector, (b) the brake pipe to the three-way union, (c) the feed pipe to the petrol pump and (d) the five-pipe assembly to the gearbox, inserting the seal plates.

10 Refit the generator cables to the regulator. Fit the brake disc cooling ducts, ensuring that they do not touch.

11 Refit the steering assembly and fit the tube for the cable harness. Adjust the position of the steering as necessary. Connect the heater hoses. Fit the coverplates for the steering.

12 Refit the exhaust downpipe to the manifold and the silencer.

13 Fit the coil and bracket assembly and connect the leads to the sparking plugs.

14 Fit the battery and connect the battery cables.

15 Fit the hydraulic reservoir and connect up the high pressure pump. Fit the suspension sphere and tighten by hand.

16 Fill the cooling system with water. Open the heater control valve and undo the bleed screw to allow air to escape.

17 Fit the air deflector panel and the front wings. Couple up the bonnet lock control and adjust the cable if necessary. Fit the air sleeves.

18 Fit the crossmember supporting the sphere wheel and attach the wheel. Lower the car to the ground.

19 Refill the engine and gearbox with the correct grade of lubricating oil.

20 After a final inspection to ensure that all components have been properly connected, fill the reservoir with hydraulic fluid and undo the screw on the pressure control valve. Start the engine, let it run for a few minutes and check for any oil or water leaks. Retighten the bleed screw so as to put the hydraulic system under pressure and check all unions for leakage.

21 Bleed the hydraulic gear selector. Operate the auxiliary clutch control lever and make successive movements

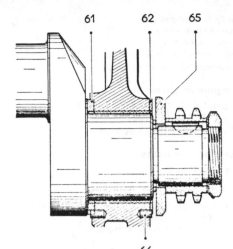

FIG 1:15 Sectional view of crankshaft rear bearing

Key to Fig 1:15
62 Bearing thrust ring   64 Pin   61 Inner bearing ring   65 Thrust washer

with the gearlever through all gears several times so as to bleed the gearbox and clutch hydraulic system.

22 Bleed the brakes, adjust the idling speeds and adjust the clutch clearance, which is sometimes necessary to readjust after running 30 or 40 miles. Adjust, if necessary, the initial advance setting.

1:15 Fault diagnosis

(a) Engine will not start

1 Defective coil
2 Faulty distributor capacitor
3 Dirty, pitted or incorrectly set contact breaker points
4 Ignition wires loose or insulation faulty
5 Water on sparking plug leads
6 Corrosion of battery terminals or discharged condition
7 Faulty or jammed starter
8 Sparking plug leads wrongly connected
9 Vapour lock in fuel pipes
10 Defective fuel pump
11 Overchoking
12 Underchoking
13 Blocked petrol filter or carburetter jets
14 Leaking valves
15 Sticking valves
16 Valve timing incorrect
17 Ignition timing incorrect

(b) Engine stalls

Check 1, 2, 3, 4, 10, 11, 12, 13, 14 and 15 in (a)
1 Sparking plugs defective or gap incorrect
2 Retarded ignition
3 Mixture too weak
4 Water in fuel system
5 Petrol tank breather choked
6 Incorrect valve clearance

(c) Engine idles badly

Check 1 and 6 in (b)
1 Air leak in manifold joints
2 Slow-running jet blocked or out of adjustment

3 Air leak in carburetter
4 Over-rich mixture
5 Worn piston rings
6 Worn valve stems or guides
7 Weak exhaust valve springs

(d) Engine misfires

Check 1, 2, 3, 4, 5, 8, 10, 13, 14, 15, 16 and 17 in (a) and 1, 2, 3 and 6 in (b)
1 Weak or broken valve springs

(e) Engine overheats

See **Chapter 5**

(f) Compression low

Check 14 and 15 in (a); 5 and 6 in (c) and 1 in (d)
1 Worn piston ring grooves
2 Scored or worn cylinder bores

(g) Engine lacks power

Check 3, 10, 11, 13, 14, 15 and 16 in (a); 1, 2, 3 and 6 in (b); 5 and 6 in (c) and 1 in (d). Also check (e) and (f)
1 Leaking joint washers
2 Fouled spark plugs

(h) Burnt valves or seats

Check 14 and 15 in (a); 6 in (b) and 1 in (d). Also check (e)
1 Excessive carbon around valve seat and head

(j) Sticking valves

Check 1 in (d)
1 Bent valve stem
2 Scored valve stem, or guide
3 Incorrect valve clearance

(k) Excessive cylinder wear

Check 11 in (a) and check (c)
1 Lack of oil
2 Dirty oil
3 Piston rings gummed up or broken
4 Badly fitting piston rings
5 Connecting rods bent

(l) Excessive oil consumption

Check 5 and 6 in (c) and check (k)
1 Ring gaps too wide
2 Scored cylinders
3 Oil level too high
4 External oil leaks
5 Ineffective valve stem oil seals

(m) Crankshaft and connecting rod failure

Check 1 in (k)
1 Restricted oilways
2 Worn journals or crankpins
3 Loose bearing caps
4 Extremely low oil pressure
5 Bent connecting rod

(n) Internal water leakage (see Chapter 5)

(o) Poor circulation (see Chapter 5)

(p) Corrosion (see Chapter 5)

(q) High fuel consumption (see Chapter 3)

(r) Engine vibration

1 Loose generator bolts
2 Rear engine supports out of adjustment
3 Exhaust pipe mountings too tight

CHAPTER 2

THE HYDRAULIC PRESSURE SYSTEM

2:1 General description

Hydraulic power for operating the brakes and often the clutch in ordinary cars is usually initiated by individual action by the driver as required, with separate fluid pressure arrangements being incorporated in particular features such as power steering equipment and automatic transmission. In the Citroen cars under description, however, a single central pressure system is employed to give a continuous source of hydraulic power when the engine is running, thus eliminating much of the physical effort involved in conventional arrangements. The engine drives a seven-cylinder pump supplying hydraulic fluid under pressure to an accumulator, from which it is bled off as required to serve particular purposes. Full use of this power source in DS cars is made by applying it to controlling a hydro-pneumatic suspension system as well as the brakes and steering, the operation of the clutch and the selection of the gears.

The supply of fluid for the hydraulic system is contained in the reservoir situated in front of the battery as shown in **FIG 2:2** and also at 45 in **FIG 2:1**. The level of the fluid should be between the minimum and maximum marks on the transparent gauge B in the former illustration, with the engine running and the car unladen stabilized at its normal height. A float switch fitted in the reservoir will light an amber warning light on the dashboard if the fluid reaches the minimum safe level. For topping up the fluid in the reservoir it is essential that only one of the fluids recommended by the manufacturers should be used, i.e., Castrol HF, Lockheed HD.19, Antar FH.6, Shell Donax D, BP Energol Hydraulic CF or Stop SP.19. Purely for an emergency or as a temporary measure either Lockheed or Castrol/Girling brake fluid may be used, but on no account use any other fluids, particularly any with a mineral base. These will rapidly make ineffective and destroy the seals and diaphragms of the hydraulic system.

The reservoir filter (47 in **FIG 2:1**) should be removed and cleaned every 6000 miles. In cars before March 1957, unscrew the cap on the reservoir outlet pipe and remove the pipe. Then unscrew the filter by the knurled part at the base of the outlet pipe. In later cars, disengage the spring retaining the outlet pipe, withdraw the pipe by pulling it upwards and remove the filter. Clean the filter by immersion in alcohol and blowing it out with compressed air **from the outside.** Refit in the reverse manner of removal. Fit a rubber joint under the cap and in later cars make sure that a seal ring is fitted on the upper part of the outlet pipe (see also **Chapter 10**).

DS 19

29

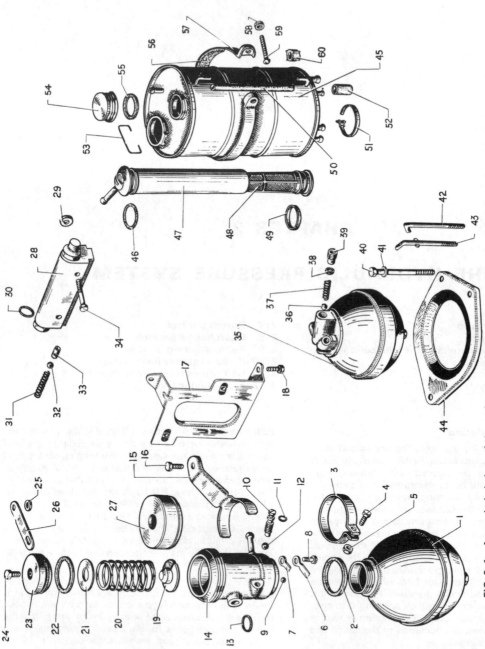

FIG 2:1   An exploded view of the main accumulator, pressure control valve, reservoir and brake accumulator

Key to Fig 2:1   1 Main accumulator   2 Rubber joint for control valve   3 Clip   4 Rubber joint for control valve, fluid passage pump to sphere   5 Nut   6 Ball retaining plate
7 Shim for thrust spring adjustment   8 Retaining plate screw   9 Ball for control valve   10 Bleed screw for pressure control valve   16 Retaining screw
11 Ring seal   12 Ball for bleed screw   13 Ring seal for control valve piston   14 Pressure control valve   15 Valve bracket   23 Cap   24 Retaining screw
17 Valve support (since September, 1962)   18 Retaining screw   19 Cup and ball   20 Spring   21 Washer   22 Rubber joint   30 Cap joint   31 Spring
25 Distance piece   26 Retaining plate   27 Nut for tightening cap   28 Pressure distribution block   29 Distance piece   38 Thrust washer   39 Screw for thrust spring
32 Ball for distribution block   33 Plunger   34 Tie-rod   35 Brake accumulator   36 Ball   37 Spring   45 Fluid reservoir   46 Ring seal   47 Filter, complete
40 Flange retaining screw   41 Washer   42 Tie-rod   43 Tie-rod   44 Flange securing brake accumulator   53 Retaining spring   54 Reservoir cap   55 Joint   56 Felt packing   57 Strap
48 Filter element   49 Sealing washer   50 Gauge tube   51 Clip   52 Rubber cap   60 Gauge tube joint
58 Nut   59 Retaining screw

The general arrangement of the hydraulic system in DS cars before 1960 is shown in **FIG 2 : 3** and for later cars in **FIG 2 : 4**. In the earlier cars the main high pressure circuit operates the suspension, the brakes, gearchanging, clutch disengagement and servo steering. An auxiliary low pressure circuit, generated from a bi-rotor pump incorporated with the belt-driven water pump, controls a starting valve which keeps the clutch disengaged for engine starting.

The high pressure system includes the reservoir, an axial piston pump, a main accumulator, front and rear brake accumulators, a distributor block, a control block for gearchanging and clutch operation, a clutch re-engagement valve, a clutch operating cylinder and front and rear suspension units with their control valves.

Referring to **FIG 2 : 3**, fluid is drawn from the reservoir by the high pressure pump which supplies the main accumulator. Pressure is controlled by a valve (see **FIG 2 : 1**) which returns fluid to the reservoir at a pressure of 2130 to 2420 lb/sq in and cuts in again at 1850 to 1990 lb/sq in. For each of the front and rear brake circuits there is one small accumulator supplied directly from the main accumulator. The operating pedal takes the form of a plunger with a small circular head and very limited movement. When depressed this opens the valves and allows fluid under pressure to be transmitted from the accumulators to each circuit with almost negligible effort. The front brake accumulator also supplies the distributor block (28 in **FIG 2 : 1**), which in turn supplies fluid to the steering servo unit, the hydraulic control block for gearchanging and clutch operation and, through non-return valves, to the suspension units. Hydraulic gear operation takes place in conjunction with the clutch release also actuated by the changespeed lever on the dash forward of the steering wheel. Control is initiated by the low pressure pump delivering fluid under pressure which varies with engine speed, gearlever movement and accelerator position. No clutch pedal is provided and clutch action begins automatically by movement of the gearlever into the required position with a light touch. A control sensitive to engine speed releases the clutch below a specified minimum speed when idling. The fast idling speed on the carburetter is set to give a slow creep when first gear is engaged but to idle slower when the footbrake is applied. An auxiliary clutch control on the facia panel overrides the automatic control and allows clutch engagement when the engine is stopped and the gearlever in neutral.

In ID19 cars gear selection is by normal manual operation with a changespeed lever located below the steering wheel. Front inboard disc brakes and the usual drum brakes mounted on the rear wheels are similar to those in the DS19, but operation is by a conventional Lockheed hydraulic system and a full-sized brake pedal.

The hydraulic system in later DS cars (see **FIG 2 : 4**) is generally similar, with the main difference that the low pressure pump is discontinued and replaced by a centrifugal clutch control unit. Also, only one front brake accumulator is fitted instead of two as formerly, with consequent modification of the pressure distribution system. The main accumulator thus supplies high pressure fluid to the gearchange and clutch control block, the centrifugal clutch control unit, the steering pressure

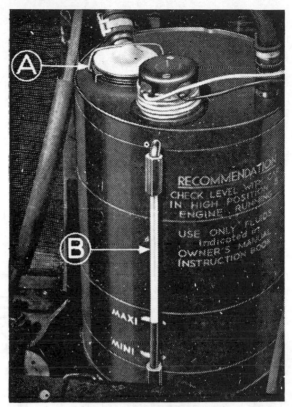

FIG 2 : 2   Hydraulic fluid reservoir

Key to Fig 2 : 2   A Filter   B Transparent gauge

distributor or servo control and the distributor block. The latter feeds the front suspension circuit supplying the front brake accumulator, also the brakes and rear suspension directly. The centrifugal clutch unit controls the clutch system pressure during starting and braking but not for gearchanging. Its purpose is to withdraw the clutch at engine speeds below approximately 1200 rev/min. At higher speeds automatic withdrawal of the clutch coincides with gearlever action in the selection of gears and taking up the drive.

2 : 2 Pressure spheres

The basic features of the power distribution system are the hydro-pneumatic pressure spheres used as accumulators and incorporated with hydraulic cylinders to act as pneumatic springs for the suspension system. The principle of their operation is that a variable flow of fluid, which is incompressible, is used to compress a volume of gas. As shown by the diagram of the main accumulator in **FIG 2 : 3**, the pressure sphere contains a flexible diaphragm which separates an inert gas in one part from hydraulic fluid acting under pressure on the other side of the diaphragm. The gas thus compressed so maintains a continuous reserve of fluid under similar pressure for the various purposes of each accumulator, used fluid being in each case ultimately returned to the reservoir for further pressurization via the fluid pump and the main

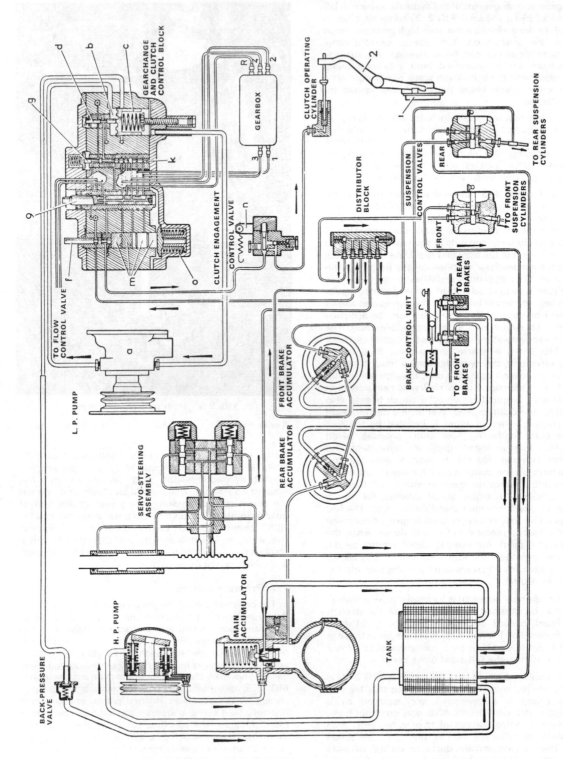

FIG 2:3 A diagrammatic view of the DS19 hydraulic circuit, 1955—60

32

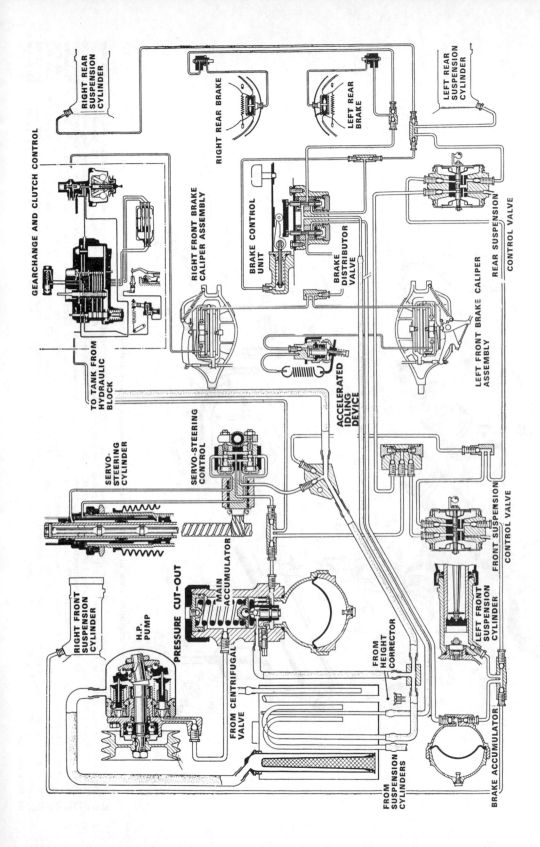

FIG 2:4 A diagrammatic view of the DS19 hydraulic system, including centrifugal clutch control valve, 1960 onwards

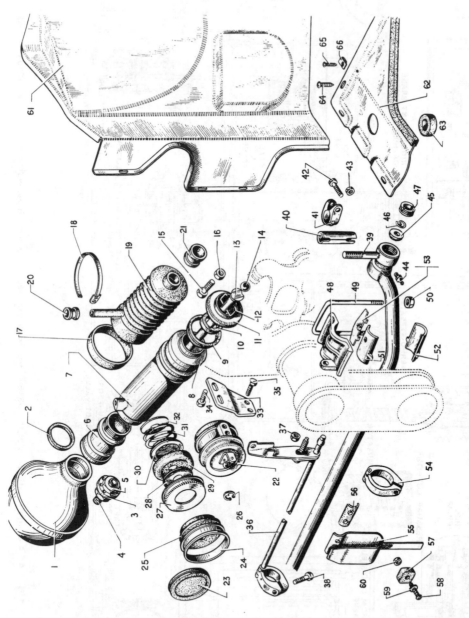

FIG 2:5   An exploded view of the front suspension pressure sphere and cylinder, height corrector and anti-roll bar

Key to Fig 2:5   1 Suspension sphere   **2** Rubber joint   **3** Damper   **4** Stud   **5** Nut   **6** Sleeve for sphere   **7** Suspension cylinder   **8** Cylinder nut with cup and joint
9 Cylinder sealing joint   **10** Felt sealing washer   **11** Cup   **12** Pin connecting piston rod with lever   **13** Piston rod   **14** Ball for piston rod   **15** Screw securing cylinder
16 Nut   **17** Protective ring under clip   **18** Clip for dust cover   **19** Rubber dust cover   **20** Protective ring under return pipe clip   **21** Protective ring under dust cover clip
22 Height corrector   **23** Rubber cover for corrector adjustment hole   **24** Retaining sleeve   **25** Sealing cup   **26** Circlip for corrector valve
27 Interior cup for tightening corrector diaphragm   **28** Cup   **29** Diaphragm   **30** Cup   **31** Spring   **32** Corrector valve   **33** Corrector bracket   **34** Screw   **35** Screw
36 Corrector control rod   **37** Nut for eccentric pin operating corrector   **38** Screw for corrector control rod   **39** Anti-roll bar   **40** Coupling sleeve   **41** Clip
42 Screw   **43** Nut   **44** Grease nipple   **45** Thrust cup and ball pin   **46** Spring for ball pin   **47** Ball pin cup nut   **48** Bearing cap   **49** U-bolt   **50** Nut
51 Nylon half bearing   **52** Nylon half bearing   **53** Adjusting shim   **54** Thrust collar   **55** Anti-rattle spring   **56** Nylon bearing   **57** Rubber stop   **58** Screw   **65** Screw
59 Washer   **60** Nut   **61** Lateral shield for suspension mechanism   **62** Lower shield for suspension mechanism   **63** Rubber washer   **64** Screw   **66** Screw
66 Retaining nut

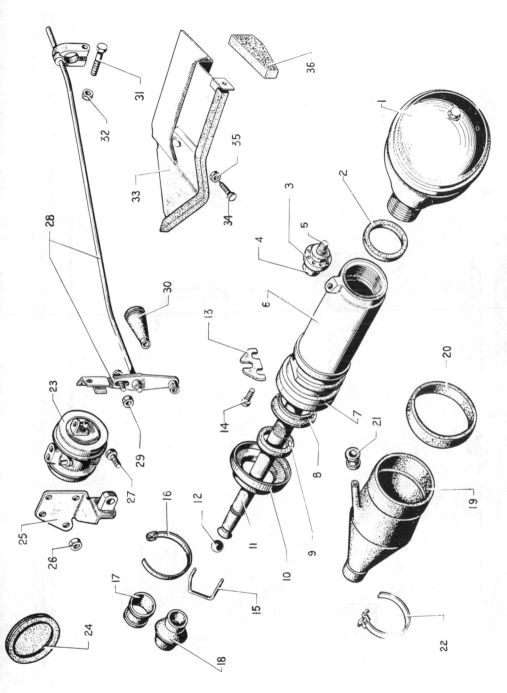

FIG 2:6   An exploded view of the rear suspension pressure sphere, cylinder and height corrector

Key to Fig 2:6   1 Suspension sphere   2 Rubber joint   3 Damper   4 Nut   5 Stud   6 Suspension cylinder   7 Nut with cup and joint   8 Sealing joint
9 Felt sealing washer   10 Cup   11 Piston rod   12 Ball   13 Retaining plate for cylinder   14 Screw   15 Pin, piston rod to lever   16 Clip for piston rod dust cover
17 Protective ring under clip   18 Piston rod dust cover   19 Cylinder dust cover   20 Protective ring under dust cover clip   21 Protective ring under clip securing
return from cylinder to reservoir   22 Clip for cylinder dust cover   23 Height corrector   24 Rubber cover for corrector adjustment control passage   25 Corrector
bracket with bearing   26 Retaining nut   27 Screw   28 Control rod for rear corrector   29 Retaining nut   30 Sealing sleeve on corrector control   31 Screw
32 Nut   33 Corrector protection panel   34 Screw   35 Retaining nut   36 Rubber sealing pad, body to corrector panel

DS 19

35

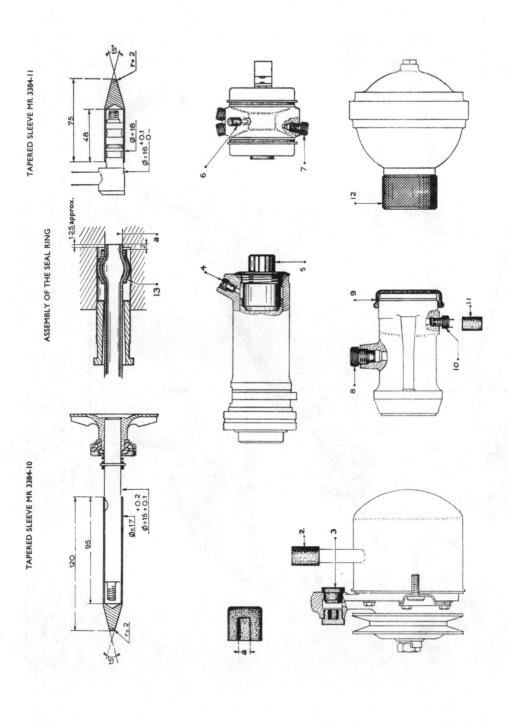

TAPERED SLEEVE MR 3384-11

15°
r=2

75
48

Ø=18
Ø=16 $^{+0.1}_{-0}$

ASSEMBLY OF THE SEAL RING

125 approx.

a
2
13

TAPERED SLEEVE MR 3384-10

120
95

Ø=17 $^{+0.2}_{-}$
Ø=15 $^{+0.1}_{-}$

r=2
15°

6
7

12

4
5

9
8
10
11

2
3

a

FIG 2:7   Tapered sleeves, sealing rings and plugs

Key to Fig 2:7 1 Caps for metal pipes with screwed unions (a: 3 mm, 4.5 mm, 6.35 mm, 8 mm)   2 Cap, pump feed pipe   3 Cap, pump outlet   4 Plug, suspension cylinder inlet union   5 Plug, suspension sphere union   6 Plug, height corrector   7 Plug, height corrector   8 Plug, pressure regulator   9 Cap, pressure regulator accumulator union   10 Plug, pressure regulator   11 Cap, pressure regulator   12 Cap for main accumulator   13 Sealing sleeve (dimensions are in millimetres)

36

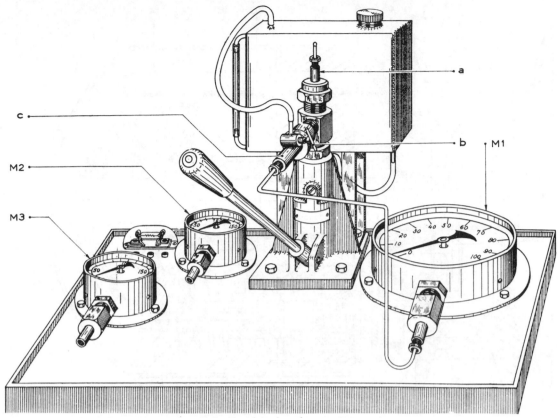

2:8 Test bench and apparatus

Key to Fig 2:8   **a** Pump orifice   **b** Bleed screw   **c** Pressure outlet   **M1, M2, M3** Pressure gauges

accumulator. A main accumulator and a brake accumulator sphere are shown in **FIG 2:1** and the suspension spheres in **FIGS 2:5** and **2:6**.

2:3 Instructions on servicing the hydraulic system

For the correct functioning of the whole of the hydraulic system it is essential that the fluid and the units of the system should be perfectly clean and strict precautions must be observed. Seals and rubber pipes must be protected from exposure to dust, light or heat. The fluid must be kept in its original container securely sealed. The use of 1 quart containers for topping up or 1 gallon containers in the case of draining or refilling is advised in order to avoid keeping many small containers.

Before starting work carefully wash the car or round the area in which the work is to be carried out. When replacing a rear suspension cylinder carefully wash the corresponding wheel arch. Before disconnecting a union carefully wash it and the surrounding area with alcohol. The overhaul of any unit is preceeded by removing the spare wheel, unscrewing the bleed screw on the pressure regulator (10 in **FIG 2:1**) and moving the manual height control lever to the low position. Additionally for work on the braking system, connect a flexible pipe (plastic or rubber) to the front brake bleed screw or to the rear bleed screw of the centrifugal regulator and to the bleed screw or the accelerated idling hydraulic control. Connect

also a pipe on a rear brake cylinder bleed screw and press on the hydraulic brake pedal until the fluid ceases to flow. If the union is situated below the level of the fluid in the reservoir, either drain the reservoir in order to avoid a loss of fluid or immediately close the pipe with the appropriate plug. Seal the open ends of all pipes with caps, of which details are given in **FIG 2:7**. Protect union flanges and plastic pipes with cellulose tape. For the rubber pipes use cylindrical pegs 50 mm long by 8 or 12 mm diameter. All plugs, caps and pegs must be carefully cleaned before using.

Prior to assembly blow through the steel pipes with compressed air. Using only alcohol, clean rubber pipes, ring seals and all hydraulic units and complete by blowing off with compressed air. Ring seals, however, should preferably be renewed. The approved method of fitting a ring seal is as follows, referring to **FIG 2:7**:

1 Moisten the seal with hydraulic fluid.
2 Fit a tapered sleeve MR.3384.11 for the union of the high pressure pump or a tapered sleeve MR.3384.10 for the spindle of the low pressure pump.
3 Fit the ring seal in position by sliding it over the tapered sleeve. Because of their design the efficiency of these seals increases with pressure. The sealing is not increased by increasing the tightening of the unions.

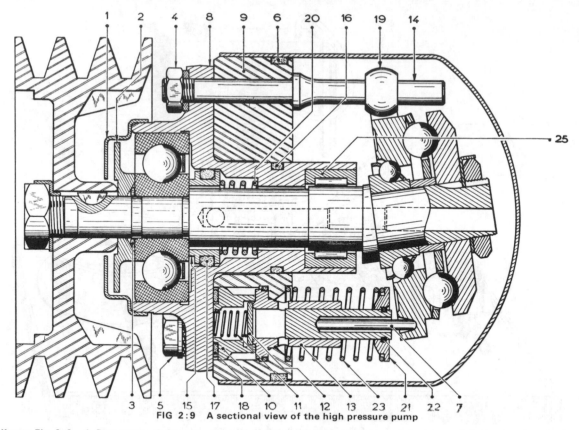

FIG 2:9 A sectional view of the high pressure pump

Key to Fig 2:9 1 Dust cover   2 Thrust washer   3 Seal ring   4 Nut   5 Screws   6 Seal ring   7 Pushrods   8 End plate
9 Pump body   10 Valve guides   11 Springs   12 Valves   13 Cylinders   14 Rods   15 Distance piece and seal assembly
16 Seal ring, end plate   17 Seal ring   18 Seal rings   19 Olive   20 Springs   21 Cups   22 Circlips   23 Return springs
25 Needle bearings

Sealing sleeves (13 in **FIG 2:7**) should be replaced after each dismantling operation and should be set back 2 mm from the end of the pipe. Centralize the pipe in the bore and make sure that the end of the pipe enters the small bore at 'a'. Screw on the union nut by hand. On certain units the axis of the bore is oblique relatively to the face of the boss for the unit. Lightly tighten the nut to a torque of 4.3 to 5.7 lb ft. This light tightening is sufficient to ensure a good seal. Excessive tightening will cause leakage.

Operations for draining, flushing and refilling the whole hydraulic system can be undertaken, but on completion it is necessary to carry out a hydraulic check. This requires specially designed equipment, either for a rapid test or for more precise procedures involving test bench operations, and it is therefore advisable that such work should be undertaken by a suitably equipped service agent. A view of the test bench employed is given in **FIG 2:8**.

2:4 Main accumulator

Details of the main accumulator 1 and the pressure control valve 14 are shown in **FIG 2:1**. To remove the accumulator, preliminary operations are to be undertaken as described in **Section 2:3**. Continue as follows:

1 Disconnect the cable from the negative terminal of the battery.

2 Remove the lefthand front suspension sphere, using a strap wrench; also the fuel pump.

3 Disconnect from the pressure regulator the outlet pipe and the overflow return pipe to the reservoir.

4 Disengage the regulator retaining clip and its support to obtain access to disconnect the pipe between the regulator and the high pressure pump.

5 Pivot the body of the regulator towards the front and the accumulator towards the rear. Withdraw the regulator/accumulator assembly from underneath the car. Disconnect the regulator from the accumulator.

Dismantling and reassembly of the regulator requires the use of a press to control the spring 20, which exerts a considerable thrust. This precaution is essential to avoid stripping the threads of the cap and it is therefore advisable that the operations should be undertaken by a service agent. In addition it is necessary for various pressure checks to be made, e.g., the initial pressure of the accumulator, the pressure of the assembly, the cutting-in and cutting-out pressures and for leakages. For these purposes service agents use the specially designed test bench (see **FIG 2:8**) complete with the necessary pipes and unions for connecting the units to be tested.

Operations for refitting the accumulator assembly are the reverse of those employed for removal, tightening the accumulator on the regulator by hand. Ensure that the rubber return pipe to the reservoir is not chafing on the brake accumulator outlet pipes. Finally unscrew the bleed screw 10, start the engine, let it run for a few minutes, retighten the bleed screw and put the systems under pressure. Check the unions for leakage and if necessary top up the level of the fluid in the reservoir.

2:5 Hydraulic pump

The hydraulic system is put under pressure by a belt-driven hydraulic pump, in which the pressure is maintained by pistons acting in seven cylinders and operated by an inclined swashplate. A typical sectional view of the pump is shown in **FIG 2:9**. Later models may differ in constructional details but the general principles remain the same. The operations entailed in the removal and dismantling of the pump are as follows:

1 Remove the spare wheel and support and the air deflection panel. Release the pressure and retighten the pressure control valve bleed screw.
2 In later cars (since September 1960) remove the belt from the centrifugal regulator assembly, as follows:
(a) Unscrew the retaining nuts and remove the tie-rod between the pump and regulator.
(b) Unscrew the nut of the regulator articulating spindle and remove the belt from the regulator and the pump.
3 Disconnect and remove the pipe between the pump and the pressure regulator.
4 Where fitted, remove the screw from the connecting pipe retaining clip on the gearbox.
5 Remove the nut from the pump fixing spindle. Unscrew the retaining nut and disconnect the pump tie-rod from the water pump. Remove the belts from the pump pulley.
6 Disconnect the pump feed pipe from the reservoir. Remove the pump fixing spindle and remove the pump. Remove the pump feed pipe. Drain all fluid from the pump.
7 Referring to **FIG 2:9**, hold the mounting bracket of the front end plate in a soft-jawed vice and remove the pulley nut, holding the pulley whilst undoing the nut. Remove the pulley and its key.
8 Disengage the steel dust cover 1, the thrust washer 2 and the ring seal 3.
9 Remove the nut 4 and the screws 5 fixing the end plate. Remove the tie-rod fixing plate.
10 Remove the pump housing, for which service agents use an extractor 2282.T, and remove the seal ring 6 from the pump body.
11 Extract the shaft from the end plate bearing. Note that if the shaft is to be renewed it is also necessary to renew the needle bearings 25.
12 Hold the pump vertically, the swashplate towards the top, and remove the shaft.
13 Disengage the pistons. Note that the pistons and cylinders are paired on assembly and must be kept in their correct order for reassembly. Use a numbered rack and commence with the piston nearest the rod supporting the swashplate. Remove the cups and springs.
14 Using a mallet, drive out the end plate 8 from the body of the pump 9, steadying the assembly by hand. When the end plate is free, turn the assembly over in order to

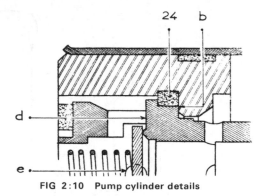

FIG 2:10   Pump cylinder details

Key to Fig 2:10   24 Seal rings. Diameter b: 18.5 ± .05 mm Face d to be level with lower part of hole e in the body

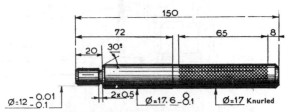

FIG 2:11   Mandrel MR.3436.10 used in assembly of high pressure pump

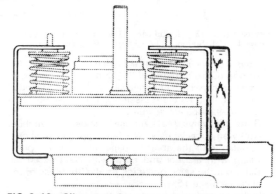

FIG 2:12   Clips used for piston assembly in the high pressure pump

avoid dropping the cylinders. Note the order of disassembly of the parts.
15 Remove the valve guides 10, the springs 11 and the valves 12. Remove the cylinders 13 in the same order as for the pistons. Keep the cylinders with their corresponding pistons and remove the cylinder seal rings. Drive out the rod 14 from the pump body.
16 Drive out the distance piece and seal assembly 15 and the end plate bearing, by using a mandrel of 17 mm diameter. A new bearing must be fitted on reassembly Disengage the seal ring 16 from the end plate and the seal 17 from the distance piece.
17 Remove the thrust bearing and the swashplate. With a magnifying glass make sure that there is no pitting or coppering of the thrust plates and ballbearings. Clean the parts with alcohol. A new thrust bearing should be

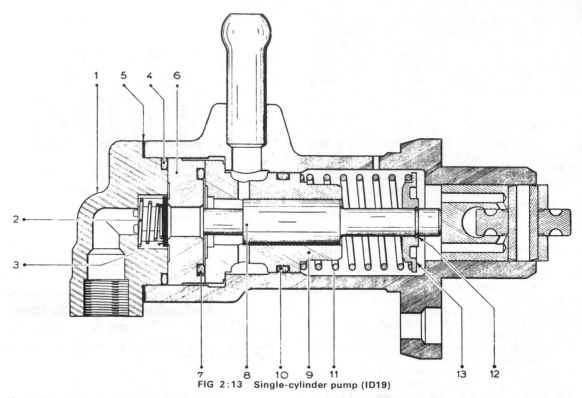

FIG 2:13 Single-cylinder pump (ID19)

Key to Fig 2:13 1 End cap 2 Valve spring 3 Valve 4 End cap seal 5 Shim 6 Seat 7 Seal 8 Piston 9 Cylinder
10 Seal 11 Spring 12 Circlip 13 Spring cup

fitted if there is any trace of defect, tightening the locking nut to a torque of $25\frac{1}{4}$ lb ft.

Unless otherwise mentioned all parts should be dipped in hydraulic fluid before reassembly. The reassembly and refitting operations are as follows:

1 Grind the valve seats on the cylinders by rubbing lightly on abrasive paper No. 600 dipped in alcohol, if possible with the abrasive paper on a surface plate. Clean with alcohol and blow with compressed air. Carry out the same operation on the front face of the distance piece 15.

2 Make sure that the cylinders are manufactured as shown in **FIG 2:10** and have a diameter 'b'=18.5 $\pm$ .05 mm. If otherwise, replace the piston and cylinder assemblies. Refit the rod 14, using a press.

3 Place the body of the pump on two V-blocks whose thickness is less than 50 mm. Fit the seal rings in the grooves of the cylinder bores. Press the seals in position if necessary.

4 Locate the cylinders 13 in position in the pump body 9 in the same order as when dismantling. Smear the collar of the cylinder with alcohol. Offer up the cylinder in the bore of the pump body and press sufficiently strongly by means of a mandrel up to the moment when it becomes locked (seal in the collar). Make sure that the face 'd' is level with the lower part of the hole 'e' in the body (see **FIG 2:10**).

5 Fit new valves 12 and the valve guides 10. The guides are only in position when they are below the level of the pump, otherwise the guides are bearing on the

valves. Fit the ring seals 18 on the guides and fit the valve springs 11.

6 Fit the end plate seal ring 16 on the hub of the front end plate. Carefully position the end plate 8 in the pump body and fit by hand. Fit the screw 5 with serrated washer. Fit the tie-rod fixing plate. Insert the serrated washer between the fixing plate and the end plate, not under the heads of the screws. Tighten the tie-rod screws to a torque of $25\frac{1}{4}$ lb ft. Provision is made for checking the valves for leakage on the test bench mentioned in **Section 2:2**.

7 Fit the seal ring 17 soaked in castor oil on the distance piece 15. Fit the spring 20 and the distance piece in the pump.

8 Check the condition of the surface of the inner cage of the bearing in the end plate. This face should show no signs of scratches, blows or markings. If grinding the face has left criss-cross marks, the bearing should be renewed. Grease this face with castor oil and offer up the bearing in the end plate with the nylon bush towards the interior of the pump. Insert the bearing in position with the aid of a press. Position the distance piece with a mandrel MR.3436.10 as shown in **FIG 2:11**.

9 Fit the cups 21 on the pistons, ensuring that the circlips 22 are in position. Dip the pistons in hydraulic fluid and fit the return springs 23. Engage the pistons in their corresponding cylinders in the order of their removal, using the clips 2284.T to hold the pistons as shown in **FIG 2:12**.

10 Fit the pushrods 7. Select a pushrod in good condition, preferably a new one, and measure with a micrometer. All the pushrods should be the same length within .05 mm.

11 Engage the shaft by hand. Fit the olive 19 in the groove in the swashplate and the rod 14. Complete the fitting of the shaft, for which service agents use a press and a mandrel 2286.T.

12 Remove the clips retaining the pistons and ensure that the pushrods enter the sockets in the swashplate and that the olive does not bind on the guide. Turn the shaft to check for freedom from stiffness.

13 Grease the bearing, fit the seal ring 3, the thrust washer 2 and the cover 1. Fit the seal 6 in the groove of the pump body. Coat the body with hydraulic fluid and locate the pump casing in position in a press.

14 Fit the key, the pulley and the lockwasher. Hold the pulley with a 19 mm box spanner and tighten the nut to a torque of $25\frac{1}{4}$ lb ft. To test the output of the pump it is necessary to employ the test bench shown in **FIG 2:8**.

For refitting the pump, operations in general are those undertaken in removal and carried out in reverse, with regard given to the following:

1 When fitting the pump on the fixing spindle the flat on the spindle faces the pulley.

2 The pulley belt must be correctly tensioned (see **Section 2:11**). Tighten the tie-rod nut using plain and spring washers, and the pump fixing spindle.

3 Refill the pump with fluid through the feed pipe. Connect the pipe to the reservoir, fit a flexible sleeve and tighten the clip.

4 Unscrew the bleed screw on the pressure regulator, start the engine and let it idle for a few minutes. Tighten the bleed screw to put the system under pressure and check for leaks. Also check the level of the fluid in the reservoir.

The same type of pump is used on ID19 cars fitted with power assisted steering, but on earlier cars eccentrically operated single-cylinder suspension pumps were employed as shown in **FIG 2:13**. Referring to **FIG 2:14**, the pump is removed as follows:

1 Release the pressure by unscrewing the bleed screw of the pressure regulator. Retighten the bleed screw.

2 Slightly unscrew the union on the control valve from the connecting pipe between pump and control valve and unscrew fully the union on the pump.

3 Remove the pump fixing screws. Withdraw the pump complete with the distance piece 1 and the paper gaskets 2 and disconnect the pipe connecting the control valve to the pump.

4 Remove the inlet pipe clamps and disconnect the pipe from the pump and from the reservoir. Remove the distance piece 1 complete with dowels 3 from the pump and remove the paper gaskets 2 between pump and distance piece.

When overhauling the pump, referring to **FIG 2:13**, if renewal is necessary of the end cap 1, the seat 6, the cylinder 9 or the pump body, it is essential to determine the precise measurement of the clearance between the end cap and the body to ascertain the thickness of the washer 5 required for a clearance of .05 to .09 mm. As the reassembly operations require some experience it is advised that this work should be carried out by a service

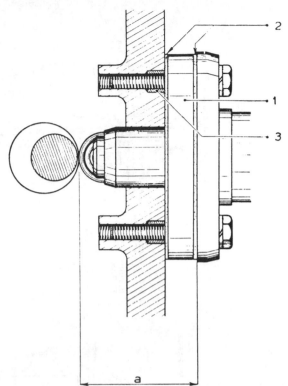

FIG 2:14 Location of single-cylinder pump

Key to Fig 2:14   1 Distance piece   2 Paper gasket
3 Dowels.   Dimension a: $40 \pm .1$ mm

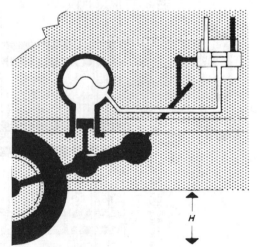

FIG 2:15 Diagram showing suspension action

agent. For refitting the pump the removal operations are undertaken in reverse. Note that where the clamp fits round the inlet pipe a rubber ring should be inserted to prevent fracture of the pipe. Before running, it is essential to prime the pump with the recommended fluid through the inlet pipe. Finally put the system under pressure and check for leaks as previously described.

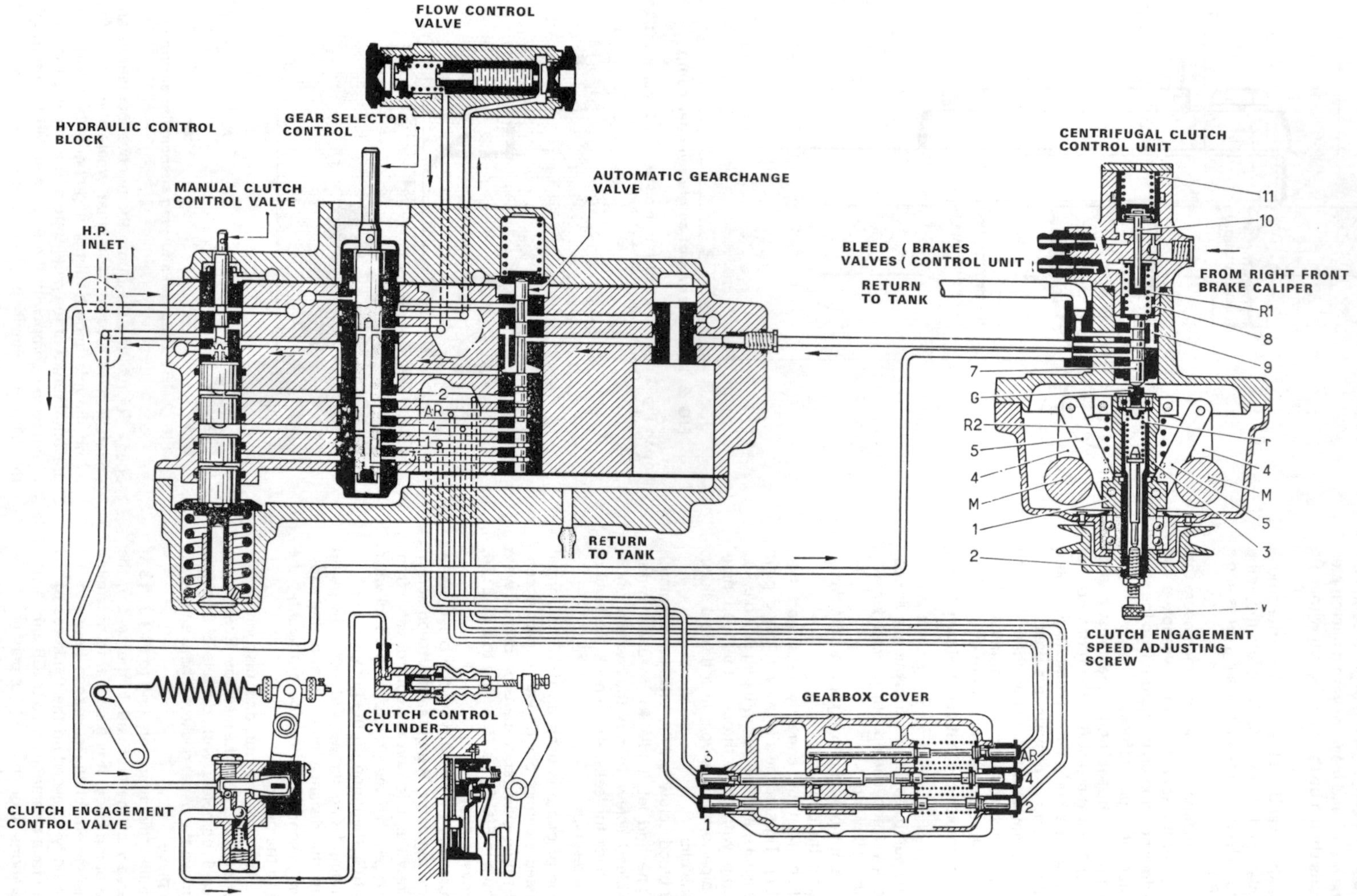

CENTRIFUGAL CLUTCH
CONTROL UNIT

11
10

FROM RIGHT FRONT
BRAKE CALIPER

R1
8
9

r
4
M
5
3

CLUTCH ENGAGEMENT
SPEED ADJUSTING
SCREW

y

7
G
R2
5
4
M
1
2

BLEED (BRAKES
VALVES (CONTROL UNIT

RETURN
TO TANK

GEARBOX COVER

AUTOMATIC GEARCHANGE
VALVE

RETURN
TO TANK

FLOW CONTROL
VALVE

GEAR SELECTOR
CONTROL

HYDRAULIC CONTROL
BLOCK

MANUAL CLUTCH
CONTROL VALVE

CLUTCH CONTROL
CYLINDER

H.P.
INLET

CLUTCH ENGAGEMENT
CONTROL VALVE

FIG 2:16   A diagrammatic view of the gearchange control with centrifugal clutch control unit

42

If a new engine or crankcase has been installed it is necessary to check that the dimension 'a' in **FIG 2:14** between the pump mounting face and the operating cam is maintained at 40 ± .1 mm. This should preferably be undertaken by a service agent using a special setting fixture 1693.T on a surface plate and fitted with a dial test indicator.

2:6 Suspension system

Suspension of each of the four independently sprung wheels is by hydro-pneumatic means instead of the conventional coil or laminated spring arrangements. The hydro-pneumatic principle is illustrated diagrammatically in **FIG 2:15**. Referring also to **FIG 2:5**, a pressure sphere, into which is screwed a piston operated hydraulic cylinder, supports the weight of each wheel. The cylinder is kept constantly supplied with fluid under pressure. The piston is connected to a suspension arm linked to the wheel so that the gas pressure in the sphere is hydraulically adjusted following the movement of the wheel, and in effect becomes a flexible pneumatic spring according to the variations imposed on the gas pressure. A two-way damper valve (3 in **FIG 2:5**) is incorporated in the neck of the spherical component where it is connected to the cylinder, to smooth out oscillations.

A further feature is that automatic height correctors 22 are provided to ensure a constant ground clearance H irrespective of the load being carried. They give added damping action. An additional manual control of the correctors enables the ground clearance to be raised to cope with rough or flooded roads or for changing a wheel. The height correctors are linked to the centres of anti-roll torsion bars 39 between each pair of springs at front and rear. As the suspension arms rise and fall, slide valve action either permits fluid under pressure to enter the suspension cylinder or to return to the reservoir if the car rises too high. In normal running on level surfaces the valves remain closed.

2:7 Clutch control

Referring to **FIG 2:3**, high pressure fluid flows through the control block via the manual control valve **f**, the starting valve **d**, the upper piston **g** of the automatic gearchange, and the clutch control valve **n** to the clutch operating cylinder. The starting valve **d** restricts flow and reduces pressure in the clutch circuit for progressive clutch engagement. The piston **c** controls the position of the valve **d**.

At idling speed the low pressure flow in the circuit passes through the calibrated port **b** in the piston **c** without any pressure rise. The valve **d** remains static, allowing the reduced high pressure flow to the clutch operating cylinder to maintain the clutch out of engagement.

Acceleration increases pressure in the low pressure system and the calibrated port **b** in piston **c** cannot pass the increased flow. Hence the pressure rises, and the piston **c** moves against spring pressure to move the valve **d** gradually into a position to cut-out the high pressure flow to the clutch. Through interaction with the clutch control valve **n** this ensures the progressive engagement of the clutch. The piston **c**, moving against the spring, uncovers a bypass port back to the reservoir to limit the pressure in the low pressure circuit. The pressure is adjustable through an adjusting screw acting on the

spring. A back-pressure valve in the return line stabilizes operation.

On later cars a centrifugal clutch control unit was fitted as shown in **FIG 2:16**. The drive is by pulley and belt from the engine to the shaft 2 to which the centrifugal weight carrier 1 is attached. The sliding hollow shaft 3 is linked to the centrifugal weights by the links 4 and to the centrifugal weight carrier by the links 5. Movement outwards, under centrifugal force, of the weights will force the hollow shaft 3 against spring pressure to allow movement of the valve 7. Adjustment of pull-away is by the adjusting screw **r** acting on the spring.

The valve 7 under control of the sliding hollow shaft 3 either isolates the clutch circuit, or connects it to the high pressure side or returns it to the reservoir. The dashpot 8 communicates with clutch system pressure through the passage 9.

The valve 7 is in equilibrium under:

1 The action of the three springs. As the movement of these springs is very small, their effect is practically constant.
2 The variable centrifugal assembly.
3 The clutch circuit pressure acting on the dashpot 8.

When the engine is stopped, the centrifugal force is nil, and the valve 7 connects a reduced high pressure to the clutch circuit.

With increasing engine speed, centrifugal force acts on the weights M and moves them outwards, allowing valve 7 to move towards the exhaust position and thus decreasing clutch circuit pressure gradually until the clutch is fully engaged.

Piston 11 is subject to front brake pressure from the righthand front caliper. Brake pressure forces the piston 11 to the bottom of its cylinder, carrying the pushrod 10 with it, changing the rating of the spring R1 and increasing pressure in the clutch circuit.

An accelerated idling speed is automatically provided for smooth take-up. It consists of an abnormally high fast-idling setting on the carburetter which, once the engine is started, will cause the car to move slowly in first or reverse unless the footbrake is applied. Application of the brake brings a linkage into operation which slows down the idling speed below that of normal clutch engagement.

2:8 Gearchange control

On DS19 cars hydraulic servo mechanism enables the selection of gears to be made with a minimum of effort. Light finger operation of the gearlever behind the steering wheel gives the required gear selection with which clutch operation is automatically combined. Moving the gearlever to the far left operates the starter switch, a lock preventing accidental use of the starter with the engine running.

Referring to **FIG 2:3**, when first or reverse gear is selected the selector valve 9 releases high pressure fluid to the gear servo. The automatic control valve **g** moves under pressure to pass high pressure to the starting valve **d**. Clutch engagement then takes place as described in **Section 2:7**.

When the selector valve 9 is moved to another gear, the previously used circuit exhausts, and a spring moves the gearbox selector rod to neutral. The piston **k** then moves to allow the automatic gearchange valve **g** to pass reduced pressure to the clutch.

A stack of pistons **m** and the spring **O** temporarily limit servo pressure to allow the gearbox pinions to synchronize. High pressure then passes to the gear servo and automatic gearchange valve **g** to connect the clutch control valve **n** with the control block.

The clutch control valve **n** is in effect a non-return valve, with a controlled leak-back. A mechanical connection between the clutch control valve and the accelerator through a spring actuates a lever acting on a ball valve in the clutch control valve, to exhaust pressure from the clutch operating cylinder. Spring tension which is adjustable controls the speed of clutch engagement. The accelerator therefore controls the action of the clutch and not engine speed.

A short pause must be made during gearchanging, to allow time for the selected gear to engage, before re-accelerating. The engine can act as a brake when going downhill, even with 'foot-off', as engine speed will maintain the clutch in engagement. Gearchange can only take place when high pressure is available for the servos, and the car cannot be parked in gear.

To avoid clutch slip or engine stall during energetic braking, a small servo cylinder links the brake circuit with the throttle valve. A manual control acting on valve **f** will engage the clutch with the engine stopped so that the starting handle can be used to turn the engine.

2:9 Servo steering control

A two-way cylinder acting on the steering rack is controlled by a two-way valve distributor and a rotary valve operated by the steering wheel shaft. Depending on the position of the rotary valve, pressure is applied to one end of the cylinder and exhausted from the other.

With high pressure available, there is no mechanical connection between the steering wheel shaft and the rack pinion, which idles on the rack during operation. A loss of pressure causes the distributor compensator to restore the mechanical connection, thus ensuring that the steering is always under the driver's control.

2:10 Brake pressure distributor

An arrangement under the brake pedal, or button, is designed to adjust the brake effort applied to front and rear brakes according to the position and amount of the load being carried in the car. The brake button has very small movement, sufficient only to open spring-loaded hydraulic valves to transmit fluid pressure to the brakes. The brake button stem movement is transmitted to the valves for front and rear braking through a carriage moving on rollers on a pivoted blade or balance beam (**r** in **FIG 2:3**) surmounting and actuating the valves. A hydraulic cylinder connected to the fluid pressure in a rear suspension accumulator contains a piston which controls the movement of the carriage along the pivoted plate. An increase in the rear load, therefore, such as extra passengers, causes the piston to move the carriage and hence the pivot point of the plate to apply a greater proportion of the braking effort to the rear wheels. Under other conditions more braking effort can be received by the front wheels.

2:11 Belt renewal and adjustments

Operations for the removal and refitting of high pressure pump belts are as follows:

1 Remove the generator and water pump belts as described in **Chapter 5**.

2 Disengage the auxiliary clutch control, pushing it to the front and then upwards.

3 Loosen the front nut of the clutch fork control rod. Disconnect the rod from the fork. Do not loosen the rear nuts to avoid having to readjust the clutch (see **FIG 6:3, Chapter 6**).

4 Loosen the nut of the high pressure pump fixing spindle and the nut of the tie-rod fixing screw on the hydraulic pump and the water pump. In cars from September, 1960, disconnect the centrifugal regulator tie-rod from the high pressure pump. Remove the belts. New belts are supplied in sets of two of identical dimensions and for this reason it is necessary to renew both belts even if one is in good condition.

5 Fit the belts on the driving pulley and then on the high pressure pump pulley, passing the belts between the clutch fork and the clutch housing. Tension the belts described later. Continue refitting operations in the reverse order to that described for dismantling.

Removal and refitting of a centrifugal regulator belt, where fitted, is as follows:

1 Unscrew the nuts of (a) the tie-rod between the high pressure pump and the regulator (b) the tie-rod reinforcing arm between the cylinder head and the regulator.

2 Unscrew the centrifugal regulator articulation spindle nut, swing the regulator towards the high pressure pump and remove the belt.

3 To refit, locate the belt on the pulleys and tension the belt as described later. Tighten the nuts loosened during removal.

Tensioning of the various belts is precisely undertaken in service workshops by a specially dimensioned lever, or a hook in the case of the centrifugal regulator belt, appropriately situated with a spring gauge attached to one end, on which a specified pull must be registered to obtain the correct belt tension. In the absence of this equipment the twin belts of the high pressure pump and the centrifugal regulator belt should be adjusted to have $\frac{1}{4}$ inch free play. Adjustment of the former is made by loosening and retightening the tie-rod to the pump and the pump bearing spindle nut, and of the latter by similar operations on the tie-rod fixing nuts and the regulator swivelling nut.

2:12 Fault diagnosis

If any irregularity of working occurs, first check that the hydraulic system is under pressure as follows:

1 With engine idling, unscrew the pressure regulator bleed screw about 1 to $1\frac{1}{2}$ turns, when the release of pressure in the control valve should be heard.

2 Screw up the bleed screw, when the valve should cut-out in less than 20 seconds. The point of cut-out is indicated by a reduction in the noise of operation.

Further checks to be made if the preliminary tests are unsatisfactory are to ensure that:

1 There is sufficient hydraulic fluid in the reservoir.

2 The filter in the reservoir is perfectly clean and in good condition.

3 Air is not being sucked in through the pump inlet pipe.

4 The belt of the high pressure pump is not slipping.

5 The bleed screw is tightened.

A complete hydraulic test of the system can be undertaken if required by a service agent using the test bench equipment described in **Section 2:2**.

CHAPTER 3

THE FUEL SYSTEM

3:1 General description

Fuel is supplied from a tank of 14 gallons capacity to a mechanically operated pump mainly of the Guiot type, although an AC/RH type is employed on some ID19 cars. Details of these pumps are shown in **FIGS 3:1** and **3:2**. A rocker arm or lever is actuated by a cam and operates a flexible diaphragm against a spring to create a partial vacuum in the pump, which enables the atmospheric pressure in the tank to send fuel through the connecting pipe to the pump. The return action of the spring then pushes the diaphragm upwards to deliver the fuel to the carburetter float chamber. When the bowl is full the float closes a needle valve, preventing further petrol supply from the pump until the carburetter requires more fuel and the needle valve opens. In the meantime the pump rocker arm is given an idling movement.

The carburetters used in DS19 cars are of the down-draught twin-choke type, in which category either a Weber 24/30.DCZC1 or DCLC, a Weber 24/32.DDC or a Zenith 24/30.EEAC carburetter may be employed. In ID19 cars a Solex 34.PBIC carburetter is used.

FUEL PUMPS

3:2 Maintenance and testing

Action of the pumps is automatic and normally no maintenance is required. If trouble is experienced with the fuel supply the first approach should be to ensure that there are no leaks or obstructions in the fuel line. Should the pump then become suspect, a quick check can be made by disconnecting the pipe at the pump outlet, engaging the auxiliary clutch control if fitted and turning the engine by the starter motor, when fuel should spurt from the outlet. Another test is to disconnect the inlet union and hold a finger over it whilst again turning the engine by the starter motor, when suction should be felt. With the pump removed from the engine it can be tested for leaks by closing the outlet to the carburetter with a plug, fitting a rubber hose on the inlet opening and immersing the whole pump in a container filled with clean petrol. Compressed air is then blown through the rubber hose at a pressure of $1\frac{1}{2}$ to $4\frac{1}{2}$ lb/sq in, when bubbles of escaping air will indicate either a defective diaphragm or leaking gaskets.

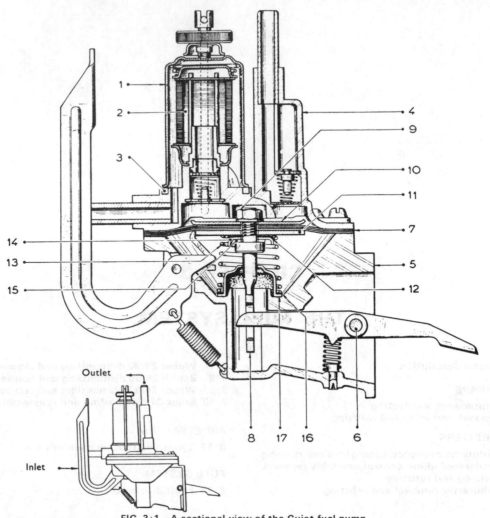

FIG 3 : 1   A sectional view of the Guiot fuel pump

Key to Fig 3 : 1   1 Filter cover   2 Filter   3 Cover gasket   4 Upper body   5 Lower body   6 Lever pin
7 Assembly of four diaphragms   8 Pushrod   9 Nut   10 Upper support washer   11 Lower support washer
12 Gasket   13 Spring   14 Cup   15 Gasket   16 Cap pressure washer   17 Sealing cap
Note:The inlet and outlet valves are located in the pump cover

3:3 Removal, servicing and refitting

To remove a fuel pump, disconnect the inlet and out-let pipes, remove the retaining nuts and withdraw the pump and its gasket.

The overhaul of a Guiot pump is undertaken as follows, referring to **FIG 3 : 1**:

1 Remove the filter cover 1 and disengage the filter 2. Extract the cover joint 3.

2 Disengage the upper part of the pump 4 from the body 5. Drive out the pin 6 from the operating lever. Disengage the diaphragm assembly 7 and the pushrod 8.

3 Unscrew the nut 9 and withdraw the serrated washer. Disengage the rod 8, the upper washer 10, the set of four diaphragms 7, the lower support washer 11, the joint 12, the spring 13, the cup 14, the joint 15, the cap pressure washer 16 and the sealing cap 17.

4 The seats of the inlet and outlet valves are set in the cover of the pump. If the valves are ineffective it will be necessary to replace the pump. Clean the components.

5 Reassemble the pump by locating the sealing cap 17 on the pushrod 8. Continue to assemble on the rod 8 in order, the cap pressure washer 16, the joint 15, the cup 14, the joint 12, the spring 13, the end with the large diameter on the washer 16. Fit the lower support washer 11, the set of four diaphragm washers 7, the upper support washer 10, the serrated washer and screw on the nut 9 without tightening.

6 Insert the diaphragm and pushrod assembly in the pump body. Fit the operating lever, press in the pin 6 and peen it lightly.

7 Make sure that the screw holes in the diaphragms correspond with the threaded holes in the pump body and tighten the nut 9.

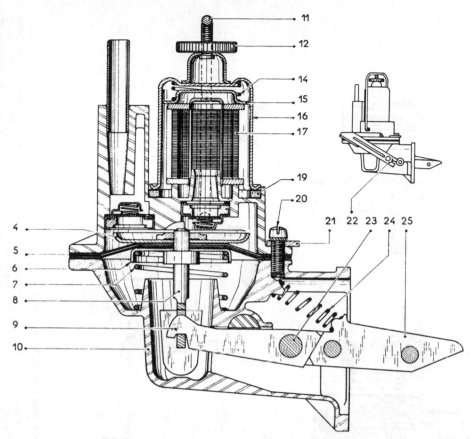

FIG 3:2 A sectional view of the AC/RH fuel pump

Key to Fig 3:2   4 Cup   5 Diaphragm assembly   6 Cup   7 Spring   8 Spindle   9 Relay lever   10 Lower body
11 U-clip   12 Nut   14 Spring   15 Cup   16 Bowl   17 Filter   19 Joint   20 Screws   21 Clip   22 Lever stop
23 Spindle   24 Spring   25 Lever   Note: The valves are incorporated in the pump cover

8 Connect the upper part of the pump 4 to the body 5. **The diaphragms should be fitted dry.** Tighten the screws without inserting washers.

9 Assemble the filter cover joint 3 and fit the filter element 2. Fit the filter cover 1 and tighten the knurled nut.

For the overhaul of an AC pump proceed as follows, referring to **FIG 3:2** :

1 Unscrew the nut 12 and remove the bowl 16. Remove the cup 15 and the spring 14 from the bowl 16. Remove the filter 17 and the joint 19 from the bowl.

2 Mark the position of the cover on the pump body. Remove the screws 20 the clip 21 and the lever stop 22 and detach the cover from the pump body.

3 Tap out the spindle 23, then remove the lever 25 and the spring 24. Unhook the relay lever 9 from the spindle 8 and remove the diaphragm assembly 5, the cups 4 and 6, the spindle 8, the spring 7 and the relay lever 9 from the pump body. Clean the parts with petrol.

4 The valve seats are incorporated in the pump cover and if the valves are unserviceable the pump should be renewed.

5 To reassemble the pump, locate the relay lever 9 and the spring 7 in the pump body. Offer up the assembly spindle 8, the diaphragm 5 and the cups 4 and 6. Hook the eye of the spindle 8 to the relay lever 9. Fit the lever 25 and the spindle 23, tightening it lightly. Fit the spring 24.

6 Make sure that the holes in the diaphragms for the screws are correctly aligned with the threaded bores in the pump body. Fit the pump cover on the body, so that the marks made when dismantling coincide. If not, position the cover so that, when allowing the U-clip to fall towards the front, the nut 12 is against the front end of the pump fixing flange. It is important that the diaphragms should be fitted dry.

7 Fit the stop 22 for the lever 25. Tighten the screws securing the cover using spring washers. Assemble the joint 19 of the bowl and the filter 17. Locate the spring 14 and the cup 15 in the bowl 16 and assemble to the pump. Lightly tighten the nut 12.

To refit the pumps, use a new cork gasket and locate the pump in position on the crankcase. Fit the front nut with a serrated or spring washer without tightening to hold the pump in position. Assemble the rear nut with shakeproof washer and tighten both nuts. Connect the inlet and outlet pipes and prime the pump with the lever.

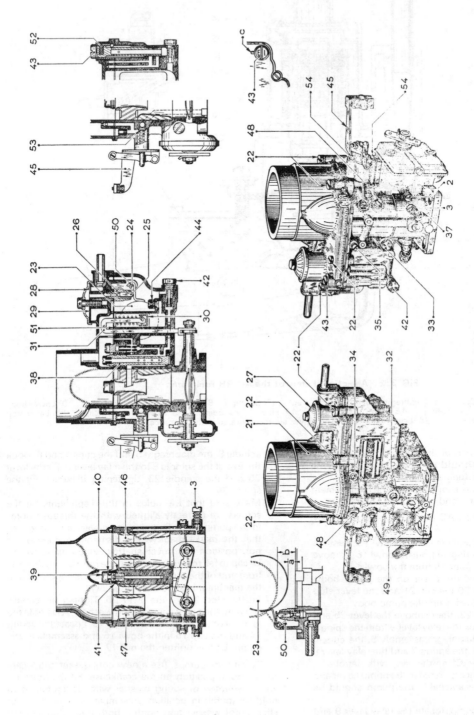

FIG 3:3   Details of the Weber 24/30 DCZC1 carburetter

Key to Fig 3:3   2 Throttle valve screw   3 Volume screw   21 Cover   22 Fixing screw   23 Floats   24 Pin   25 Needle valve   26 Needle valve seat   27 Cover
28 Joint   29 Filter gauze   30 Accelerator pump   31 Connecting rod   32 Main jet   33 Main jet   34 Slow-running jet   35 Slow-running jet   37 Volume screw spring
38 Emulsion tubes   39 Pump delivery valve   40 Joints   41 Pump jet joint   42 Starter jet   43 Starter corrector (24/30 DCLC)   44 Pump inlet valve   45 Choke control
46 Venturi sleeve   47 Venturi sleeve   48 Screws   49 Throttle valve stop screw   50 Stop   51 Accelerator pump retaining plate   52 Starter corrector housing
53 Choke control seating   54 Screws

CARBURETTERS

3:4 Routine maintenance, tuning for slow-running

Ordinary maintenance work necessary to keep the carburetters in good working order is mainly concerned with the periodic cleaning of jets and float chambers which can be performed without extensive dismantling and which is described in the general instructions given later for the overhaul of the particular carburetters concerned.

Adjustments for slow-running should be carried out with the engine hot, the choke control fully closed and the ignition control in the midway position. The adjustments to be made are critical in DS cars with relation to the automatic control of clutch and gearchange operation, and it is essential that a revolution counter is employed which may be either mechanical or electrical. Service agents use a mechanical instrument 2434.T with drive 2423.T or 2433.T driven by the high pressure pump pulley. Alternatively an electrical revolution counter 2436.T may be used, which is connected to the output yellow terminal of the upper coil with two-coil ignition. When using the mechanical revolution counter, to compensate for either belt slip or irregular engine performance the bleed screw of the pressure control valve should be unscrewed or the manual height control lever placed in the low position

In DS19 cars before March, 1956, with an accelerator control with two rods, adjust the slow-running to 550 rev/min. First ensure that the accelerator works normally and that the spring returns the throttle butterfly to the closed position. Referring to **FIG 3:3** showing details of the Weber 24/30 carburetter, proceed as follows:

1 Adjust the screw 2 of the throttle valve and the volume screw 3 controlling the richness of the mixture for idling. Set the screw 2 to give the minimum opening of the secondary throttle which will allow the engine to idle evenly.

2 Turn the volume screw 3 to increase the richness of the mixture to give the high speed at the throttle opening already determined. In order to reduce the speed to that desired unscrew the screw 2.

3 After each alteration to the setting of the secondary throttle valve screw 2 give the throttle a flick open and shut to ensure that the throttle returns fully to the stop on the screw.

4 Remove the tube between the carburetter and the air cleaner silencer. Press the accelerator pedal right down. If necessary adjust the maximum opening of the throttle valve by adjusting only on the inside accelerator control rod on the engine side. Connect the tube to the carburetter.

5 Press down the accelerator slightly to the point where increased resistance is felt on the control. Hold the accelerator in this position. Check the speed of the engine, which should be from 950 to 1000 rev/min. If necessary adjust the outside accelerator control rod. On no account must the inside rod be adjusted.

In cars between March, 1956 and March, 1961 with a single rod accelerator control and accelerated idling, refer to **FIG 3:4** and proceed as follows:

1 Unhook the spring 13 by removing it from the support tube 14. Pull the spring upwards to disengage it from the accelerator control.

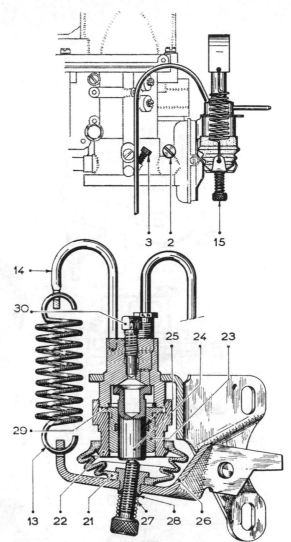

FIG 3:4 Accelerated idling control assembly

Key to Fig 3:4   2 Mixture screw   3 Throttle screw
13 Spring   14 Support tube   15 Adjusting screw
21 Dust cover   22 Cap   23 Cylinder   24 Piston
25 Seal   26 Lever   27 Spring   28 Washer   29 Seal
30 Bleed screw

2 Adjust the slow-running on a Weber carburetter as described in the preceding operations.

3 On a Zenith carburetter (see **FIG 3:5**), adjust the slow-running screw 36 and the screw 30 controlling the richness of the mixture for idling, then continuing as previously described.

4 Check the maximum opening of the throttle valve as in the previous Operation 4. Adjust the accelerator rod (see previous Operation 5).

5 To adjust the accelerated idling (see **FIG 3:4**) hook the spring 13 in position by pressing on the support tube 14. Adjust the screw 15 in order to obtain a speed which exceeds the speed at which the clutch drags by

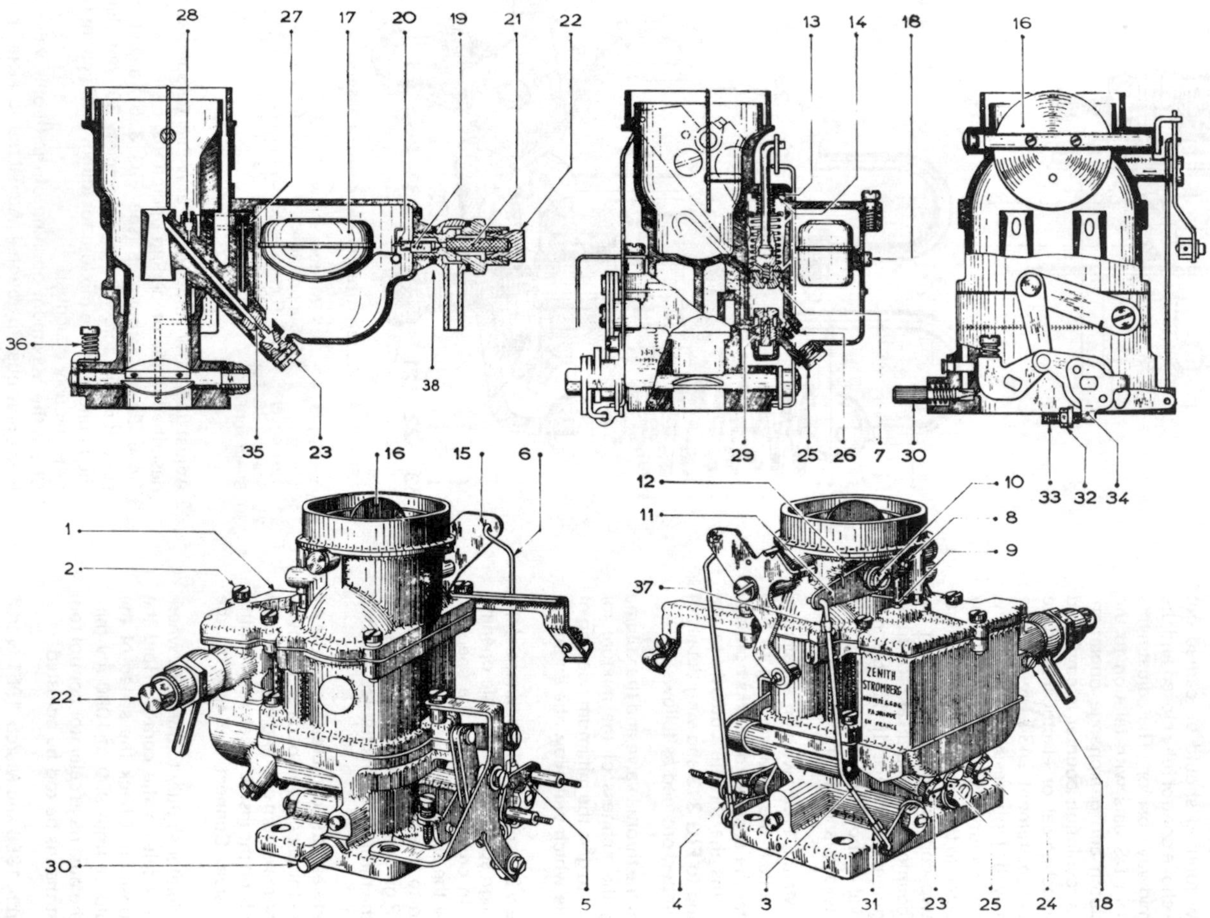

FIG 3:5 Details of the Zenith 24/30 EEAC carburetter

Key to Fig 3:5   1 Cover   2 Fixing screws   3 Connecting rod   4 Retaining clip   5 Throttle control   6 Connecting rod   7 Accelerator pump   8 Pin   9 Rod
10 Screw   11 Lever   12 Spring   13 Rubber washer   14 Steel washer   15 Choke control lever   16 Choke   17 Float   18 Pin   19 Needle valve   20 Connecting pin
21 Filter   22 Plug   23 Plug   24 Plug   25 Plug   26 Pump inlet   27 Slow-running jets   28 Emulsion tubes   29 Pump delivery valve   30 Volume screw   31 Retaining clip
32 Locknut   33 Screw   34 Butterfly stop   35 Main jets   36 Slow-running screw   37 Retainer   38 Joint

150 rev/min (900 $\pm$ 25 rev/min). In practice this adjustment should be carried out after the adjustment of the clutch drag (see **Chapter 6**).

In cars since March, 1961, with accelerated idling incorporated in the carburetter, refer to **FIG 3 : 6** showing details of the Weber 24/32 carburetter and proceed as follows to adjust the slow-running:

1 Without using force, screw in the accelerated idling adjusting screw 39. Turn the secondary butterfly stop screw 35 in order to obtain a speed of approximately 550 rev/min. Also turn the mixture adjustment screw 37 in one direction or the other slowly in order to obtain the maximum speed.

2 Slowly unscrew the stop screw 35 in order to bring the speed to 550 to 600 rev/min. If the running is unstable, again very slowly turn the mixture adjustment screw 37.

3 Before adjusting the accelerated idling it is necessary to adjust the clutch drag. Start the engine, engage first speed and accelerate very lightly, when the clutch drag of the car should be between 700 and 750 rev/min. If otherwise, stop the engine and unlock the locknut of the adjusting screw on the pulley end of the centrifugal regulator. If the clutch drags at a speed less than 700 rev/min tighten the screw. Unscrew it if the clutch drags at a speed greater than 750 rev/min. Lock the locknut.

4 To adjust the accelerated idling, unscrew the screw 39 with the engine idling, until a speed between 875 and 925 rev/min is obtained.

On ID19 cars fitted with a Solex 34 carburetter (see **FIG 3 : 7**), the slow-running adjustment is made as follows:

1 Screw, without forcing, the mixture screw 29 to the bottom and then unscrew it one and a half turns. This is intended to clear the pipe if partially obstructed.

2 Adjust this screw so as to obtain the highest engine speed with the engine running smoothly and regularly.

3 Adjust screw 4 of the butterfly until a speed of 550 to 600 rev/min is obtained.

3 : 5 Accelerated idling control assembly removal, servicing and refitting

To disconnect the accelerated idling control assembly (see **FIG 3 : 4**) in DS19 cars, first release the pressure in the front brake system by means of the bleed screw 30 at the rear of the assembly. Then for cars before January, 1959, proceed as follows:

1 Disconnect the clips retaining the slow-running feed pipe to the rear support of the lefthand brake unit and also to the closing plate of the inlet manifold.

2 Unscrew the assembly support from the carburetter and remove the assembly and pipe from the car. Note that on later cars it is unnecessary to remove the feed pipe, disconnecting it only from the accelerated idling control.

Referring to **FIG 3 : 4**, dismantling and reassembly operations are as follows:

1 Remove the support 14 from the body of the assembly, then remove the spring 13 from the lever 26. Remove also the adjusting screw 15, the spring 27 and the washer 28 from the lever 26.

2 Disengage the dust cover 21 from the cap 22 and from the lever 26. Unscrew the cap 22, holding the assembly by its support, and remove the assembly of the cylinder 23 and the piston 24. Disengage the seal 29 between the cylinder and body.

3 Disengage the piston 24 from the cylinder 23. Remove the ring seal 25 from the cylinder 23 using a small brass wire hook. Remove the bleed screw 30.

4 Clean the parts with alcohol only. Do not use trichlorethylene. In the case of slight scratches being found on the piston a light rubbing with No. 600 abrasive paper smeared in alcohol is permitted. Clean with alcohol and blow with compressed air. When refitting the parts they should be smeared with hydraulic fluid. Reassemble the components in the reverse order of their removal.

Refitting operations are as follows, noting that on cars before January, 1959 it is preferable to fit a later type of accelerated idling control:

1 Offer up the control, inserting the washers between the carburetter and the support. Place the assembly in position at the top of the slots and tighten the fixing screws, using plain and spring washers.

2 In cars since January, 1959, connect the feed pipe to the control assembly.

3 In earlier cars, locate the rubber guides and fixing plates on the pipe. Offer up the pipe and connect the unions of the control assembly and lefthand brake unit. Fix the rear clip fixing the feed pipe to the inlet manifold closing plate with spring washers under the heads of the screws. Fix the front clip fixing the feed pipe to the rear support of the lefthand brake unit. Insert a lockwasher or place a washer under the head of the fixing screw. Lock the two upper fixing screws of the brake unit using locking wire so as to avoid rotation in the unscrewing direction, or turn over the lockwashers. Make sure that the rubber guide for the pipe is in position in the fixing clip on the lefthand brake unit.

4 Bleed the control assembly as described for bleeding the brake system in the Chapter covering the brakes. Check for leakage by pressing on the brake pedal and retaining the pressure for a few minutes.

5 Referring to **Section 3 : 4**, check the slow-running requirements of 550 to 650 rev/min and the clutch drag at 700 to 750 rev/min. Adjust the accelerated idling speed to a speed of between 875 to 925 rev/min.

3 : 6 Carburetter removal and refitting

Operations to remove the carburetters fitted on DS19 cars are as follows:

1 Disconnect the petrol feed pipe from the carburetter. Loosen the clip fixing the tube between the carburetter and the air filter and remove the tube. Disconnect the choke control.

2 In cars before March, 1961, disconnect the accelerated idling control, taking care of the washers between the control and the carburetter.

3 In cars since March, 1961, disconnect the carburetter union of the tube to the lefthand brake unit.

4 Disconnect the cruciform coupling controlling the throttle valves on the carburetter. Remove the carburetter together with its gasket.

The Solex carburetter on ID19 cars is removed by following Operations 1, 2 and 3. Disconnect also the accelerator control cable and the vacuum pipe union.

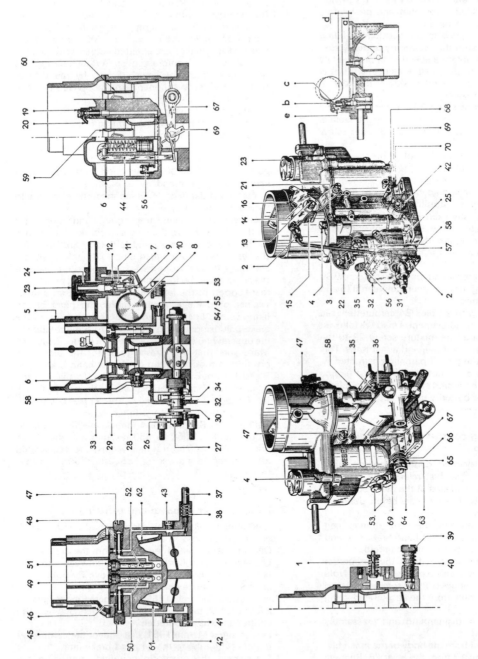

FIG 3:6 Details of the Weber 24/32 DDC carburetter

Key to Fig 3:6 1 Accelerated idling valve 2 Retaining plates 3 Rod 4 Screw 5 Cover 6 Joint 7 Pin 8 Float 9 Needle valve 10 Hook 11 Needle valve seat 12 Joint 13 Screw 14 Spring 15 Return spring 16 Spring 19 Accelerator pump delivery valve 20 Pump jet 21 Screw 22 Lever 23 Cap 24 Filter 25 Joint 26 Safety washer 27 Nut 28 Butterfly control lever 29 Spacing washer 30 Lever 31 Screw 32 Cover 33 Spacing sleeve 34 Primary toothed quadrant 35 Butterfly stop screw 36 Spring 37 Slow-running adjusting screw 38 Spring 39 Accelerated idling adjusting screw 40 Spring 41 Duct inspecting screw 42 Duct inspecting screw 43 Duct inspecting screw 44 Connecting rod 45 Jet carrier 46 Slow-running jet 47 Jet carrier 48 Slow-running jet 49 Air jet 50 Emulsion tube 51 Air jet 52 Emulsion tube 53 Plugs 54 Main jet 55 Main jet 56 Accelerator pump 57 Safety tongue 58 Screws 59 Aligner 60 Aligner 61 Choke 62 Choke 63 Safety washer 64 Nut 65 Spring washer 66 Circlips 67 Pump control lever 68 Nut 69 Nut 70 Spring washer **a, b, c, d, e** Adjustments for float level (see text)

52

Refitting is undertaken by following the removal operations in reverse order. When coupling up the accelerated idling control on DS cars, insert a plain washer between the accelerated idling control and the carburetter and the second plain washer and the spring washer under the heads of the screws.

3:7 Weber 24/30 dismantling and reassembly

Referring to **FIG 3:3**, dismantling operations on Weber 24/30 carburetters are undertaken as follows:

1 Unscrew the fixing screws 22 and raise the cover 21 vertically in order to disengage the floats 23. Remove the paper joint.
2 Remove the floats 23 by withdrawing the pin 24. Remove the needle valve 25 and unscrew the needle valve seat 26. If any part is defective, renew the assembly.
3 Remove the cover 27 from the filter. Disengage the joint 28 and the filter gauze 29. Clean the parts with petrol and blow through the channels with compressed air.
4 Remove the accelerator pump 30 by drawing out the connecting rod 31.
5 Remove the main jets 32 and 33, the slow-running jets 34 and 35 and the volume screw 3 with its spring 37. Remove the emulsion tubes 38.
6 Remove the pump delivery valve 39. Be careful not to mislay the joints 40 and 41.
7 Remove the starter jet 42 and the corrector 43 (24/30.DCLC). Remove the pump inlet valve 44 and the complete choke control 45.
8 Detach the screw 48 and remove the primary and secondary venturi sleeves 46 and 47.
9 Clean the parts in petrol and blow out the passages in the carburetter and the different jets carefully with compressed air. Never use wire or anything which may enlarge the jets. Note that it is essential that the disassembly of the carburetter should be limited to the operations described, as otherwise it may be made unusable. Do not disturb the adjustment of the stop screw 49 of the throttle valve in the first body. The adjustment is carried out by the makers and is peculiar to each carburetter.

Reassembly is undertaken as follows:

1 Fit the seat 26 of the needle valve 25 with its aluminium joint and assemble the needle valve 25 in position.
2 Locate the floats 23 in position and fit the pin 24. For the floats to be at their correct levels, the dimension 'a' between the float and the surface of the cover should be 5 $\pm$ .5 mm with the cover 21 of the carburetter turned towards the front. Finally ensure that the movement 'b' of the float 23 is 12 $\pm$ .5 mm. If necessary modify the position of the stop 50.
3 Locate the filter gauze 29 in position, the joint 28, the cover 27 and the screw. Tighten the screw, fitting a joint under the head. If the filter was fitted with a rubber joint it must be replaced by joint of a newer type.
4 Assemble the accelerator pump 30 and engage the retaining plate 51 as far as possible.
5 Assemble the primary venturi slow-running jet 34, the primary venturi main jet 32, the secondary venturi slow-running jet 35, and the secondary venturi main

jet 33. Fit copper joints under the heads of the jet carriers. Fit the volume screw 3 and the spring 37.
6 Fit the emulsion tube assemblies on the primary and secondary venturi sides. Note that on the secondary venturi side the DCZC1 carburetter has a 240 air jet and the DCLC carburetter a 230 air jet.
7 Fit the pump jet 41 and the delivery valve 39, fitting the joint 40 between the pump jet and the head of the valve.
8 Fit the starter jet 42 with an aluminium joint under the head. Fit the starter corrector 43 (DCLC carburetter) in its housing 52.
9 Assemble the pump feed valve 44 and the primary and secondary venturi sleeves 46 and 47. Tighten the screws 48.
10 Check that there is no dirt on the seating 53 of the choke control 45 and fit it in place. Tighten the screws 54.
11 Fit the joint of the cover 21 and engage the cover vertically on the body. Tighten the fixing screws 22 with serrated washers under the heads.
12 On the 24/30 DCLC carburetter, the correct working of the starter is dependent upon the temperature. Hence turn the corrector 43 so that the letter E in summer or the letter I in winter is on the same side as the mark C shown on the righthand side of **FIG 3:3**

3:8 Zenith 24/30 dismantling and reassembly

Referring to **FIG 3:5**, dismantling operations on the Zenith 24/30 carburetter are undertaken as follows:

1 Disengage the connecting rod 3 and the retainer 37. Turn the throttle control 5 in order to disengage the connecting rod 6 after having removed the retaining clip 4.
2 Remove the retaining screws 2 and lift the cover 1 vertically in order to avoid damage to the accelerator pump 7. Remove the paper joint from the cover.
3 Remove the pin 8, the screw 10, the lever 11, the spring 12 and the piston from the accelerator pump.
4 Disengage the rubber washer 13 and the steel washer 14 from the rod 9.
5 Remove the connecting rod 6 from the control lever 15 of the choke 16. Clean the parts with petrol.
6 Remove the float 17 with the needle valve 19 by unscrewing the pin 18. The needle valve 19 is attached to the float 17 by the connecting pin 20.
7 Remove in the following order the plug 22, the filter 21, the plugs 23, 24 and 25, the pump inlet jet 26, the slow-running jets 27, the emulsion tubes 28, the accelerator pump delivery valve 29, the spring and volume screw 30, the retaining clip 31, the connecting rod 3 and the main jets 35.
8 Clean the parts with petrol and blow through with compressed air. Do not use wire to clean the jets.

Reassembly operations are in the main the reverse of those undertaken when dismantling. Particular features to observe are:

1 To regulate the closing of the butterfly of the first body, unscrew the locknut 32 and the screw 33 until the butterfly is totally closed. Then bring the screw 33 into contact with the stop 34 and tighten the screw 33 exactly $\frac{3}{4}$ of a turn. Tighten the locknut 32.

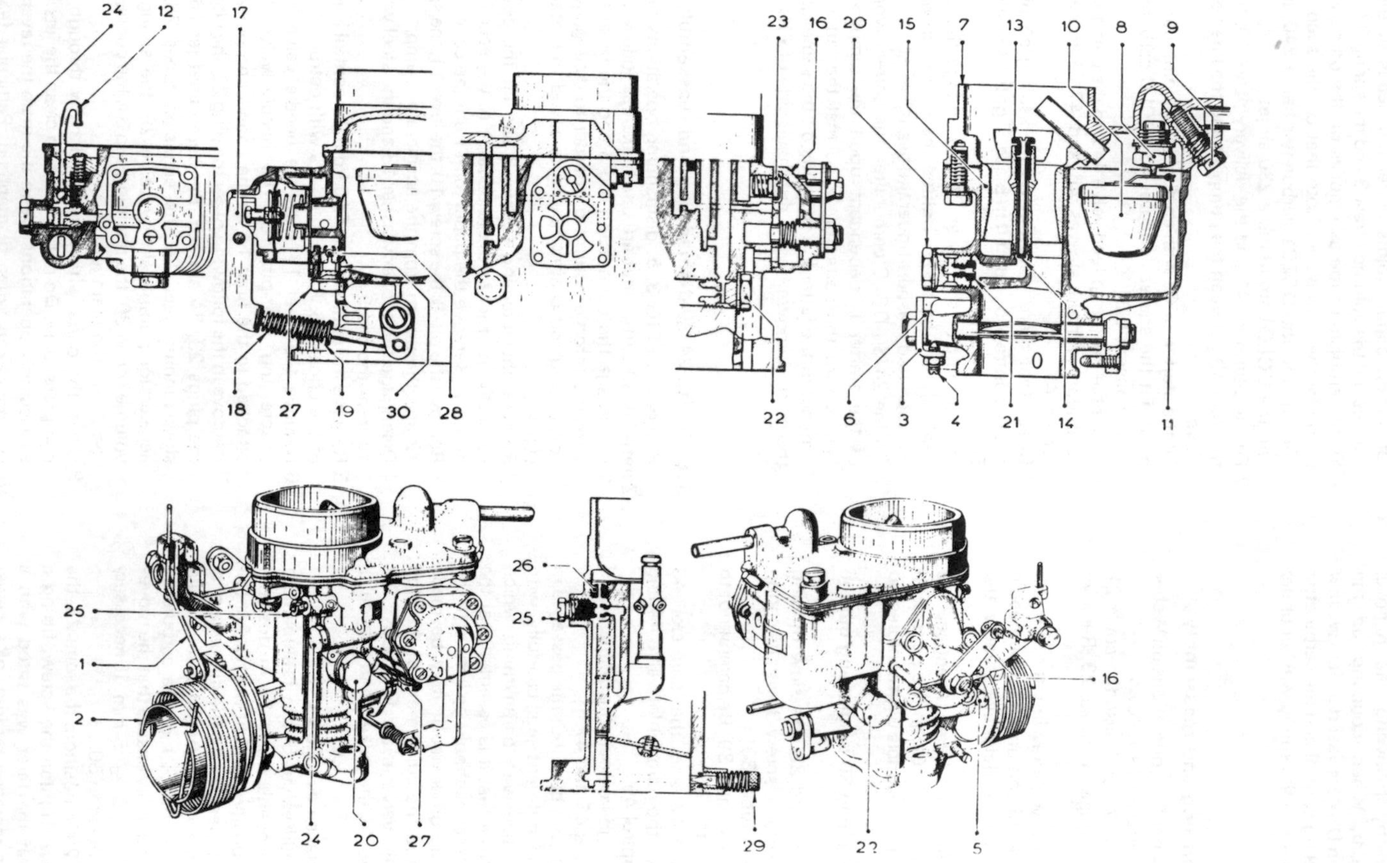

FIG 3:7 Details of the Solex 34 PBIC carburetter

Key to Fig 3:7 1 Spring 2 Throttle control 3 Support 4 Butterfly regulating screw 5 Throttle stop screw 6 Washer 7 Float chamber cover 8 Needle valve 9 Filter plug 10 Float 11 Float spindle 12 Injector 13 Air correction jet 14 Emulsion tube 15 Choke tube 16 Accelerator pump 17 Pump lever 18 Spring 19 Washer 20 Main jet carrier 21 Main jet 22 Starter petrol jet 23 Starter air jet 24 Pump jet 25 Slow-running jet 26 Idling air bleed 27 Ball seat 28 Pump inlet valve ball 29 Volume control screw 30 Pump valve filter

2 Adjustment of the fuel level is carried out with the carburetter fitted on the car and the cover removed. Operations are as follows:

(a) Operate the fuel pump by hand, until the level of the fuel is stabilized in the float chamber.

(b) Using a straightedge measure the distance between the joint face for the cover on the float chamber and the upper level of the petrol. This dimension should be taken at four different points and the average should be between 13 and 16 mm.

(c) If the average dimension is less than 13 mm, increase the thickness of the joint 38. If the average is greater than 16 mm, reduce the thickness of the joint 38.

3:9 Weber 24/32 dismantling and reassembly

Referring to **FIG 3:6**, dismantling operations on the Weber 24/32 carburetter are undertaken as follows:

1 Remove the accelerated idling control apparatus and remove the joint between the apparatus and the carburetter. Remove the accelerated idling valve 1 complete, the retaining plates 2, the rod 3 and the screw 4. Remove the cover 5 complete and its joint 6.

2 Remove the pin 7 and disengage the float 8, the needle valve 9 and its hook 10. Remove the joint 6, also the needle valve seat 11 and its joint 12.

3 Remove the screw 13 and disengage the choke control lever 14, the return spring 15 and the spring 16 for the adjustment of the choke shutter opening.

4 Remove the screw 21 and disengage the lever 22 supporting the choke control sheath.

5 Remove the pump delivery valve 19 and its jet 20. Remove the cap 23 and disengage the filter 24.

6 Disengage the safety washer 26 and remove the nut 27, the butterfly control lever 28, the spacing washer 29 and the lever 30.

7 Remove the screw 31 and disengage the cover 32, the spacing sleeve 33 and the primary toothed quadrant 34.

8 Remove the butterfly adjusting screw 35 and its spring 36, but do not remove the butterfly adjusting screw 25.

9 Remove the slow-running adjusting screw 37 and its spring 38, also the accelerated idling adjusting screw 39 and its spring 40.

10 Remove the duct inspection screws 41, 42 and 43.

11 Remove the accelerator pump by drawing out the connecting rod 44.

12 Remove the jet carrier 45 and slow-running jet 46 from the primary body, also the jet carrier 47 and slow-running jet 48 from the secondary body.

13 Remove the air jet (automatic) 49 from the primary body and the emulsion tube 50, also the air jet (automatic) 51 from the secondary body and the emulsion tube 52.

14 Remove the plugs 53. Remove the main jet 54 from the primary body and the main jet 55 from the secondary body. Remove the valve from the pump 56.

15 Disengage the safety tongue 57. Remove the screws 58 securing the chokes 61 and 62. Remove the aligners 59 and 60. Disengage the choke 61 from the primary body and the choke 62 from the secondary body.

16 Disengage the safety washer 63 and remove the nut 64. Remove the spacing washer 65 the circlips 66 and the pump control lever 67. Remove the nut 68 and its spring washer, then disengage the cam 69 controlling the pump and the spacing washer 70.

17 Clean the parts in petrol and blow out the passages in the carburetter and the different jets carefully with compressed air. The same remarks apply as in the first Operation 9 of **Section 3:7**.

Reassembly operations are in general the reverse of those undertaken when dismantling. Particular features to observe are:

1 To adjust the level of the float, referring to the diagram on the righthand side of **FIG 3:6**, with the cover turned over the distance 'a' between the float (at each side) and the cover joint must be 8 $\pm$ .5 mm. If not, set the strips 'b'. The strip 'c' must rest perpendicular to the centre line of the needle valve 9. With the cover in its normal position the distance 'd' between the float at each side and the cover joint must be 13 $\pm$ .5 mm. If not, set the strip 'e'.

2 Note that the emulsion tubes 50 and 52 are identical, as are also the aligners 59 and 60.

3:10 Solex 34 dismantling and reassembly

Referring to **FIG 3:7**, dismantling operations on the Solex 34 carburetter are undertaken as follows:

1 Remove the spring 1 of the throttle control 2 controlling the opening of the throttle (cars before October 1960) and disconnect the throttle control 2 from the carburetter. Remove the support 3 of the regulating screws 4 and 5 and remove the washer 6.

2 Remove the top float chamber cover 7 from the carburetter. Remove the paper gasket. Remove the needle valve 8 and the filter plug 9 from the top of the cover. Remove the float 10 and its spindle 11 from the carburetter.

3 Remove the screws retaining the injector 12 and paper gasket. Remove the air correction jet 13 and withdraw the emulsion tube 14. Remove the choke tube locking screw and the choke tube 15.

4 Remove the accelerator pump 16 from the carburetter body. Remove the pump lever pin 17, the spring 18 and the washer 19. Disconnect the accelerator pump (secured by four screws) from the carburetter and withdraw the gasket. Note that if a pump diaphragm is damaged, a new pump must be fitted. Never remove the diaphragm.

5 Remove the main jet carrier 20 and remove the main jet 21 from the carrier 20. Remove the starter petrol jet 22 and the starter air jet 23. Remove the pump jet 24, the pilot jet 25 and the idling air bleed 26. Remove the seat 27 of the pump inlet valve ball 28 and the volume control screw 29.

6 Clean the parts and blow compressed air through the ducts and the jets. Thoroughly clean the filter plug 9 and the filter 30 of the pump valves 28. Do not use wire to clean the jets.

Reassembly operations are in general the same as those applied to dismantling but in reverse order. New copper gaskets should be fitted to the needle valve 8, the pump inlet valve 28, the pump jet 24 and the starter jets 22 and 23. New paper gaskets are required for the accelerator pump 16, the pump injector 12 and the float chamber cover 7, also a new fibre washer for the main jet carrier 20.

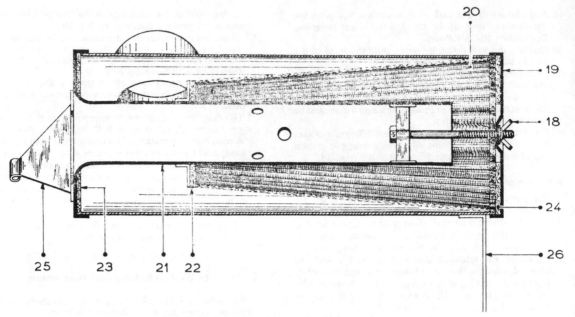

FIG 3:8 A sectional view of the Vokes air cleaner

Key to Fig 3:8   18 Wingnut   19 Cover   20 Filter element   21 Interior tube assembly   22 Felt joint   23 Felt joint
24 Felt joint   25 Rear fixing plate   26 Front fixing plate

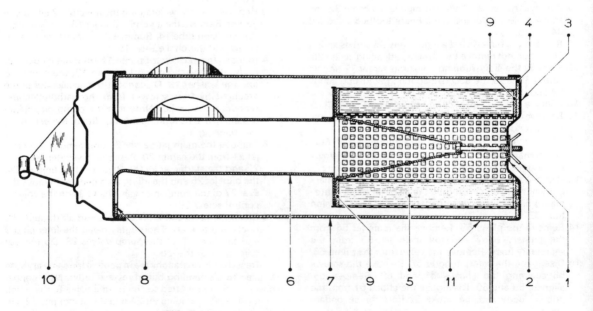

FIG 3:9 A sectional view of the Miofiltre air cleaner

Key to Fig 3:9   1 Wingnut   2 Shakeproof washer   3 Front cover   4 Felt joint   5 Filter element   6 Tube assembly
7 Body   8 Rear cover felt joint   9 Cork joint   10 Rear fixing plate   11 Front fixing plate

AIR CLEANERS

3:11 Types and routine maintenance

On both DS19 and ID19 cars one of two types of air cleaners, or 'air filter silencers' may be fitted, either a Vokes or a Miofiltre type. To remove an air cleaner, loosen the clip on the tube between the air cleaner and the carburetter. Disconnect the tube and in cars before September, 1960, remove the fixing nuts and disengage the air cleaner. In later cars remove the rear retaining nuts from the air cleaner, disengage the retaining strap towards the rear and remove the air cleaner.

An air cleaner element should be removed for inspection and cleaning after each 4000 miles of normal running. In the case of the Vokes type (see **FIG 3:8**), unscrew the wingnut 18, remove the cover 19 and remove the interior tube 21 together with the filter element 20. Remove the filter element 20 from the interior tube 21. Clean the parts. Hold the filter element vertically and release the dust covers by tapping gently with the hand on the ends.

When reassembling the filter element 20 make sure that the felt joints 22 and 23 are securely attached in position. If not, re-attach them with a good adhesive. Engage these parts in the body of the air cleaner. Put the cover 19 in position together with its felt joint 24. Position the rear fixing plate 25 in relation to the front fixing plate 26 and tighten the wingnut 18 and plain washer. For efficient operation the filter element should be under pressure at the two ends, on the felt joints 22 and 24. Make sure that the element is sufficiently compressed by the cover, if not add a second felt washer 22 and attach it to the first one with a good adhesive.

In the case of the Miofiltre type (see **FIG 3:9**), unscrew the wingnut 1 and remove the shakeproof washer 2. Remove the front cover 3 together with its felt joint 4 and disengage the filter element 5 with the cork joint 9. Remove the rear cover and tube assembly 6 from the body 7. Clean the parts. Wash the filter element 5 in petrol. Brush the filter element 5 then blow with compressed air. Then soak the element in engine oil and leave to drain. Reassembly is undertaken by following the dismantling operations in reverse. Make sure that the felt joint 8 for the rear cover is firmly attached in position, otherwise re-attach with adhesive. Also ensure that the filter element 5 is applied correctly to the felt joint 4. If not, add a second felt washer and stick it to the first one.

FUEL SYSTEM

3:12 Fault diagnosis

(a) Leakage or insufficient fuel delivered

1 Air vent in tank restricted
2 Petrol pipes blocked
3 Air leaks at pipe connections
4 Pump or carburetter filters blocked
5 Pump gaskets faulty
6 Pump diaphragm defective
7 Pump valves sticking or seating badly
8 Fuel vaporizing in pipe lines due to heat

(b) Excessive fuel consumption

1 Carburetter needs adjusting
2 Fuel leakage
3 Sticking controls or choke device
4 Dirty air cleaner
5 Excessive engine temperature
6 Brakes binding
7 Tyres under-inflated
8 Idling speed too high
9 Car overloaded

(c) Noisy fuel pump

1 Air leak on suction side and at diaphragm
2 Obstruction in fuel pipe
3 Clogged pump filter

(d) No fuel delivery

1 Float needle stuck
2 Vent in tank blocked
3 Pipe line obstructed
4 Pump diaphragm stiff or damaged
5 Inlet valve in pump stuck open
6 Bad air leak on suction side of pump

CHAPTER 4

THE IGNITION SYSTEM

4:1 Operating principles

In early DS19 cars until July 1959 the ignition system is one in which low-tension current is supplied from the battery to two contact breakers in the same housing (see **FIG 4:1**) and thence to two twin-spark coils. From the opposite ends of each coil high-tension current is supplied to two sparking plugs. As shown in the relative wiring diagram in the Appendix, one coil is connected to the plugs in cylinders 1 and 4 and the other coil to the plugs in cylinders 2 and 3. The result is that in each pair of cylinders an effective firing spark is created at the top of the compression stroke in one cylinder at the same time as an ineffective spark occurs at the top of the exhaust stroke in the other cylinder. This system has no distributor in the normal sense, ignition timing being mechanically controlled according to engine speed by the centrifugal action of weights in the contact breaker housing and by a manual control on the facia panel which enables adjustments to be made for different grades of fuel or for changing conditions while driving. Later DS cars after July, 1959, were fitted with either Ducellier or SEV distributors of conventional design, as used in all ID19 cars, although early models had no vacuum control. The manual control continued to be employed until March,

1961, on DS cars and until April, 1962, on ID cars. In both types of cars a 6-volt system was used until March, 1961, and a 12-volt system in later production.

4:2 Distributor maintenance, contact point adjustment

The distributor, where fitted, must always be kept clean and dry, neglect of which is sometimes the cause of difficult starting in damp weather. As necessary, the cap should be unclipped and the inside and outside of the distributor wiped with a dry cloth. Occasionally, say every 5000 miles or six months, remove the cap, lift out the rotor and apply two drops of engine oil to the felt pad where fitted in the centre of the cam. Do not over-lubricate any part of the distributor, otherwise lubricant may reach the contact breaker points, resulting in burning and difficult starting.

To adjust the contact points in an SEV or Ducellier distributor, remove the cap and rotor arm and turn the engine with the starting handle so that the heel of the moving contact breaker arm is on the highest point of the cam. In the SEV distributor then slacken the fixed contact locking screw 25 in **FIG 4:3** and turn the eccentric screw 29 until the distance between the contact points is

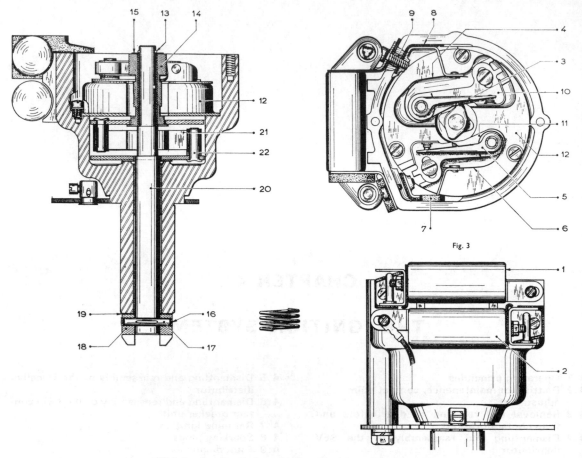

FIG 4:1 Sectional views of the twin contact breaker unit

Key to Fig 4:1   1 Upper capacitor   2 Lower capacitor   3 Moving contact   4 Spring   5 Moving contact   6 Spring
7 Insulator   8 Insulator   9 Insulating sleeve   10 Fixed contact carrier   11 Fixed contact cárrier   12 Contact carrier plate
13 Circlip   14 Cam   15 Thrust washer   16 Spring   17 Pin   18 Driving dog   19 Adjusting washer   20 Shaft
21 Centrifugal advance weights   22 Weight spindle

Fig. 3

.4 mm. Tighten the locking screw and recheck the gap. In the Ducellier distributor, slacken the screw 17 in **FIG 4:4,** insert a screwdriver into the slot in the plate 18 and move the plate as necessary to obtain a contact gap of .4 mm. Tighten the locking screw and recheck the gap. In each case refit the rotor arm squarely, press it firmly down and refit the cap.

With the twin contact breakers employed in the two-coil ignition system in earlier DS19 cars, access is difficult because of the amount of equipment packed under the bonnet, and it is necessary first to remove the induction manifold as described in **Section 4:3.** The contact points of each breaker can then be set to .4 mm, or an average of the two gaps of .4 mm, as for the distributor breakers. But this work may be more appropriately undertaken by a service agent, as in addition to the removal operations special test equipment is required to turn the breakers on a graduated scale if their correct synchronization has to be established.

4:3 Removal and refitting of distributors and twin contact breakers

To remove and refit a distributor, operations are as follows:

1 Disconnect (a) the leads from the sparking plugs and coil (b) the earth lead from the distributor (c) the vacuum pipe from the carburetter.

2 Undo all the fixing screws of the distributor control lever or contact plate (see 12 in **FIG 4:2**) and remove the distributor.

3 To refit, first turn the engine to bring the No. 1 piston (nearest the radiator) to the end of its compression stroke.

4 Insert a 6 mm diameter rod in the hole provided on the lefthand side of the clutch bellhousing under the generator, which partly covers the hole. Turn the engine slowly in its own direction of rotation until the rod engages in the recess in the flywheel. The engine is then at the firing point at 10 deg. advance. **Remove the rod from the flywheel.**

5 Remove the cover and lower the distributor into the housing, turning the rotor to ensure that the shaft dog engages correctly in that of the driving shaft.

6 Connect the leads to the coil and the earth lead to the capacitor 2 in **FIG 4:2**.

7 Adjust the advance control as described in **Section 4:7**. Refit the cover, connect the leads to the sparking plugs and refit the vacuum pipe 7 between the distributor and the carburetter.

The removal and refitting of a twin contact breaker unit is undertaken as follows:

1 Drain the water from the radiator and the cylinder block and use the stop shown in **FIG 1:4** to hold the bonnet open.

2 Disconnect the battery and the sparking plug leads.

3 Remove the hose between the carburetter and the air filter and disconnect the petrol feed pipe from the carburetter, also the heater pipe from the inlet manifold.

4 Remove the ignition coils and bracket assembly.

5 Disconnect the accelerator control from the butterfly control, then disengage the former from its spindle on the scuttle and turn it to the left.

6 Remove the screw retaining the accelerated idling control pipe to the hot spot coverplate on the inlet manifold. Remove the accelerated idling control and the carburetter as described in **Chapter 3**.

7 Take out the two rear upper studs of the inlet manifold and remove it. Remove the dipstick.

8 Disconnect the primary leads, the earth lead and the retaining screw to withdraw the contact breaker unit.

9 To refit the unit, connect the earth lead and locate the contact breaker in its housing. Turn the shaft to ensure that the driving dog engages correctly.

10 Set the firing point by using a 6 mm diameter rod as described in Operation 4 of the preceding instructions for distributors.

11 Set the manual ignition control in the midway position, counting the number of clicks.

12 Reconnect the battery and connect the primary leads on the contact breaker. Connect a test lamp on the red terminal of the lower coil and switch on the ignition.

13 Turn the body of the contact breaker until the contacts break. When the lamp lights at the moment of breaking, tighten the screw fixing the contact breaker in position. Switch off the ignition. Disconnect the test lamp and fit the cover on the contact breaker.

14 Refit the inlet manifold with new gaskets, coating the two rear upper studs with a good sealer.

15 Refit the carburetter and accelerated idling control as described in **Chapter 3**. Reassemble the remaining components in the reverse order of their removal. When refitting the cooling system open the vane of the heater.

16 Adjust the slow-running if necessary as described in **Chapter 3**. Finally check that the heater pipe to the inlet manifold is warm.

4:4 Dismantling and reassembly of the SEV distributor

With the distributor removed from the engine as described in the last Section, dismantling is undertaken as follows:

1 Remove the distributor cover and the rotor. Referring to **FIG 4:3**, disconnect the primary contact strip 1. Remove the capacitor 2 and terminal 3. Disconnect the earth lead from the distributor body and remove the distributor cover retaining springs 27.

2 Remove the retaining spring 4 of the locking pin 5 of the dog 6. Drive out the pin 5. Remove the dog 6 and the clearance adjustment washers 7.

3 Remove the vacuum unit 8, diaphragm control rod 9 and the pilot rod 10.

4 Gently tap the lower end of the spindle to release the contact support plate assembly 12. Rotate the spindle in order to release the contact support plate.

5 Remove the contact support plate thrust ring 14 from the distributor body. Remove the clearance adjustment washers. Unhook the springs 15, remove the rollers 17, the cam 18 and the friction washer.

6 Remove the flat ring 19, the spade terminal 20, terminal 21, contact 22, contact support 23 and the insulating washer 24.

7 Inspect and clean the components with trichlorethylene, blowing off with compressed air. If the surfaces of the contact points are pitted or worn the contacts should be renewed. The capacitor should be checked, but its precise testing requires specialized equipment and the simplest test for a suspected capacitor is by substitution.

To reassemble the distributor, procedure is as follows:

1 Locate the thrust ring 14 of the contact support plate 12 in the body of the distributor. Locate the contact support 23 on the plate 12 together with the screw 25 and the terminal of the primary wire, but do not tighten the locking screw.

2 Also on the contact support fit the contact 22 and the insulating washer 24. Fit the contact spring between the support and the terminal of the primary wire and tighten the nut.

3 Attach the terminal 20 to the contact support 23 and tighten the locking screw 25, using a spring washer. Place the flat ring 19 on the plate.

4 Oil the spindle and place it in the body of the distributor, using two adjusting washers.

5 Fit the driving dog 6, ensuring that the hole for pin 5 in the shaft is offset. Place the pin in position temporarily and insert an adjusting washer 7 between the dog and the distributor. Make sure that the spindle turns freely and that the longitudinal play or end float does not exceed .4 mm. If it does then use another adjusting washer.

6 Drive in the pin and place the pin retaining spring 4 in position, ensuring that the direction of the winding of the spring is lefthand. If not, turn the spring round to reverse the winding.

7 Locate the friction washer on the spindle. Place the cam 18 in position, noting that with the small side of the dog towards the operator the groove in the cam will be on the right.

8 Fit the rollers 17 with the smaller ends upwards. Fit the springs 15 of the advance weights 16.

9 Place the contact support plate assembly 12 in the distributor body on the ring 14. Lubricate the balls with vaseline. Connect the earth lead by means of the screw 26.

10 Fit the pilot rod 10, the diaphragm control rod 9 and the retainer ring on the support plate driving peg.

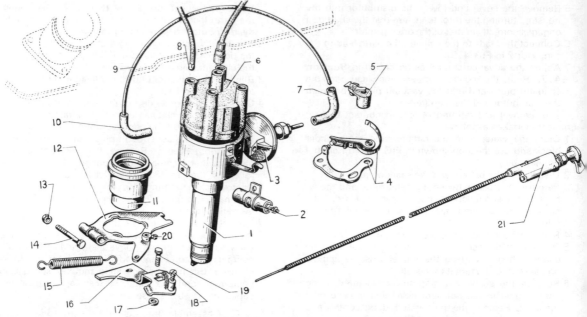

FIG 4 : 2   A part exploded view of a distributor and ignition controls

Key to Fig 4 : 2   1 Distributor, SEV or Ducellier   2 Capacitor   3 Vacuum unit   4 Contact breaker parts   5 Rotor arm
6 Distributor head   7 Rubber connection for vacuum pipe   8 Sparking plug lead with end piece   9 Vacuum pipe   10 Vacuum
pipe connection   11 Distributor housing   12 Distributor lever   13 Nut   14 Screw   15 Distributor return spring   16 Bracket
with trunnion securing distributor   17 Shakeproof washer   18 Screw securing sheath for ignition control   19 Retaining screw
20 Screw securing cable   21 Ignition control

11 Fit the primary terminal 3, the primary contact strip 1, the primary wire to the coil and the capacitor 2.

12 Connect the vacuum diaphragm 8 to the control rod 9 and tighten the diaphragm fixing screws, using spring washers.

13 Fit the distributor cover retaining springs 27 and adjust the nuts 28 to make contact with the flat ring 19. Make sure that the contact support plate assembly 12 can rotate.

14 Slacken the locking screw and adjust the distance between the contact points to .4 mm by turning the eccentric screw 29. Tighten the locking screw.

15 Locate the rotor squarely on the cam, ensuring that the lug is correctly engaged in the groove. Press firmly down. Refit the cover.

4:5 Dismantling and reassembly of the Ducellier distributor

With the distributor removed from the engine as described in **Section 4 : 3**, dismantling is undertaken as follows:

1 Remove the distributor cover and the rotor. Referring to **FIG 4 : 4**, disconnect the wire 1 from the primary terminal 2. Remove the contact support 6 and the capacitor by taking out the screw 3.

2 Remove the screw 4, the spring 5 and the contact support 6. Raise the sector 7 retaining the diaphragm control rod 8, disengage the vacuum unit 9 and disengage the sector 7 from the rod 10.

3 Remove the screw 11, the spring 12 and the earth lead from the distributor. Remove the primary terminal 2.

4 Remove the connecting clip 13, the fibre washer 14 and the movable contact 15, together with the primary wire 16. Remove the rod 10 and the lower thrust washer. Remove the screw 17 and the contact plate 18.

5 Remove the circlip 19 and the washer 20. Disengage the cam 21 with its plate 22 and remove the lower adjusting washer.

6 Remove the spring 23 and the pin 24 locking the spindle 25. Remove the driving dog 26, the celoron washer 27, the spindle 25, the spacing washer 28 and the celoron washer 29.

7 To dismantle the spindle 25, remove the circlips 30 and disengage the balance weights 31, the distance washers 32 and the springs 33 from the plate 34.

Clean the parts with trichlorethylene and proceed to reassemble as follows:

1 Place the distance washers 32 on the spindle 25 and locate the balance weights 31 in position. Hook on the springs 33 and fit the circlips 30. Place the celoron washers on the spindle and locate the assembly in the distributor.

2 Locate the celoron washer 27 on the spindle and fit the driving dog 26. Provisionally fit the pin and ensure that the spindle turns freely. Check that the end float does not exceed .4 mm, if necessary fitting a spacing washer 28 between the shoulder 'a' of the spindle and the celoron washer 29.

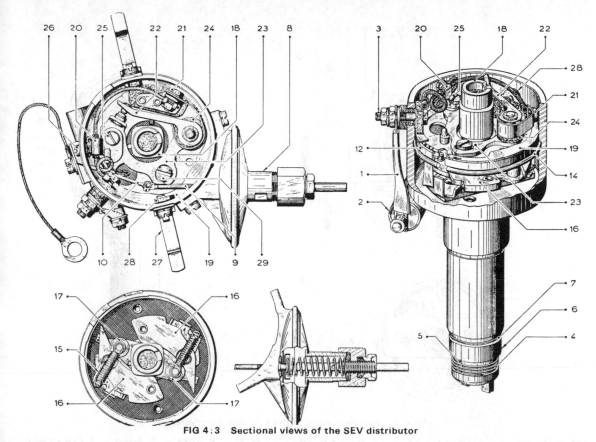

FIG 4:3   Sectional views of the SEV distributor

Key to Fig 4:3   1 Primary contact strip   2 Capacitor (condenser)   3 Primary terminal   4 Retaining spring   5 Locking pin   6 Drive dog   7 Clearance adjustment washers   8 Vacuum diaphragm   9 Diaphragm control rod   10 Pilot rod   12 Contact plate assembly   14 Contact plate thrust ring   15 Springs   16 Advance weights   17 Rollers   18 Cam   19 Flat ring   20 Spade terminal   21 Terminal   22 Contact   23 Contact support   24 Insulating washer   25 Fixed contact locking screw   26 Screw   27 Cover retaining springs   28 Nuts   29 Eccentric screw

3 Fit the assembly again, lubricate the spindle with vaseline and fit the pin 24 and the spring 23. Ensure that the direction of the winding of the spring is left-hand, or otherwise turn the spring round to reverse the winding.

4 Fit the cam 21, inserting a distance washer. The slot in the cam 21 should be opposite the narrow side of the drive dog 26. Fit the washer 20 and the circlip 19.

5 Fit the contact plate 18 and tighten the screw 17 with a plain washer under the head. Fit the rod 10, inserting a thrust washer. Fit the movable contact 15 by engaging the spring 35 between the body of the contact 15 and the insulated stop 36. Place the assembly in the distributor.

6 Fit the spring 12 and tighten the screw 11 fixing the spring and the contact support 6, inserting the terminal of the earth lead and a spring washer.

7 Offer up the vacuum unit 9 and fit the sector 7 and the rod 8.

8 Fit the spring 5 and tighten the screw 4 fixing the spring 5 to the vacuum unit 9 and the contact support 6, using a spring washer.

9 Fit the capacitor, placing a shakeproof washer between the flange 37 fixing the suction unit 9 and the

flange 38 retaining the capacitor. Tighten the screw 3 using a spring washer.

10 Engage the terminal of the primary wire 16 between the head of the terminal 2 and the insulating sleeve 39. Put this assembly in position in the distributor and fit on the terminal 2 the insulating washer 40, a plain washer, the eyelet of the wire 1, a plain washer and the nut 41 tightening the terminal 2.

11 Adjust the contact gaps to .4 mm. Loosen the screw 17 and move the contact plate 18 in the direction required. Tighten the screw 17.

12 Locate the rotor squarely on the cam. Make sure that the dowel is engaged in the slot in the cam, and press firmly down. Refit the cover.

4:6 Dismantling and reassembly of the twin contact breaker unit

Referring to **FIG 4:1**, dismantling operations are as follows:

1 Remove the cover. Remove the upper capacitor 1 and the lower capacitor 2 with their bracket.

2 Remove the moving contact 3 with its spring 4 and the moving contact 5 with its spring 6. Do not mislay the insulators 7 and 8. Remove the insulating sleeves 9.

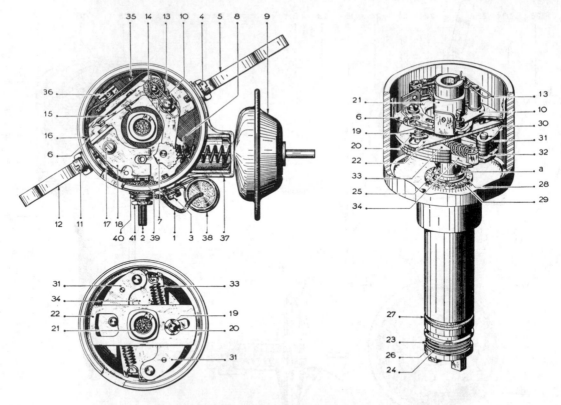

FIG 4:4 Sectional views of the Ducellier distributor

Key to Fig 4:4   1 Primary terminal wire   2 Primary terminal   3 Screw   4 Screw   5 Spring   6 Contact support
7 Sector   8 Diaphragm control rod   9 Vacuum unit   10 Rod   11 Screw   12 Spring   13 Connecting clip   14 Fibre
washer   15 Movable contact   16 Primary wire   17 Screw   18 Contact plate   19 Circlip   20 Washer   21 Cam
22 Plate   23 Spring   24 Locking pin   25 Spindle   26 Drive dog   27 Washer   28 Spacing washer   29 Washers
30 Circlips   31 Balance weights   32 Distance washers   33 Springs   34 Plate   35 Spring   36 Insulated stop
37 Vacuum unit flange   38 Capacitor flange   39 Insulating sleeve   40 Insulating washer   41 Terminal nut

If the surfaces of the contact points are badly pitted the contacts should be renewed.

3 Remove the fixed contact carriers 10 and 11. Remove the contact carrier plate 12.

4 Remove the circlip 13, the cam 14, the thrust washer 15 and the centrifugal advance weights 21.

5 Remove the spring 16 retaining the pin 17 of the driving dog 18. Remove the driving dog and the adjusting washer 19. Remove the shaft 20 from the contact breaker.

6 Clean the parts with trichlorethylene and blow off with compressed air. Make sure that the base of the contact breaker is drilled. If not drill a 3 mm dia. hole in the base of the body.

7 To reassemble, fit the shaft 20 previously oiled, into the body of the contact breaker. Fit the adjusting washer 19 and the driving dog 18 on the shaft. The direction of fitting the driving dog is immaterial. Press in the pin 17.

8 The end float of the shaft should be approximately .1 mm. Renew the adjusting washer 19 if necessary in order to obtain this clearance.

9 Fit the retaining pin 17 and the spring 16. Make sure that the direction of winding of the spring is lefthand, as shown in **FIG 4:1**, in order to avoid oil leakage.

10 Oil the centrifugal balance weight spindles 22 and fit the advance weights 21 on the spindles. Fit the cam 14 on the shaft 20 previously oiled, and the spindles in the centrifugal balance weights 21. Fit the thrust washer 15 and the circlip 13.

11 Put the contact carrier plate 12 in position. Insert spring washers under the heads of the screws.

12 Locate the fixed contact carriers 10 and 11 in position, inserting a plain and a spring washer under the heads of the screws and tightening provisionally.

13 Place the insulating sleeves 9 in position, also the moving contacts 3 and 5 with their springs 4 and 6. Insert the insulator 7 with the edges turned over the current feed for the moving contacts 5.

14 Check the capacitors before assembly as described in the first Operation 7 in **Section 4:4**.

15 Offer up the lower capacitor 2 and attach the current feed. Insert the insulators 8 with the edges turned over under the current feed for the moving contact 3.

16 Offer up the upper capacitor 1 and attach the current feed. Fit the earthing supports of the capacitors on the body of the contact breaker. Insert shakeproof washers under the heads of all retaining screws.

17 Set the contact points of each breaker to .4 mm. Fit the contact breaker cover with serrated washers under the heads of the screws. If it is required finally to bench test the contact breaker, the assistance of a service agent possessing the special apparatus mentioned in **Section 4:2** should be obtained.

4:7 Retiming the ignition

To adjust the ignition advance in DS19 cars before March, 1961, proceed as follows:

1 Put the auxiliary clutch control lever in the engaged position, by pushing forward and then locking in that position by pushing towards the top. The clutch is then in the engaged position.

2 Insert a 6 mm diameter locating pin into the special hole in the clutch bell housing. Turn the engine slowly using the starting handle until the pin falls into the recess in the flywheel. In this position the engine is at the firing point (10 deg. on the flywheel).

3 Fit the lead from a test lamp on the capacitor terminal (red terminal, blue cable) of the lower coil, with the lamp bracket connected to earth.

4 Switch on the ignition. Turn the manual ignition control until the distributor is in the midway position, by putting the control in the 'retard' position and then, by counting the clicks, setting the lever in the middle position of its effective movement.

5 Loosen the screw retaining the distributor. Find the point at which the contact breaker points open, at which moment the lamp should light. Tighten the fixing screw. Note that this operation is made easier by removing the coil and bracket assembly and allowing the assembly to rest on the suspension sphere.

6 Switch off the ignition, remove the test lamp. Remember to remove the locating pin and to move the auxiliary clutch control lever into its original disengaged position.

For DS19 cars since March, 1961, fitted with a distributor, procedure is as follows:

1 Put the engine at the firing point as described in the previous Operations 1 and 2. The engine is then at 12 deg. advance.

2 Screw the adjusting rod until the distributor lever is in the fully advanced position, the distributor lever being in contact with the fixed stop. Then unscrew the adjusting rod exactly two turns, which will allow an eventual increase in the advance of 3 deg.

3 Loosen the screw of the distributor control lever and switch on the ignition. Connect the lead of a test lamp to the capacitor terminal and connect the lamp bracket to earth. Separate the contact points by rotating the body of the distributor anticlockwise. The lamp will light at the moment the contacts separate. Tighten the screws securing the control lever to the distributor.

4 Remove the test lamp and switch off the ignition. Move the auxiliary clutch control lever to its original disengaged position.

FIG 4:5 Plug covering hole for access to rear sparking plug

To adjust the ignition advance in ID19 cars, first put the engine at the firing point as previously described for DS19 cars and **remove the rod from the flywheel.** Then for cars before April, 1962, proceed as follows:

1 Place the advance lever on the facia panel two notches before the fully retarded position. Unscrew the screw securing the control cable on the distributor lever. Place this control lever so that the stop cut into the casing retaining plate is at the end of the notch in the control lever (retard side).

2 Hook on the distributor return spring and secure the control cable to the control lever, without altering its position.

For later ID19 cars the operations are the same as those described for DS19 cars since March, 1961, except that there is no auxiliary clutch control lever to operate.

4:8 Sparking plugs

The sparking plugs specified by the manufacturers for both DS19 and ID19 cars are the Marchal 35B type. The plugs should be removed every 3000 miles or so to check the gaps, also the insulators for cracks and the electrodes for excessive burning. Note that a rubber cap has to be removed from the scuttle flange (see **FIG 4:5**) to give access to the sparking plug on No. 4 cylinder. Remove as far as possible all deposits of carbon and oil from the insulation and electrodes, using only a hard wood spatula and nothing metallic for this job. The sparking plug gaps should be set to between .7 mm and .8 mm (.027 inch and .031 inch) by bending only the side electrode. Use new gaskets when refitting the plugs and remember to refit the cap on the scuttle hole.

Plugs can be cleaned and tested under working pressure on a blasting machine used by most service agents. A deposit of brown to greyish tan colour is the normal condition of a plug used for a mixed period of high and low speed driving. Wet black deposits indicate oil fouling and dry fluffy black deposits are caused by too rich a mixture or misfiring. Badly eroded electrodes will will be a sign of overheating. Excessive idling or low speeds may keep temperatures so low that normal deposits are not burned off.

4:9 Fault diagnosis

(a) Engine will not fire

1 Battery discharged
2 Contact breaker points dirty, pitted or out of adjustment
3 Distributor cap dirty, cracked or 'tracking'
4 Carbon brush inside distributor cap not in contact with rotor
5 Faulty cable or loose connection in low-tension circuit
6 Distributor rotor arm cracked
7 Faulty coil
8 Broken contact breaker spring
9 Contact points stuck open

(b) Engine misfires

1 Check 2, 3, 5 and 7 in (a)
2 Weak contact spring
3 High-tension plug and coil leads cracked or perished
4 Sparking plug loose
5 Sparking plug insulation cracked
6 Sparking plug gap incorrect
7 Ignition timing too far advanced

CHAPTER 5

THE COOLING SYSTEM

5:1 Principle of system

The engine is watercooled by water circulating through the radiator and through water passages in the cylinder block. The cooling system is thermostatically controlled and works under slight pressure, maintained by the spring loading of the radiator cap, which enables a higher temperature to prevail before the water boils. Circulation of the water is by thermosyphon action assisted by a centrifugal water pump bolted to the front face of the cylinder block. A belt drive from a pulley on the end of the camshaft serves the generator and water pump, on the end of which is an eight-bladed nylon fan running in a ducted cowl behind the radiator. In DS19 cars before September, 1960, the low pressure hydraulic pump then used forms an integral part of the water pump assembly (see **FIG 5:1**) and the two are jointly operated. In later DS19 cars and in all ID19 cars the water pump consists of the pump alone of the same basic design.

5:2 Maintenance, flushing, antifreeze, belt tension

Service attention is directed mainly to ensure that the radiator is kept clear of sediment and that the coolant level is topped up as necessary. When checking the water level, do not remove the radiator cap immediately after stopping the engine when it is hot, when the radiator will be slightly under pressure. Start by turning the cap a quarter of a turn so as to bring the cap on to its safety catch and wait while the pressure falls before removing it completely. If the engine is very hot it is advisable to wait until it has cooled down. Radiator hoses and clamps should be periodically inspected for signs of leakage and the radiator cleaned externally to remove dirt, leaves or insects. The fan belt tension should be checked every 5000 miles.

The system should occasionally be flushed out. To drain the system the car should be standing on level ground, the radiator cap removed and the drain taps in the radiator and cylinder block opened. Retain the coolant if it contains antifreeze. Insert a hose from a freshwater tap into the filler neck and allow water to flush through the system with the drain taps open, continuing the operation until the water comes out clear.

In extreme cases the radiator may be removed for reverse flushing under pressure through the bottom hose connection. To remove the radiator after draining the system, first remove the spare wheel and then disengage the air duct from the radiator by removing the two right-hand screws and slackening the two lefthand ones.

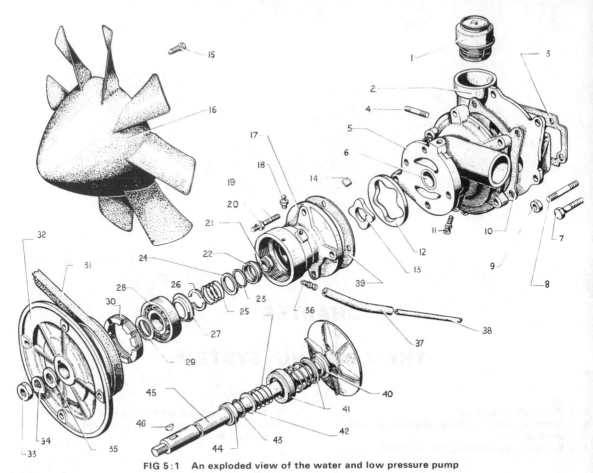

FIG 5:1   An exploded view of the water and low pressure pump

Key to Fig 5:1   1 Thermostat   2 Water pump cover   3 Cover joint, pump to cylinder head   4 Stud securing hot water outlet pipe on pump cover   5 Water pump body   6 Bush   7 Screw securing water pump   8 Stud securing water pump   9 Nut   10 Joint, water pump to cover   11 Union for drain tube   12 Wheel, low pressure pump   13 Pinion, low pressure pump   14 Pinion key   15 Screw securing fan   16 Fan, nylon, eight blades   17 Low pressure pump body   18 Grease nipple for pump ballbearing   19 Screw or stud securing water and low pressure pump bodies   20 Nut   21 Friction washer   22 Cage for ring seal   23 Ring seal   24 Washer   25 Ring seal compression spring   26 Locking ring for ballbearing   27 Retainer   28 Ballbearing, pump spindle   29 Adjusting washer   30 Castellated ring nut   31 Belt driving water pump and generator   32 Pulley with double groove for pump and fan   33 Nut   34 Lockwasher   35 Washer   36 Union for overflow pipe   37 Rubber overflow pipe   38 Nylon overflow pipe   39 Joint, water pump to low pressure pump   40 Washer for sealing gland   41 Seal for water pump   42 Washer for spring   43 Ring seal   44 Cage for ring seal   45 Spindle and impeller for water pump   46 Key for pump pulley

Disconnect the upper hose from the radiator and the lower hose from the steel pipe. Disengage the tie-rod, remove the screws fixing the radiator to the front crossmember and withdraw the radiator. When the cleaning operations are completed, refit the radiator in the reverse manner of its removal, making sure that it is centred so that the fan blades do not touch the cowl. The hoses should be renewed if they show any signs of cracking or interior fouling.

When refilling the system, close the two drain taps and add the coolant slowly to avoid the possibility of air locks. An air bleed screw in the pump casing should be opened when filling and closed when water starts to flow through the bleed orifice. If an antifreeze solution formerly in the cooling system has been retained it may be returned when refilling, but if the available amount is not sufficient to fill the system do not add plain water. Otherwise the solution will be weakened and the freezing point raised. Add additional antifreeze liquid as required. A test may be made with a hydrometer, a 20 per cent solution at 15.6°C (60°F) normally having a specific gravity of 1.032 and a 25 per cent solution a specific gravity of 1.040.

The capacity of the cooling system is 11 litres (approx. 19 pints) of liquid. Antifreeze added by the makers consists of a 20 per cent solution giving protection against 24° of frost (8°F). If antifreeze has not been added, then for this degree of protection 4 pints of water must be drawn from the radiator and 4 pints of ethylene-glycol antifreeze of a reputable make must be added. If a 25 per cent solution giving protection against 34° of frost (—2°F) is desired, 5 pints of water must be drawn

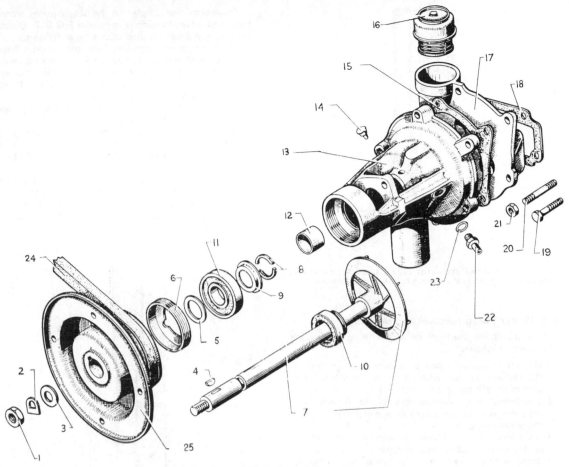

FIG 5:2   An exploded view of the water pump

Key to Fig 5:2   1 Pulley nut   2 Lockwasher   3 Washer   4 Key securing pulley   5 Washer(s)   6 Ring nut locking
ballbearing   7 Pump shaft fitted with impeller   8 Locking segments   9 Cup   10 Sealing washer   11 Ballbearing
12 Porous bronze bush for pump body   13 Water pump body   14 Oiler for pump body sleeve   15 Cover joint   16 Thermostat
17 Pump cover   18 Joint, cover to cylinder head   19 Screw securing water pump   20 Stud securing cover   21 Nut
22 Water outlet union   23 Joint   24 Belt driving water pump and generator   25 Pulley

off and 5 pints of antifreeze added on cars containing
no antifreeze. On a car already having a 20 per cent
solution in the cooling system it will be necessary to
draw off one pint and add one pint of antifreeze. The
manufacturers warn owners against the use of alcohol
as an antifreeze constituent and advise that a check on
the antifreeze solution in the cooling system should be
made each year at the approach of cold weather.

Twin V-belts were used in DS19 cars before September, 1960, to drive the water pump, low pressure
pump, generator and fan, later DS19 cars and all ID19
cars having only one belt. Renewal of the belt or belts
is undertaken by first slackening the screws attaching
the generator and tie-rod, then moving the generator
as far as possible towards the engine. A single belt can
now be released from the driving pulley and from the fan.
Where two belts are used, disengage the first belt by
passing it between the blades of the fan. Bend one fan
blade slightly, but take special care in cold weather when

the fan is more fragile. Disengage the second belt by
first passing it into the front groove of the pulley. New
belts are provided in sets of two, because the belts are
paired with identical dimensions and it is therefore
necessary to renew both belts even if one is in good
condition. Fitting is undertaken as in removal, except in
reverse order of operations.

Adjustment of a belt to its correct tension is important,
as a loose fan belt will cause it to slip on the pulleys,
resulting in engine overheating and the failure of the
generator to charge the battery. If the belt is too tight,
excessive wear may occur on the generator and water
pump bearings and the belt itself may be damaged.
Adjustment is made by moving the generator on its
mountings. Generally the belt tension should be such as
to allow it to be depressed $\frac{1}{2}$ inch midway between the
water pump and generator pulleys. More precise tensioning can be obtained with the use of the special tools
described in **Section 2:11, Chapter 2.**

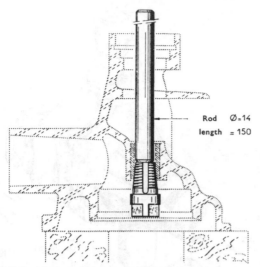

FIG 5:3 Threaded extractor 2291.T used for removing bronze bush from water pump (dimensions in mm)

Rod   ∅=14
length = 150

5:3 Water pump removal and refitting

Operations for the removal and refitting of a water pump are as follows:

1 Drain the radiator as previously described. Disconnect the radiator tie-bar, without disconnecting the feed pipe to the HP pump and remove the fan.
2 Disconnect the adjusting rods of the dynamo and high pressure pump from the water pump. Slacken the water pump belt(s).
3 Disconnect the feed and return pipes from the low pressure pump where incorporated.
4 Disconnect the water pump feed pipe and remove the pump. Scrape the joint face.
5 Note that since October, 1957, the water pumps in DS19 cars are fitted with a new type impeller and new cover which has a water passage of different section. If renewing a former pump, the later type, fitted with an impeller marked with No. DS.231-7 on the outer face, must be fitted with the new cover having a groove on the water outlet.
6 Refit the pump in the reverse order of the removal operations. When fitting the fan, tighten the retaining screws to a torque of **not more than** 7.2 lb ft.

5:4 Water pump dismantling and reassembly

Details of the water and low pressure pump assembly are shown in **FIG 5:1**. For the overhaul of this unit it is necessary that perfect sealing is obtained before refitting, which entails among other matters lapping operations on the thrust washers. Also, if a thrust washer has to be renewed, the pump body has to be heated in a furnace or by other means to specified temperature limits. Special tools are required and for this work it is advised that the assistance of a suitably equipped service agent should be obtained.

Operations are simpler on the water pump alone, an exploded view of which is shown in **FIG 5:2**. Dismantling and reassembling procedures are as follows:

1 With the pump removed from the cylinder head as previously described, turn back the locking tabs and remove the pulley fixing nut 1. Remove the lockwasher 2 and washer 3. Remove the pulley, the key 4 and the adjusting washer or washers 5.
2 Remove the nut 6 from the pump body. A special spanner 1634.T is available if required.
3 Drive out the spindle 7 and impeller by tapping on the end with a bronze drift. Note the arrangement of the retaining segments 8. Remove the cup 9 and the seal 10.
4 Remove the ballbearing 11. The bearing can be released by hand but use a drift if necessary.
5 Remove the bush 12, for which service agents use a threaded extractor tap 2291.T (see **FIG 5:3**). Clean the parts.

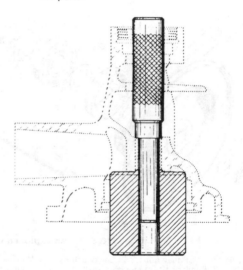

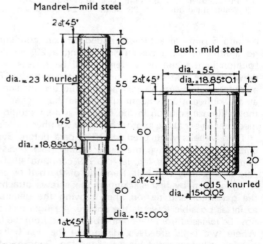

Mandrel—mild steel

2 at 45'
dia. 23 knurled
55
145
dia. 18.85±0.1
10
60
1 at 45'
dia. 15±0.03

Bush: mild steel
dia. 55
2 at 45'   dia. 18.85±0.1   1.5
60
20
2 at 45'   knurled
dia. 15 +0.15 +0.05

FIG 5:4 Mandrel and dolly ring MR.3676.270 used for fitting bush in water pump (dimensions in mm)

6 The pump body bush is made of porous bronze. Before assembling, immerse this bushing in engine oil for several minutes until the bronze is thoroughly impregnated. Under no circumstances must this bronze bush be rebored as its permeability will then deteriorate. In addition it must not be pierced when the grease nipple is positioned. Make sure that the bearing face of the packing gland on the pump is neither pitted nor scored. Fit the bush 12, using a press, into the pump body with the aid of a suitable mandrel (see **FIG 5:4**).

7 Moisten the seal 10 with castor oil and locate it on the pump shaft 7. Fit this assembly in the pump body.

8 Locate the retaining segments 8 in position with grease and place the cup 9 on the pump shaft 7.

9 Fit the ballbearing 11 in position in the pump body using a tube, also the ring nut 6 locking the ballbearing 11.

10 Fit the pulley adjusting washer 5, the key 4, the pulley 25, the washer 3, the locking washer 2 and the pulley retaining nut 1.

5:5 Thermostat removal and refitting

To remove the thermostat 16 in **FIG 5:2**, open the radiator drain tap and partially drain off the water to a level below the bottom of the thermostat housing in the water pump. Keep the water in a clean receptacle if it contains antifreeze. Disengage the water return pipe from the pump cover, also the clip retaining the thermostat in the flexible pipe. Remove the thermostat, using a screwdriver if necessary to remove any deposits around the flange until the thermostat becomes free to be taken out. Take care not to damage the instrument by prising it out if it does not come away easily.

In order to test a thermostat, suspend it and a thermometer in a container of water and heat the water. Ensure that neither the thermostat nor the thermometer rests on the bottom of the container. The valve should commence to open at a temperature of between 72° and 76°C (162° and 169°F). Also when shaken in water at a temperature of 90°C (194°F) the valve should be completely open in less than 20 seconds. If the thermostat does not satisfy these conditions it must be renewed.

Finally relocate the thermostat in its housing, refit the clip and the water return pipe and fill up the cooling system, maintaining an antifreeze solution if employed at its required level of concentration.

5:6 Fault diagnosis

(a) Internal water leakage

1 Cracked cylinder wall
2 Loose cylinder head nuts
3 Faulty head gasket (see **Chapter 1**)

(b) Poor circulation

1 Radiator core blocked
2 Engine water passages restricted
3 Low water level
4 Loose fan belt(s)
5 Defective thermostat
6 Perished or collapsed radiator hoses

(c) Corrosion

1 Impurities in the water
2 Infrequent draining and flushing

(d) Overheating

1 Check (b)
2 Sludge in crankcase
3 Faulty ignition timing (see **Chapter 4**)
4 Low oil level in sump
5 Tight engine
6 Choked exhaust system
7 Binding brakes (see **Chapter 10**)
8 Slipping clutch (see **Chapter 6**)
9 Incorrect valve timing (see **Chapter 1**)
10 Retarded ignition (see **Chapter 4**)
11 Mixture too weak (see **Chapter 3**)

CHAPTER 6

THE CLUTCH

6:1 Construction and operation

The clutches fitted to all engines are of the single dry plate type bolted to the flywheel and enclosed in a housing attached to the cylinder block and crankcase. As shown in **FIG 6:1**, the clutch assembly consists of two main units, a pressure plate assembly 2 and the clutch disc 1. The disc plate has riveted friction facings and incorporates coil-type cushioning springs. A splined hub slides on the splines of the gearbox mainshaft.

In DS19 cars the operation of the clutch is automatically performed by hydraulic action along with gearchanging and there is no clutch pedal. As stated in **Chapter 2**, a low pressure pump was used to operate the system until 1960, when later cars were fitted with a centrifugal clutch control unit. In ID19 cars, depression of the clutch pedal operates a mechanical linkage and cable (see **FIG 6:2**), by which the fork 13 in **FIG 6:1** moves the release collar 20 and its ballbearing towards the flywheel to apply pressure on the three release levers or toggles 9. The reverse action of the levers turning on their pivots disengages the clutch, by withdrawing the pressure plate 2 from contact with the clutch disc 1 against the pressure of the springs 12.

6:2 Adjustments of mechanical linkage

Correct adjustments of pedal travel in ID19 cars and the clearance of the fork control rod from the clutch housing are essential to be maintained in order to ensure the required clearance between the clutch release levers and the release bearing. Referring to **FIG 6:2**, the height of the pedal should be 148+5—0 mm from the underside of the pedal with the rubber pad removed to the top of the felt carpet under the rubber carpet, as shown at 'a' in the illustration. To alter the height of the pedal, unscrew the locknut, turn the stop screw 13 as required and then retighten the locknut.

The clearance between the rear end of the fork control rod 2 and the clutch housing should be a minimum of 1 mm as shown by 'j'. To obtain this dimension, move the threaded sleeve 9 by adjusting the nuts 8. To adjust the clutch clearance, measure exactly the clearance 'j'. Now obtain an assistant to depress the clutch pedal by hand until it is felt that the thrust comes into contact with the toggles. Measure the new clearance. The difference between the two dimensions should be from 1.75 to 2.25 mm. If otherwise, slacken the locknut 15, adjust the nuts 1 and 11 as required, and finally retighten the locknut 15 and the nut 1.

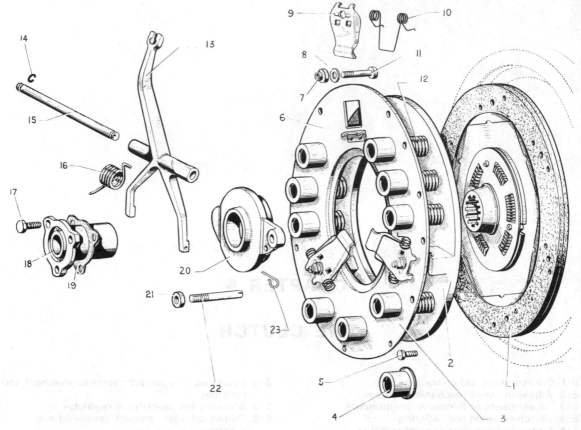

FIG 6:1   An exploded view of the clutch

Key to Fig 6:1   1 Clutch disc   2 Pressure plate   3 Carrier plate   4 Spring cup   5 Screw   6 Carrier plate   7 Nut   8 Washer   9 Clutch toggle   10 Toggle return spring   11 Screw for toggle adjustment   12 Clutch springs   13 Clutch withdrawal fork   14 Circlip   15 Fork shaft   16 Fork return spring   17 Screw   18 Ballbearing hub   19 Paper joint for ballbearing carrier   20 Release collar and ballbearing housing   21 Nut   22 Guide pin for ballbearing   23 Spring pin retaining ballbearing

6:3 Adjustments of hydraulic components

The elements of the clutch hydraulic system in DS19 cars on which adjustment checks may be necessary to ensure the continued effective operation of the system include the idling or slow-running, clutch clearance, clutch drag and also the clutch engagement control. For the adjustment of slow-running and accelerated idling reference should be made to **Chapter 3.** Adjustment of the clutch clearance is made as follows:

1 Put the hydraulic system under pressure, then stop the engine. It will be necessary to run it again whenever the pressure falls.
2 Locate the starting handle in position and have it turned by an assistant. Referring to **FIG 6:3,** untighten the nut 1 and unscrew the nuts 2 and 3. Stop when the engine begins to be turned by the handle. Then start the engine and remove the starting handle, leaving the extension in position. If the starting handle extension is pushed into engagement with the starting dog, it will be repelled by the rotating dog.

3 Unscrew the nut 1 and retighten the nut 2, moving the nuts a fraction of a turn each time. This pre-adjustment is completed when the starting handle extension is pushed into engagement with the starter dog and is stabilized without ratcheting over the dog on the primary shaft.
4 For final adjustment slacken the nut 1 by one to two turns, so as to obtain a clearance between the nut and the fork of 1 to 2 mm. Tighten the nut 2 and tighten the locknut 3.

Adjustment of clutch drag should be carried out after checking and adjusting the clutch clearance. The engine should be hot, the choke control closed and the manual ignition control in the midway position, with the car resting on a level surface. The use of a revolution counter (see **Section 3:4** in **Chapter 3**) for this operation is indispensable and it may therefore be necessary to obtain the assistance of a service agent. Referring to **FIG 6:4,** disconnect the spring 1 connecting the accelerator control to the clutch engagement control lever 9 from the accelerator control. In cars before

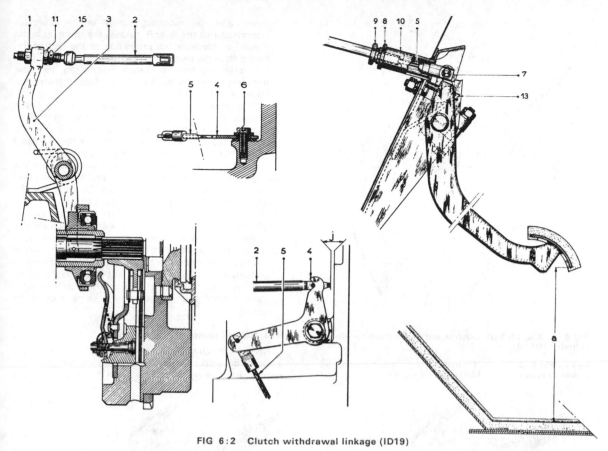

FIG 6:2 Clutch withdrawal linkage (ID19)

Key to Fig 6:2 1 Adjusting nut 2 Fork control rod 3 Clutch release arm and fork 4 Bell crank 5 Cable 6 Shouldered spindle 7 Pedal shaft lever 8 Adjusting nuts 9 Threaded sleeve 10 Support 11 Adjusting nut 13 Pedal stop screw 15 Locknut a Pedal height j Fork control rod clearance

March, 1961, disconnect the support tube (see 14 in **FIG 3:4, Chapter 3**) from the accelerated idling control or in later cars screws in, without using force, the knurled accelerated idling adjusting screw on the carburetter.

To check the adjustment of the clutch drag in cars before March, 1961, when accelerating **very slowly** the clutch drag should occur between 600 and 750 rev/min. If otherwise, proceed as follows:

1 Stop the engine. Referring to **FIG 6:5**, remove the plug 10 in the hydraulic gear selector, loosen the screwed sleeve 11 (acting as a locknut) and turn the screw 12 to adjust the piston for automatic clutch control. If the speed of engagement is below 700 rev/min, screw up the screw. Unscrew it if the speed of engagement is above 750 rev/min.

2 Tighten the body 11 at the same time holding the screw 12. The position of the head of the adjusting screw should give a dimension 'c' of between 17 and 25 mm from the base of the body 11.

3 If this dimension is greater than 25 mm, it may be due to either too great a clearance between the piston and cylinder causing leakage, to the seizure of the spring spring of the control piston or to the hole in the piston being partially blocked.

4 If the dimension is less than 25 mm, it can be due to a weak control piston spring. If the adjustment is found to be unstable, check the operation of the control valve.

The adjustment of clutch drag in cars later than March, 1961, is described in **Section 3:4** of **Chapter 3**. The adjusting screw is shown at 24 in **FIG 6:9**.

Operations for the adjustment of the clutch engagement control are as follows:

1 Referring to **FIG 6:4** showing the accelerator control with two rods, stop the engine and press the accelerator right down. There should now be a clearance at 'd' (see centre illustration) of 1 to 2 mm between the pin 6 and the hook of the spring, with the pin resting on the lower part of the slot. If necessary, adjust the length of the spring by moving its end in the trunnion 7.

2 Where the accelerator control has one rod, stop the engine and press the accelerator pedal right down. The hook of the spring should be fitted without strain or without clearance on the pin 6 with the pin resting at the lower part of the slot 'a'. If necessary, adjust the length of the spring by moving its end in the trunnion 7.

3 In cars between December 1956 and July 1959 with one control rod the spring has a diameter of 13.2 mm. With the engine stopped, the accelerator pedal right

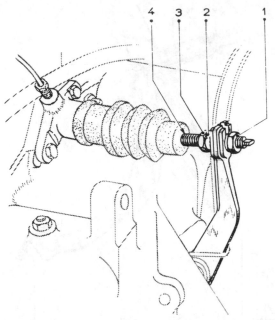

FIG 6:3 Clutch fork control rod connection to clutch cylinder (DS19)

Key to Fig 6:3   1 Front nut   2 Adjusting nut
3 Adjusting nut   4 Clutch fork control rod

down and the retaining screw in the trunnion slackened, pull the lever 9 towards the spring as far as it will go. Measure the protrusion of the end of the spring from the trunnion. Hold the lever 9 and pull on the spring so that its former protrusion from the trunnion is exceeded by 6 mm, then tighten the retaining screw.

4 In later cars with one control rod, the spring has a diameter of 15.5 to 16.1 mm. To fit this spring in place of the former spring, adjust as in Operation 3 to give a final protrusion of the end of the spring either the same as or 1 mm less than the former protrusion.

It is sometimes necessary to make these adjustments (idling, clutch drag, clutch clearance and clutch engagement) again after a few dozen miles. To carry out the clutch engagement adjustment on the road:

1 On a level road, change from first to second gear at 20 mile/hr and completely release the accelerator pedal. Clutch engagement should occur without a jerk.

2 On a level road at 56 mile/hr in fourth gear, maintain the accelerator pedal in the same position and change to third gear. Clutch engagement should occur without a jerk. If a jerk occurs, tighten the clutch engagement control spring. If there is a delay, loosen the spring.

6:4 Clutch removal and refitting

Before the clutch can be removed a considerable amount of work is required to remove the gearbox, necessitating taking the engine out of the car as described

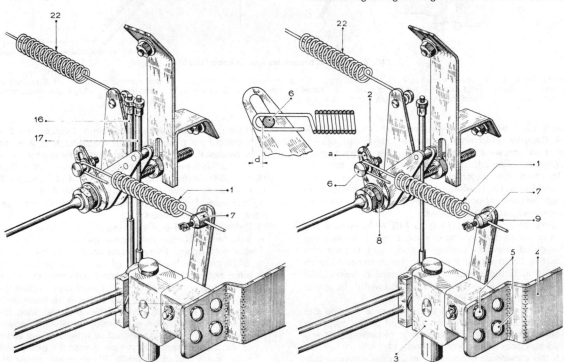

FIG 6:4   Clutch engagement and accelerator controls

Key to Fig 6:4   1 Spring, accelerator control to clutch engagement control   2 Connecting lever   3 Clutch engagement control   4 Securing bracket to body   5 Screws   6 Pin   7 Trunnion   8 Nut   9 Control lever   16 Inner control rod   17 Outer control rod   22 Accelerator control return spring   **a** Slot   **d** Clearance (see text)

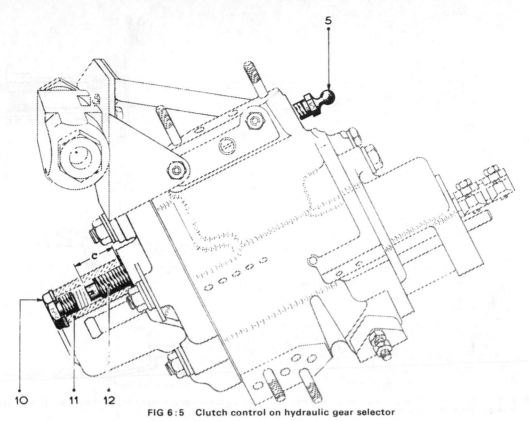

FIG 6:5 Clutch control on hydraulic gear selector

Key to Fig 6:5   5 Bleed screw   10 Plug   11 Screwed hexagonal sleeve   12 Adjusting screw for clutch control piston

in **Section 1:9, Chapter 1.** Removal operations among other matters include the removal of the radiator, the steering assembly, the generator, the front wheels and the flexible couplings, as well as various hydraulic details in DS cars. The clutch is then withdrawn by disconnecting it from the engine flywheel as described in **Chapter 1** with details of inspection requirements for the flywheel.

The clutch disc or driven plate should be examined for excessive wear and signs of overheating. Check that the friction linings are secure and free from oil. A polished glaze on the linings is normal, but they should be light in colour with the grain clearly visible. A much darker colour obliterating the grain is a sign of oil on the linings, which can cause clutch slip or possibly difficulty in disengagement. If this condition is found or if the linings are worn down near to the rivet heads, it is advised that the complete disc assembly should be renewed in preference to riveting new linings on the existing assembly. It should be ensured that the damper springs are firmly attached and serviceable, also that the hub splines are not excessively worn. Further dismantling of the pressure plate assembly is not advised, as a special fixture and equipment are necessary for reassembly and it follows that the work is more suitably to be undertaken by a service agent. At the same time, if the driving plate is worn it can under certain circumstances be ground on a lathe. Dimensions are critical, however, because rectification of the surface

causes loss of pressure on the clutch disc and if badly worn the plate must be renewed. Refitting the clutch to the flywheel is described in **Chapter 1.**

In mechanically-operated clutches, details of the clutch control linkage are shown in **FIG 6:2.** Removal and refitting operations are as follows:

1 Unscrew the nut 1 and disengage the rod 2 from the clutch fork 3 and the lever 4.

2 Remove the screw securing the lever 4 to the clutch housing. Disconnect the lever 4 from the front socket of the cable 5. Remove the lever 4 and the shouldered spindle 6.

3 Disconnect the cable 5 and its sheath from the sheath retaining boss on the clutch housing. Disconnect the rear socket of the cable 5 from the pedal shaft lever 7.

4 Unscrew the nut 8 and remove the threaded sleeve 9 from the support 10. Remove the control cable assembly.

5 When refitting, connect the rear socket of the cable 5 to the pedal shaft lever 7.

6 Place the threaded sleeve 9 in position on the support 10 and screw up the nut 8 without tightening it.

7 Place the cable 5 and sheath in position on the retaining boss on the clutch housing.

8 Connect the lever 4 to the front socket of cable 5 and place the lever 4 and the shouldered spindle 6 in position after first greasing them lightly. Tighten the fixing nut.

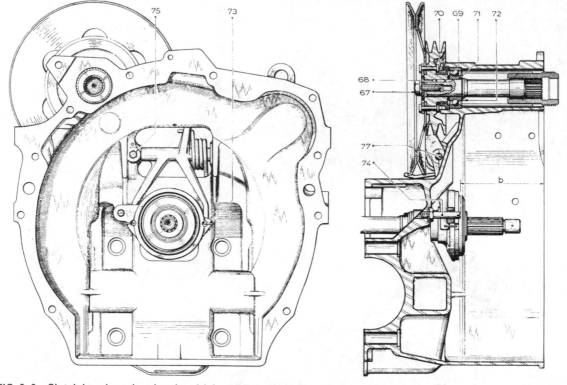

FIG 6:6 Clutch housing, also showing driving pulley and shaft on DS19 cars. Details for ID19 cars are similar except for a single-groove driving pulley

Key to Fig 6:6   67 Pulley retaining screw   68 Key for pulley   69 Adjusting washer   70 Ring nut   71 Ballbearing
72 Oil retaining washer   73 Springs retaining thrust ballbearing   74 Thrust guide screw   75 Locking screw for clutch fork
spindle   77 Circlips retaining spindle

9 Connect the rod 2 to the lever 4 and to the clutch fork 3. Screw on the nuts 1 and 11 without tightening them.
10 Adjust the clutch control as described in **Section 6:2**.
Renewal of a clutch fork or a thrust ballbearing in either DS or ID cars is undertaken as follows:
1 With the gearbox detached, remove the rubber closing plate for the fork opening. Disengage the fork control rod from the fork, either as in the previous Operation 1 or in DS19 cars by unscrewing the nuts 2 and 3 in **FIG 6:3**.
2 Referring to **FIG 6:6**, remove the retaining springs 73 and the thrust ballbearing.
3 Remove the locknut and screw 75 (or two circlips in later cars) retaining the clutch fork spindle 77. Detach the spindle, the spring and the fork.
4 Reassembly consists of the same operations but in reverse order.

6:5 Clutch engagement control removal, servicing and refitting

Referring to **FIG 6:4**, removal of the clutch engagement control is undertaken as follows:
1 Release the pressure in the hydraulic system (see **Chapter 2**) and remove the coils and bracket assembly where fitted.

2 Disconnect the pressure inlet union from the pressure distribution block.
3 Disconnect the union plates from the hydraulic gear selector and from the clutch engagement control. Remove the seal plates.
4 Unhook the clutch engagement control spring 1, from the accelerator connecting rod 2. Remove the clutch engagement control 3 and its bracket.
5 Remove the bracket 4 from the clutch engagement control. Remove only the two screws 5 which project beyond the others. Also, in order not to interfere with the adjustment, do not remove the control spring unless renewing the clutch engagement control.
6 Referring to **FIG 6:7**, remove the connecting screws 6 from the body 7 and from the bearing block 8. Disengage the bearing block from the body. Do not lose the ball 9.
7 Remove the upper and lower plugs 10 and 11. Disengage the spring 12, the piston 13 and the ball 14. Remove the seals 15, 16 and 17.
8 Clean the parts, using alcohol exclusively, and blow out with compressed air.
9 Reassemble by first making sure that the lever 18 is tight on the spindle. If not, renew the clutch engagement control. Also make sure that the lever 19 is tight on the spindle, otherwise weld at one point.

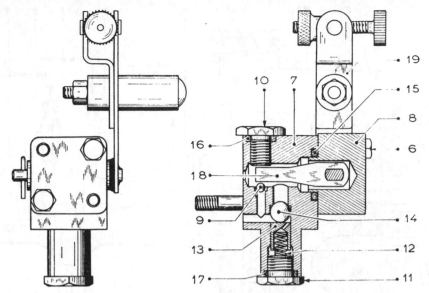

FIG 6:7　A sectional view of the clutch engagement control

Key to Fig 6:7　　6 Connecting screws　　7 Body　　8 Bearing block　　9 Ball　　10 Upper plug　　11 Lower plug　　12 Spring
13 Piston　　14 Ball　　15 Seal　　16 Seal　　17 Seal　　18 Lever　　19 Lever

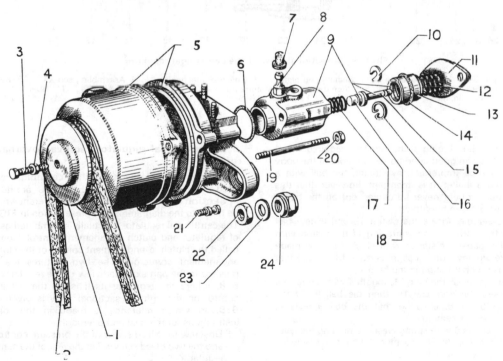

FIG 6:8　A part exploded view of the centrifugal regulator

Key to Fig 6:8　　1 Pulley　　2 Belt　　3 Adjusting screw　　4 Locknut　　5 Centrifugal regulator　　6 Ring seal between
centrifugal regulator and clutch engagement control　　7 Cap for bleed screw　　8 Bleed screw　　9 Clutch engagement control
10 Washer retaining plunger 15　　11 Retaining flange　　12 Return spring for piston 13　　13 Control piston for plunger 15
14 Piston ring seal　　15 Plunger for clutch engagement control　　16 Circlip for 10　　17 Return spring for clutch engagement
control slide valve　　18 Thrust cup for slide valve return spring　　19 Assembling stud, regulator and engagement control　　20 Nut
21 Overflow pipe connection　　22 Nut securing regulator on water pump body　　23 Adjustment washer　　24 Nut

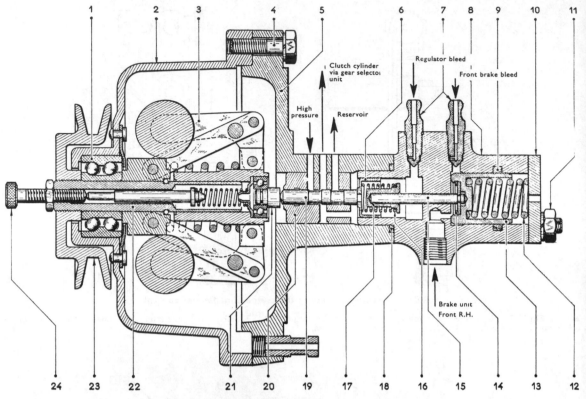

FIG 6:9 A sectional view of the centrifugal regulator

Key to Fig 6:9 1 Front bearing 2 Bearing end plate 3 Governor mechanism 4 Assembling screws 5 Regulator body 6 Dashpot 7 Bleed screws 8 Clutch disengagement corrector body 9 Seal 10 Rear plate 11 Nuts 12 Spring 13 Piston 14 Circlips 15 Rod 16 Spring 17 Cup 18 Seal 19 Slide valve 20 Support 21 Pad 22 Sleeve 23 Pulley 24 Adjusting screw

10 To remake the seating of the ball 14 if required, insert a ball that is in good condition in the bore of the body and make an impression by striking the ball with a drift and a mallet. It is important, however, that this procedure should never be carried out on the ball 9 but a new assembly fitted.

11 To reassemble, locate the piston 13 and a new ball 14 in the body. A light surfacing of the piston with abrasive paper moistened with alcohol can be made if there are any signs of slight seizure. Make sure that there is no obstruction in the hole.

12 Fit the spring 12, the plug 11, together with a ring seal 17. Insert the ring seal 15, then the ball 9. Fit the bearing block 8, ensuring that the ball 9 rests in position on its seating.

13 Fit the screws 6 with spring washers, holding the lever 18 on the ball 9. Fit the plug 10 together with its square section seal 16.

Refit the control as in removal with the operations in reverse order. Make certain that the oil holes in the seal plates correspond with those in the joints. Finally hook the clutch engagement control spring (see **FIG 6:4**) on the accelerator connecting rod and adjust the clutch engagement control as described in **Section 6:3**.

6:6 Centrifugal regulator removal, overhaul and refitting

The principles of operation of the centrifugal regulator used in DS19 cars after September, 1960, are described in **Section 2:7** of **Chapter 2**, where reference may also be made to the diagrammatic representation in **FIG 2:16**. The centrifugal regulator is actually a combined assembly of regulator and clutch engagement control (sometimes called the clutch re-engagement control or the clutch disengagement corrector). The two features are distinguished in the part exploded view of the regulator in **FIG 6:8**, where the regulator itself is on the left and the control on the right. A sectional view is given in **FIG 6:9**, to which reference is made in the following instructions for removal and overhaul.

1 Unscrew the bleed screw of the pressure control valve and the two bleed screws 7 at the rear of the centrifugal regulator.

2 From the regulator disconnect (a) the pipe to the right-hand brake unit, (b) the pipe assembly flange to the hydraulic gear selector, removing the seal plates and (c) the tie rod to the high pressure pump.

3 Unscrew the nuts from the reinforcing arm forming a tie rod between the cylinder head and the centrifugal

regulator. Remove the nut from the swivelling pin and disengage the belt (see **Section 2:11, Chapter 2**).

4 Withdraw the centrifugal regulator and the pulley adjusting washer on the swivelling pin.

5 Remove the two nuts 11, the rear plate 10 and disengage the spring 12.

6 Remove the body 8 of the clutch disengagement corrector. Hold the dashpot 6 in order to avoid it dropping under the action of the spring 16.

7 Remove the dashpot 6, the spring 16, the cup 17 and the joint 18. Remove the piston 13 by pushing on the rod 15 and remove the joint 9. Remove the circlips 14 to disengage the rod 15 together with its lockwasher.

8 The bore of the clutch disengagement corrector body 8 and the dashpot 6 must be free from scratches, otherwise the assembly of the body and dashpot must be renewed. Also renew the piston 13 if there are any traces of damage, scratches or seizure. Renew the joints 9 and 18 when reassembling. Reassemble in the reverse order of dismantling, using a new seal 9 previously dipped in hydraulic fluid.

9 To renew the governor mechanism, remove the assembling screw 4 and disconnect the rubber bearing and plate 2 from the body 5.

10 A clamp 2229.T is used as shown in **FIG 6:10**. Engage the mechanism 3 in the clamp, tighten the screw and hold the pulley in a vice. Unscrew the mechanism from the pulley by turning the end piece and remove the pulley from the vice.

11 Screw on the pulley by hand until in contact with the bearing 1 in **FIG 6:9**.

12 Using the clamp and vice as in removal, tighten the mechanism on the pulley to a torque of approximately 14 lb ft. Refit the end plate.

13 Proceed to refit the regulator in the reverse manner of its removal described in Operations 1 to 4.

14 The pulley may be aligned if required by a service agent equipped with specially designed fixtures for the purpose, by which the correct thickness of the pulley adjusting washer is determined.

15 Refit and tension the belt (see **Section 2:11, Chapter 2**) and bleed the centrifugal regulator as described in the following Section.

6:7 Bleeding the centrifugal regulator

To bleed the centrifugal regulator, release the pressure by unscrewing the bleed screw of the pressure control

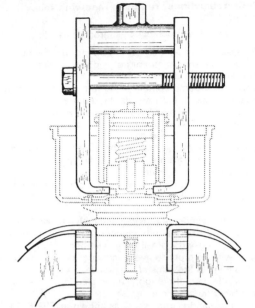

FIG 6:10 Clamp No. 2229.T used for renewing centrifugal regulator mechanism

valve (see 14 in **FIG 2:1, Chapter 2**) and fitting a flexible pipe, transparent for preference, on the front bleed screw of the regulator (see **FIG 6:9**). Put the other end of the pipe in the hydraulic reservoir.

Start the engine and set the speed between 1500 and 2000 rev/min, by turning the throttle adjusting screw with the accelerated idling control spring unhooked in cars before March, 1961, or by turning the accelerated idling adjusting screw in later cars. Unscrew the centrifugal regulator bleed screw. Then very slowly reduce the speed of the engine to between 500 and 600 rev/min. Let the engine idle for about two minutes, then tighten the bleed screw.

The rear bleed screw on the regulator is used for bleeding the clutch disengagement corrector. Fit a pipe on this bleed screw as for the other one, with the free end in the reservoir. Release the pressure and proceed as described for bleeding the brakes in **Chapter 10**. Adjust the slow-running and the accelerated idling (see **Chapter 3**) also the clutch drag as described earlier in **Section 6:3**.

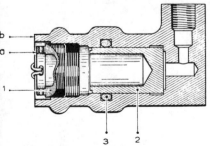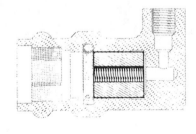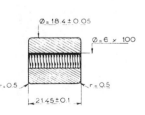

FIG 6:11 A sectional view of the clutch cylinder and the mandrel used for renewing the seal. Dimensions are in mm

Key to Fig 6:11   1 Nut retaining piston   2 Piston   3 Ring seal   **a** Face of nut   **b** Face of cylinder

6 : 8 Clutch cylinder removal, renewing seal, refitting

To remove the clutch cylinder, proceed as follows:

1 Release the pressure in the clutch cylinder by means of the auxiliary clutch control and disconnect the tie rod on the high pressure pump.
2 Loosen the pump spindle fixing nut, remove the belt and work the pump towards the outside. Disconnect the pressure feed pipe from the clutch cylinder.
3 Referring to **FIG 6 : 3**, remove the front nut 1 on the clutch fork control rod 4.
4 Remove the screws fixing the clutch cylinder and withdraw the assembly. Remove the control rod and dust cover from the cylinder.
5 Referring to **FIG 6 : 11,** using circlip pliers remove the circlip or splitpin and remove the nut 1 retaining the piston 2.
6 Wrap the cylinder and piston assembly in a cloth, and blow out the piston with compressed air. Remove the ring seal 3 using a small brass wire hook. Do not use steel wire, in order to avoid scratches on the cylinder or damage to the sides of the groove.
7 Clean the parts thoroughly, using alcohol exclusively, and blow out with compressed air.
8 Using a mandrel (not sold) as shown in **FIG 6 : 11,** moisten the seal with hydraulic fluid and insert it in the bore of the cylinder. Position it with the aid of the piston. Remove the piston and then the mandrel, using a screw.
9 Coat the cylinder bore and piston with hydraulic fluid, insert the piston and push it to the bottom of the cylinder.
10 Screw in the nut 1 until the face 'a' of the nut is either level with or recessed not more than .5 mm from the face 'b' of the cylinder. Refit the dust cover and control rod assembly.

11 Refit the clutch cylinder in the reverse manner of its removal. Adjust the tension of the pump driving belt (see **Chapter 2**) and the clutch clearance (see **Section 6 : 3**). Bleed the hydraulic gear selector unit (see **Chapter 7, Section 7 : 5**).

6 : 9 Fault diagnosis

(a) Clutch drag or spin

1 Excessive play at clutch fork
2 Oil or grease on linings
3 Flywheel face not running true
4 Misalignment between engine and gearbox
5 Clutch disc hub binding on splines
6 Clutch disc distorted
7 Pressure plate distorted
8 Disc linings broken
9 Foreign matter in clutch

(b) Fierceness or snatch

1 Check 2, 3, 4, 6 in (a)
2 Worn clutch linings

(c) Clutch slip

1 Check 2 and 3 in (a)
2 Check 2 in (b)
3 Weak pressure springs
4 Insufficient clearance at clutch fork

(d) Judder

1 Check 2, 3 and 6 in (a)
2 Pressure plate not parallel with flywheel face
3 Contact area of friction linings not evenly distributed

(e) Rattles and knocks

1 Broken damper springs in clutch disc
2 Badly worn splines in disc hub
3 Worn release bearing
4 Loose flywheel

CHAPTER 7

THE TRANSMISSION AND DRIVE SHAFTS

7:1 General description

One of the main features of the front wheel drive system is that the engine, gearbox, differential and final drive gearing are assembled as a complete unit. Power generated by the engine is transmitted to the gearbox through the flywheel and clutch at the front end of the crankshaft. From the clutch the drive is taken up by the upper of the two parallel shafts in the gearbox shown in **FIG 7:2** which carry the gearwheels providing changes of engine speed and power according to driving requirements. There is also an intermediate reverse gear layshaft which is brought into operation to reverse the drive when necessary. A final drive pinion is located on the rearward end of the lower shaft, continuing the drive through the crownwheel and differential assembly to the differential and drive shafts and the front wheels.

The gearbox has four forward ratios and one reverse, with synchromesh engagement of the upper three forward gears normally used with the car in motion. In DS19 cars a light touch on the gearlever behind the steering wheel gives selection of gears by hydraulic servos directing fluid under pressure into any one of five hydraulic cylinders in the gearbox cover. The lever engages first or reverse if pushed away from the driver, reverse being to the right of the first gear position after forcing the lever through a stop. A straight pull back engages second gear, followed by a curving movement to the right into third and top gears. Engagement is effected by three selector forks and shafts in the gearbox for first and second gears, third and fourth gears and also the reverse gear.

The principles governing the operation of hydraulic gear selection in DS19 cars are described in **Chapter 2**. It should be noted that when the car is at rest a gear should never be engaged when the engine is running on the choke, as the relatively high engine speed will then cause sudden engagement of the clutch. Also, before changing from second to the unsynchronized first gear it is advised that the car should be stationary or at least proceeding extremely slowly. Errors of synchronizing judgement with the car in motion and with the gear system under high servo pressure could be disastrous.

In ID19 cars the gearbox arrangements are similar to those shown in **FIG 7:2** except for the selector shaft 61 and the hydraulic cylinders in the cover, which are replaced by the selector mechanism shown in **FIG 7:13**. This mechanism is operated by a cable control from the gearlever behind the steering wheel after depression of the clutch pedal. Pulling the lever towards the driver and

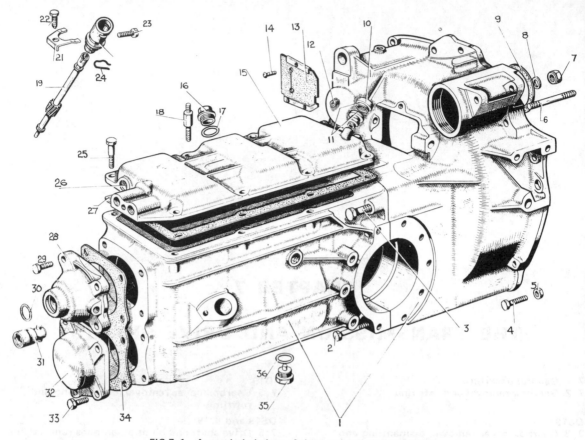

FIG 7 : 1   An exploded view of the gearbox housing (DS19)

Key to Fig 7 :1   1 Gearbox casing   2 Screw assembling gearbox and clutch housing   3 Screw assembling gearbox and clutch housing   4 Screw, clutch housing to engine   5 Nut   6 Stud   7 Nut   8 Washer   9 Paper joint   10 Filter for breather   11 Breather assembly   12 Air vent plug   13 Rubber closing plate, clutch withdrawal opening   14 Screw   15 Gearbox cover for hydraulic control   16 Filler plug   17 Washer   18 Shouldered stud for cover and pipe assemblies   19 Speedometer drive pinion   20 Socket for speedometer pinion   21 Clamp for pinion socket   22 Screw   23 Screw for cable   24 Locking clip for speedometer cable   25 Screw, centring and securing cover   26 Expanding sealing washer   27 Paper joint for cover   28 Front bearing cap for mainshaft and starting handle dog   29 Screw   30 Ring seal   31 Starting handle dog   32 Front bearing cap for bevel pinion shaft   33 Screw   34 Double joint   35 Drain plug with magnetized dowel   36 Copper joint

then upwards or downwards engages first and second gear respectively. Pushing the lever upwards or downwards engages third or fourth gears. Reverse is obtained by pushing the lever completely forwards and then downwards.

In both types of cars the differential gear transmits the drive from each side of the transmission casing through universal joints to the constant velocity joints at the front road wheels. The constant velocity joints are specially designed to transmit uniform rotary movement over the wide angle of movement of the front wheels and are sometimes considered analogous to three-dimensional ballbearings.

7:2 Gearbox removal and refitting

Considerable work is entailed in removing the gearbox as it is necessary first to remove the complete engine and gearbox assembly from the car, for which the operations were described in **Chapter 1**. The gearbox (see **FIG 7 :1**) may then be disconnected from the engine by removing the clutch housing fixing screws. After such servicing operations as may need attention the gearbox is refitted to the engine and the whole assembly re-installed in the car, again as described in **Chapter 1**. Before removing the gearbox or the hydraulic gear selector in DS19 cars, however, if difficulty is experienced in operating the gears it should be ensured that the pressure distribution is correct for each gear by first raising the front of the car with the engine running at accelerated idling. Then with the aid of an assistant engage first gear and observe the movement of the clutch fork, which should move slowly towards the rear (engaged position). Proceed similarly for the remaining four gears. If the fork remains in the de-clutched position, checks must be made on the operating pressures, the hydraulic gear selector and the gear control cylinders with the aid of the test bench shown in **FIG 2 :8** in **Chapter 2**, for which the assistance of a service agent should be

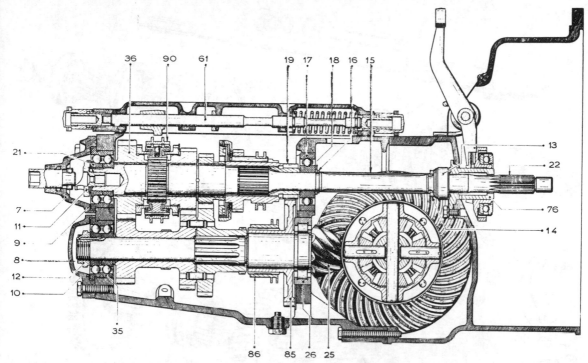

FIG 7:2 A sectional view of the gearbox fitted with cover for hydraulic gear selection

Key to Fig 7:2 7 Mainshaft bearing cap   8 Pinion shaft bearing cap   9 Adjusting shims   10 Adjusting shims   11 Starting handle dog   12 Locknut   13 Rear oil seal   14 Washer   15 Distance tube   16 Circlip   17 Rear mainshaft bearing   18 Distance piece   19 First-speed pinion   21 Front mainshaft bearing   22 Mainshaft   25 Bevel pinion   26 Bearing   35 Pinion shaft front bearing   36 Fourth-speed loose pinion   61 Selector shaft   76 Clutch thrust bearing hub support   85 First-speed loose pinion   86 Sliding pinion   90 Third and fourth-speed synchromesh

obtained. Also check the adjustment of the slow-running, as in **Chapter 3**, as well as the clutch clearance, the clutch drag and the clutch engagement control, all as described in **Chapter 6**.

The internal components of the gearbox are shown in **FIGS 7:2** and **7:3**. Servicing operations on the mechanism are necessarily limited by the facilities available for precise reassembly after dismantling and which are only ordinarily to be found in a well-equipped service workshop. Dismantling operations present no serious difficulties but reassembly needs observance of very precise limits for clearances and fits in both the differential gear (see **FIG 7:4**) and final drive. The precise adjustment of the bevel pinion 25 in **FIG 7:2**, for example, is of very great importance because an incorrect setting of the gear teeth will result in noisy operation and reducing the life of the gear. The setting dimension is specified between the centre line of the differential shaft and the ground end of the pinion and varies with each crown-wheel and pinion. Its significance is shown by its being engraved by the makers in millimetres and hundredths of millimetres on each pinion. In addition there have been a number of changes of design of gearwheels made from time to time, which have to be taken into account if renewal of gears becomes necessary. All of this requires special tools and workshop equipment as well as practical experience and it follows that the complete stripping

and reassembly of a gearbox should be undertaken only by a qualified service agent.

Operations which can be undertaken without serious difficulty and which are described later in this Chapter include the dismantling and reassembly of gearbox covers and selector assemblies, also the various hydraulic units contributing to the general gearbox and clutch system.

DS19:

7:3 Gearbox cover removal, dismantling and refitting

Removal of the gearbox cover is undertaken by disconnecting the five-pipe control assembly from the cover and then removing the retaining screws and lifting the cover vertically from the gearbox. Referring to **FIG 7:5**, continue as follows:

1 Remove the third and fourth speed selector fork thrust pads to avoid dropping them downwards, then completely remove the cover together with the control pipe assembly.

2 Remove the fixing clamps 20 from the control cylinders at each end of the cover, together with the clamp adjusting washers 99. Remove the cylinders and pipe assemblies, also the adjusting washers 59.

3 Take out the screws fixing the forks so that they slide freely on the shafts. Check that all the shafts are in their neutral position.

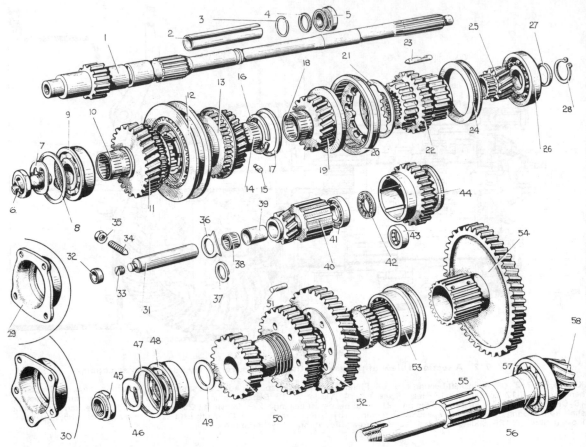

FIG 7:3   An exploded view of the gear components

Key to Fig 7:3   1 Mainshaft   2 Distance piece for sealing ring   3 Circlip   4 Spacer for sealing ring   5 Sealing ring
6 Dog nut for starting handle   7 Lockwasher   8 Front bearing adjusting washer   9 Double ballbearing   10 Cage for needle
bearings   11 Fourth-speed mainshaft pinion with dogs   12 Synchromesh for third and fourth-speed pinions   13 Third-speed
mainshaft pinion with dogs   14 Cage for needle bearings   15 Dowel for half washers between second and third-speed pinions
16 Half washer   17 Lockwasher   18 Cage for needle bearings   19 Second-speed pinion   20 Second-speed synchromesh
21 Internally-toothed ring for adjusting synchromesh   22 Reverse speed mainshaft pinion   23 Set of 12 meshing plungers
24 Sliding collar operating plungers   25 First-speed pinion   26 Rear mainshaft bearing   27 Spacing washer   28 Circlip
securing bearing   29 Housing for front mainshaft bearing   30 Housing for front pinion shaft bearing   31 Intermediate reverse
pinion shaft   32 Cap for hole for reverse speed shaft   33 Threaded plug   34 Grubscrew securing shaft   35 Locking nut
36 Stop washer with lug   37 Adjusting washer   38 Cage for needle bearings   39 Distance piece   40 Intermediate reverse
pinion   41 Ballbearing   42 Needle thrust bearing   43 Ballbearing   44 Reverse speed sliding pinion   45 Locking nut
46 Lockwasher   47 Washer   48 Double ballbearing   49 Spacing washer   50 Third and fourth-speed gear train   51 Dowel
between third and fourth-speed train and second and reverse speed pinion   52 Second and reverse speed pinion on drive pinion
shaft   53 First-speed sliding collar   54 First-speed pinion on drive pinion shaft   55 Distance piece   56 Locking ring
for rear roller bearing   57 Drive pinion rear bearing   58 Bevel pinion

4 Remove the spring cup 60 from the fourth speed
selector shaft 61, for which service agents use the
spring compressor 1798.T shown in **FIG 7:6**. Slide
the shaft towards the front until the front cup 62 is on
the small diameter of the shaft at 'a'. Compress the
spring and remove the cup 62.

5 Remove the shaft, the spring and the rocker 63. Disengage the selector fork 64 and carry out the same
operation for the other selector shafts.

6 Knock out the expanding washers 65 and remove the
locking plungers 66. Take care not to lose the cylinder
adjusting washers 59 and the adjusting washers 99
of the clamps 20.

To renew the control cylinder ring seals, proceed as
follows:

1 Mark each piston and its corresponding cylinder and
drive out the pistons from the cylinders with compressed air. Hold the cylinders in a cloth in order to
avoid the pistons being suddenly ejected.

2 Remove the ring seals from the cylinders, using a brass
wire hook.

3 Carefully clean the cylinders and pistons by immersion
in clean alcohol and blow out the parts with compressed air. Smear the cylinders and pistons with
hydraulic fluid.

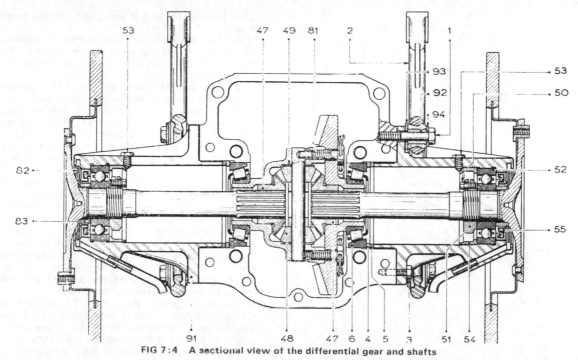

FIG 7:4 A sectional view of the differential gear and shafts

Key to Fig 7:4 1 Screws for support arm 2 Support bracket 3 Bearing fixing screws 4 Adjusting washer 5 Distance washer 6 Tapered roller bearing 47 Planet wheel 48 Satellite wheels 49 Thrust washers 50 Retaining screw for 51 51 Locknut 52 Differential bearing 53 Retaining screw for 54 54 Bearing locknut 55 Oil seal 81 Differential housing screws 82 Oil retaining washer 83 Thrust washer 91 Casing 92 Distance piece 93 Large diameter washer 94 Washer

4 Using a mandrel (not supplied by the makers) as shown in **FIG 7:7**, insert it into each cylinder in turn. Offer up the seal smeared with hydraulic fluid and put it in position in the groove of the cylinder, using a reversed piston. Remove the mandrel by means of a screw.

5 Smear the cylinders and pistons with hydraulic fluid and engage the pistons in their corresponding cylinders.

When assembling the cover, check the selector fork return springs, the length of which under a load of 54 to 56 lb should be 68 mm. Continue as follows:

1 Fit the first and second speed selector shaft 77 through the rear of the cover. Fit the return spring without the cup, then the selector fork 78 using the spring compressor. Insert the selector shaft locking plunger 66.

2 Fit the reverse selector shaft 79, its return spring and the selector fork 80.

3 Insert the third and fourth speed selector shaft 61 and its return spring. Fit the selector shaft plungers 66, the rocker 63 and the third and fourth-speed selector fork 64.

4 Tighten the locking screws on the selector forks. Lock the screws with wire so as to prevent any rotation in direction of unscrewing.

5 Fit the fork return spring thrust cups with the aid of the compressor shown in **FIG 7:6.**

6 Refit the cylinders and pipe assemblies, the adjusting washers and the fixing clamps in the reverse order of their removal.

7 Fit the cover on the gearbox as follows:

(a) Make sure that the selector fork shafts and the sliding pinions are in the neutral position.

(b) Attach a new paper cover joint on the cover with grease. Also attach the third and fourth-speed selector fork thrust pads in position with grease.

(c) Locate the cover in position on the gearbox. Make sure that the selector forks are correctly positioned in the grooves of the sliding pinions and that the first-speed control lever is engaged in the first and second-speed selector fork.

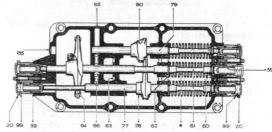

FIG 7:5 A sectional view of the gearbox cover used with hydraulic control

Key to Fig 7:5 20 Cylinder clamps 59 Adjusting washers 60 Spring cups 61 Third and fourth-speed selector shaft 62 Front cups 63 Tongue or rocker 64 Third and fourth-speed selector fork 65 Expanding washers 66 Locking plungers 77 First and second-speed selector shaft 78 Selector fork 79 Reverse selector shaft 80 Selector fork 99 Clamp adjusting washers a Small diameter of shaft

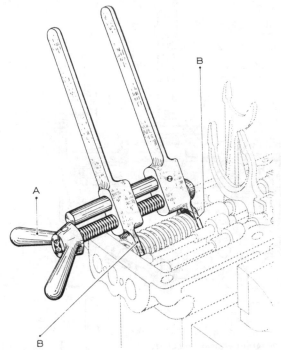

FIG 7:6 Compressor No. 1798.T used for assembling and dismantling selector shaft springs

Key to Fig 7:6   A Wing nut   B Compressor forks

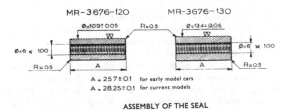

MR-3676-120   MR-3676-130

∅=109±005   R=0.5   ∅=134±005

∅=6 × 100   ∅=6 × 100

R=0.5   R=0.5

A   A

A = 257±0.1   for early model cars
A = 28.25±0.1 for current models

ASSEMBLY OF THE SEAL

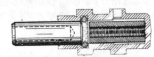

FIG 7:7 Assembly mandrels for control cylinder ring seals (dimensions in mm)

(d) Fit the cover on the gearbox with the two centring screws, then with the other screws and studs.

Adjustments of the engagement of the gears are made by varying the thickness of the adjusting washers (59 in **FIG 7:5**) between the control cylinders and the gearbox cover. In order to carry out this operation the selector fork return spring thrust cups should not be fitted prior to fitting the cover on the gearbox. Procedure is as follows:

1 To adjust the fourth-speed control cylinder, use the help of an assistant to bring the base of the third-speed synchro as far as possible into contact with the thrust washers of the pinion (see **FIG 7:3**) by pushing the selector shaft 61 and holding the shaft in this position. It is necessary to obtain a clearance of .1 to

.3 mm between the face of the synchro and the thrust washer.

2 To do this, locate the rear pipe assembly in position but do not fit the adjusting washer between the fourth-speed control cylinder and the joint face on the gearbox cover.

3 Hold the pipe assembly and with feeler gauges measure the clearance at several points between the control cylinder and the gearbox cover. If the resulting dimension is, say, 1.35 mm, then to obtain the required clearance of .1 to .3 mm it will be necessary to fit an adjusting washer with a thickness between 1.35–.3 mm and 1.35–.1 mm, i.e. between 1.05 mm and 1.25 mm.

4 To adjust the third-speed control cylinder, proceed as in Operations 1 to 3 after having engaged the fourth-speed as far as possible. In this case push the shaft 61 towards the front.

5 To adjust the first-speed control cylinder, put the third and fourth-speed shaft in the neutral position. Engage the second speed as far as possible by pushing on the shaft 77. Then proceed as in Operations 1 to 3 to obtain a clearance between the synchro and the reverse pinion of between .30 and .65 mm.

6 Fit on each cylinder the washers determined as described. Remove the cover and pipe assembly, fit the pipe assembly clamps and fit the fork return spring cups with the aid of the compressor. Refit the cover on the gearbox as described in the previous Operation 7.

7:4 Hydraulic gear selector removal and refitting

A general description of the operation of the hydraulic gear selector, to which is attached the gear changespeed control, is given in **Chapter 2**. Details of the unit as used in conjunction with a centrifugal regulator and showing two types of changespeed units are given in **FIG 7:8**. The arrangement of the combined gearlever and auxiliary clutch control lever assemblies in relation to the hydraulic gear selector is shown in **FIG 7:9**. Movement of the gearlever operates a control rod which is connected to the hydraulic gear selector actuating mechanism, resulting in fluid pressure being transmitted through the pipe assembly 1 to operate the pistons at the front and rear of the gearbox which control the gears. Moving the gearlever to the far left operates the starter switch 15. If difficult gear engagement is experienced, the checks described in **Section 7:2** should be made before removing the unit.

Removal requires firstly the detachment of either the facia board or the changespeed control cover in cars supplied before and after September 1961, respectively. Procedures are as follows:

1 To remove the facia board, first disconnect the battery. Take out the screws of the facia board cover and remove the anchor plates.

2 Remove the screws fixing the facia surround, access as necessary being obtained by removing the upper part of the glove box. Detach the nuts fixing the facia board, disconnect the speedometer cable and wires and remove the board.

3 Remove the changespeed control cover by taking out the finisher fixing screws and withdrawing the finisher on the steering wheel arm.

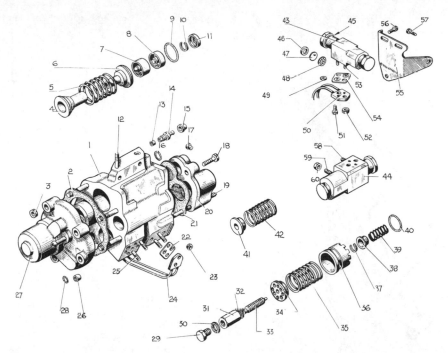

FIG 7:8   Part exploded views of the hydraulic gear selectot and the gear changespeed regulator

Key to Fig 7:8   1 Hydraulic gear selector and clutch control, with gear changespeed control. Front cover arrangement as used with centrifugal regulator   2 Front cover joint   3 Front cover nut   4 Thrust washer for synchronizing piston return spring   5 Return spring for synchronizing pistons   6 Thrust washer for synchronizing piston return spring   7 Synchronizing piston for third-speed   8 Synchronizing piston for second and fourth-speeds   9 Ring seal for synchronizing pistons of hydraulic gear selector   10 Split rubber ring between auxiliary clutch control cylinder and rear cover   11 Rubber joint between auxiliary clutch control cylinder and rear cover   12 Stud securing pipe assemblies   13 Joint for bleed screw   14 Bleed screw   15 Cap   16 Ring seal for selector slide valve   17 Rubber plug for setting hole   18 Screw securing rear cover   19 Stud securing gearlever assembly on hydraulic gear selector   20 Rear cover   21 Rear cover joint   22 Seal plate, gear change-speed control pipe assembly   23 Securing nut   24 Feed pipe assembly gear changespeed control   25 Studs securing pipe assembly   26 Aluminium stop for gear selector pistons   27 Front cover   28 Ring seal   29 Plug for locknut of adjusting screw   30 Copper joint   31 Locknut for adjusting screw   32 Copper joint   33 Adjusting grubscrew for automatic clutch control   34 Shouldered thrust washer for automatic clutch control piston   35 Return spring for automatic clutch control piston   36 Automatic clutch control piston   37 Circlip locking automatic clutch control valve   38 Thrust collar for valve spring   39 Automatic clutch control valve spring   40 Ring seal between automatic clutch control piston and rear cover   41 Thrust washer for gear control spring   42 Automatic gear control valve spring   43 Gear changespeed control attached perpendicular to hydraulic gear selector   44 Gear changespeed control attached parallel to hydraulic gear selector   45 Ring seal for plug   46 Distance piece   47 Disc jet with central or eccentric hole   48 Filter   49 Ring seal for plug   50 Feed pipe assembly   51 Screw securing feed pipe assembly   52 Nut securing pipe assembly   53 Studs for pipe assembly   54 Seal plate   55 Bracket   56 Screw securing gear change-speed control   57 Screw securing bracket   58 Stud   59 Stud   60 Nut

Put the manual height control lever in the low position and release the hydraulic pressure by slackening the bleed screw on the pressure control approximately half a turn. On early models without the manual height control, raise the front of the car with the wheels resting on the ground. Further operations are as follows:

1 Unscrew the lefthand suspension sphere. Place a cloth under the union in order to avoid spilling the fluid.

2 Disconnect the pressure feed pipe from the pressure distribution block at the second union from the right in cars before 1960.

3 Disconnect the union plates from the clutch engagement control where fitted and from the hydraulic gear selector. Remove the pipe assembly from the fixing studs. Remove the seal plate.

4 Referring to FIG 7:9, disconnect the union plate of the gearbox pipe assembly 1 without bending the pipes. Remove the seal plates.

5 In cars before September, 1960, disconnect the rubber pipe 2 feeding the low pressure pump and remove the low pressure pipe assembly 10. In later cars disconnect the overflow return pipe and the pipe assembly between the centrifugal regulator and the hydraulic gear selector.

6 Remove the rubber grommet in the steering tunnel and through the hole 'a' untighten the screw 3 in the coupling of the selector lever to the sliding valve of the hydraulic gear selector. Do not slacken the screw 4 in order to avoid moving the flange 5.

7 Disengage the speedometer cable from the seal plate on the hydraulic gear selector. On early models it is necessary to disconnect the plate.

8 Slacken the screw 6 on the auxiliary clutch control rod trunnion 13. Remove the nuts 7 from the studs attaching the hydraulic gear selector to the selector

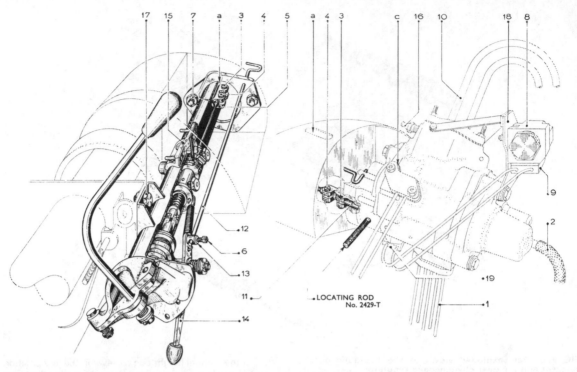

FIG 7:9 Gear selection and auxiliary clutch control lever assemblies connected to the hydraulic gear selector (front cover arrangement for low pressure pump) and gear changespeed regulator

Key to Fig 7:9   1 Five-pipe assembly to gearbox   2 Low pressure feed pipe   3 Screw in the coupling of the selector lever to the sliding valve of the hydraulic gear selector   4 Clamp screw   5 Selector clamp   6 Trunnion screw   7 Nuts and studs fixing the hydraulic gear selector to the selector lever assembly   8 Gear changespeed control or regulator   9 Pipe assembly retaining flange   10 Low pressure pipe assembly   11 Sliding valve   12 Auxiliary clutch control rod   13 Trunnion   14 Auxiliary clutch control lever   15 Starter switch   16 Bleed screw   17 Bracket screw   18 Bracket   19 Pipe assembly retaining flange   **a** Access hole, closed with rubber plug, for screw 3

lever assembly and disengage the hydraulic gear selector.

9 To refit the unit, first put the sliding valve 11 in the first-speed position by pulling and turning the valve until the hole in the valve corresponds with that of the rear cap on the hydraulic gear selector. Fit the 3.94 mm rod No. 2429.T in the locating hole. It should be possible to insert the rod approximately 30 mm, turning the sliding valve half a turn if necessary. Put the gear selector lever in the first-speed position.

10 Locate the hydraulic gear selector in place. With care, then pass the auxiliary clutch control rod 12 through the hole in the selector flange and into the trunnion 13 of the auxiliary clutch control lever. Engage the sliding valve 11 in the selector clamp 5.

11 Attach and tighten the nuts 7 on their studs. Make sure that the lever is in the first-speed position and tighten the screw 3 of the clamp 5.

12 **Withdraw the rod** No. 2429.T from the hydraulic gear selector. Refit the rubber plugs in the locating hole and the steering tunnel hole.

13 Push the rod 12 of the auxiliary clutch control as far as possible towards the hydraulic gear selector and the lever 14 towards the driver. Lock the screw 6 of the trunnion 13. Check that the sockets are connected

to the terminals of the starter switch 15. Fit the pressure pipe to the distribution block in earlier cars and engage the union flanges on the clutch engagement control and on the hydraulic gear selector. Fit new seal plates, ensuring that the rubber rings are located correctly in relation to the fluid holes. Tighten the pipe union on the pressure distribution block.

14 Connect up the gearbox pipe assembly 1 to the hydraulic gear selector. Insert a new seal plate, again checking that the holes are correctly positioned.

15 In cars before September, 1960, connect the flange of the low pressure pipe assembly 10 to the hydraulic gear selector. Insert a new seal plate, with correct location of the rubber joints. Connect the rubber pipe 2 feeding low pressure fluid to the hydraulic gear selector. Insert a rubber bush and fit a clip.

16 In later cars connect the overflow return pipe and the pipe assembly from the centrifugal regulator to the hydraulic gear selector.

17 Fit the rubber grommet and the speedometer cable on the hydraulic gear selector or fit the fixing plate. Refit the facia board or the changespeed control cover.

18 Start the engine, let it idle for a few minutes. Tighten the bleed screw and put the manual height control in the normal running position in order to put the

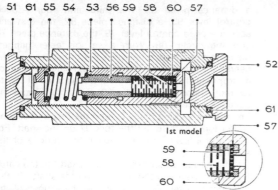

51 61 55 54 53 56 59 58 60 57

1st model

59
58
60

FIG 7:10 A sectional view of the gear changespeed control

Key to Fig 7:10
51 Plug   52 Plug   53 Piston
54 Spring   55 Spring adjusting screw   56 Screw
57 Filter   58 Disc restrictor   59 Disc restrictor
60 Distance pieces   61 Ring seal

systems under pressure. Check the joints for leakage. Change into each gear in succession in order to check the sealing of the flanges.

19 Bleed the hydraulic gear selector, for which it is necessary to apply the parking brake, raise the front of the car on stands and start the engine. Pass the gearlever successively through each gear. Operate the auxiliary clutch control several times with the gear selector lever in the neutral position and continue this operation for ten to fifteen minutes.

20 Adjust the slow-running, the clutch clearance, the clutch drag and the clutch engagement control as described in **Chapters 3** and **6**.

To remove the gear changespeed control (see 9 in **FIG 7:9**) release the pressure in the hydraulic system and put the auxiliary clutch control lever in the de-clutched position. Remove the feed pipe assembly and seal plates, then remove the unit from either its bracket 18 or its direct attachment in some cars to the hydraulic gear selector. Refitting is a reversal of the removal operations and on completion bleed the hydraulic gear selector as described in Operation 19 in the previous Section.

The components of the gear changespeed control are shown in **FIG 7:10**. Note that it is essential not to alter the spring adjusting screw 55. Otherwise the flow through the changespeed control will be changed, which will bring about fluctuations in the operation of the gears and will even cause damage to the gearbox. The rate of fluid flow can be checked and adjusted by a service agent with the aid of a hydraulic test bench unit No. 2298.T.

ID19:

7:5 Gearbox cover removal, dismantling and refitting

Before the gearbox cover in ID19 cars can be removed various connecting assemblies have to be detached as described in **Section 1:2, Chapter 1,** including the gearchange control and connecting tube. In more detail, referring to **FIG 7:11,** the operations concerned are as follows:

1 Disconnect the connecting tube 1 from the control tube 5 on the gearbox cover, retaining the rubber

gasket 6 and the two distance washers 10. Disconnect the connecting tube 1 from the bracket on the sidemember.

2 Disconnect the end piece 14 of the control rod 2 from the lever of the connecting tube.

3 Unscrew the fixing collars from the suspension reservoir. Pull the selector cable towards the front, lift the suspension reservoir and withdraw the connecting tube 1 also towards the front.

4 Disengage the circlip 9 and remove the key 8. Remove the pin coupling the cable 3 to the locking lever 16 and take care of the locking ring.

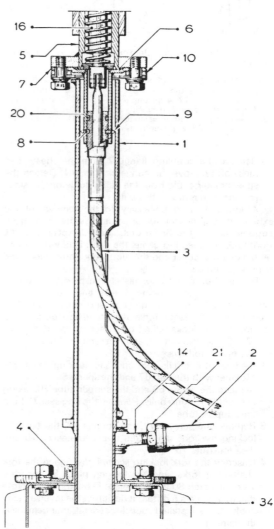

FIG 7:11 A sectional view of the manual type of gearchange control

Key to Fig 7:11   1 Connecting tube   2 Control rod
3 Cable   4 Bearing   5 Control tube   6 Rubber gasket
7 Coupling flange   8 Key   9 Circlip   10 Distance washers   14 Control rod end piece   16 Locking lever
20 Sealing ring   21 Locknut   23 Cup   24 Ball   25 Ball
26 Cup   27 Bellcrank lever   28 Fulcrum   29 Hollow fulcrum   34 Sidemember bracket

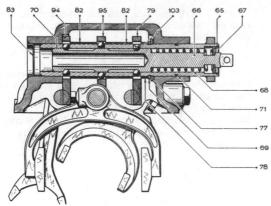

FIG 7:12 Gearchange selector mechanism for manual operation

Key to Fig 7:12   65 Circlip   66 Locking lever   67 Cup
68 Locking lever spring   69 Circlip   70 Support tube
71 Ring seal   77 Adjusting shim   78 Distance piece
79 Lever, first and second-speed   82 Distance piece
83 Sealing cap   94 Reverse lever   95 Third and fourth-
speed lever   103 Eighteen balls

5 Remove the coupling flange 7 from the sheath end
piece and remove the connecting tube 1. Detach the
speedometer cable from the cable guide on the sidemember and remove the guide.

Attention is also necessary to the removal of the
exhaust downpipe, the lower adjusting nuts of the front
support rods of the brake units (see **Chapter 10**), the
front brake connecting cable, the earth lead where fitted
on the gearbox cover and the rubber end thrust block and
support assembly.

The gearbox cover and gasket can now be removed
after releasing the retaining screws and studs. Lift the
cover vertically from the gearbox and remove the slide
blocks from the selector forks of the third and fourth-gears
to prevent the blocks falling off. Referring to **FIGS 7:12**
and **7:13,** the dismantling and reassembly of the cover is
carried out as follows:

1 Remove the circlip 65 and the locking lever 66,
together with the cup 67 and the spring 68.
2 Remove the circlip 69 and the support tube 70, taking
care of the locking balls. Remove the ring seal 71 from
the support tube.
3 Remove the screws 72, the springs 73, the balls 74
locking the fork shafts, the threaded sleeves 75 and
their locknuts 76.
4 Unscrew the fork locking screws, disengage the fork
shafts, the forks, and the locking plugs 81 together
with the catch 80 in cars before February, 1961. Note
that in later cars a different design of the reverse gearshaft 101 is installed, but the general arrangement is
the same.
5 Remove the adjusting shim 77, the distance pieces 78
and 82 and the levers 79, 94 and 95 from the fork
control lever shaft. Remove the sealing cap 83.
6 For reassembly, the two mandrels shown in **FIG 7:14**
are used to adjust the lateral clearance of the levers
controlling the selector shafts. Fit the mandrel A from
the righthand side of the gearbox cover. Fit the
reverse speed control lever 94 as shown in **FIG 7:13,**

a distance piece 82, the third and fourth-speed
control lever 95, a distance piece 82, the first and
second-speed control lever 79, the distance piece 78
and the circlip 69. With a set of feeler gauges,
measure the distance between the thrust face on the
gearbox cover and the circlip 69 and select a shim of
appropriate thickness to obtain a clearance of .15 to
.25 mm. Remove the circlip 69, the shim 77 and the
distance piece 78.
7 Engage the locking plugs 81 and the first and second
speed fork shaft 96. Fit the fork 97 on the shaft. Put
the control lever 79 in position in the groove of the
shaft 96.
8 Fit the third and fourth-speed fork shaft 99, the catch
80 where used and the fork 100 on the shaft 99. Put
the control lever 95 in position in the groove of the
shaft 99. Tighten the screw fixing the fork.
9 With the shafts 96 and 99 in the neutral position, push
the reverse gearshaft 101 towards the rear of the cover.
Engage the fork 102 on the shaft and put the lever 94
in position in the groove of the shaft.
10 Tighten the screws fixing the forks 97 and 102. Lock
the screws with wire to avoid unscrewing. Fit the
locking balls 74, the springs 73 and the screws 72 with
copper joints under the heads.
11 Fit the distance piece 78 and the shim 77 on the
mandrel A. Fit the ring seal 71 on the support tube 70
and fit the mandrel B in the support tube.
12 Put the 18 balls 103 in the tube 70, greased to keep
them in position. The shafts of the forks being in the
neutral position, engage the assembly of the mandrel
B and the tube 70 in the cover of the gearbox, pushing

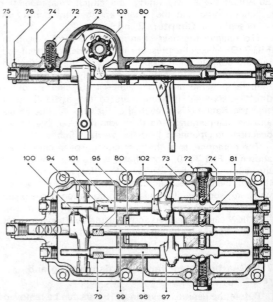

FIG 7:13 Sectional views of the gearbox cover used with manual control

Key to Fig 7:13   72 Screws   73 Springs   74 Locking
balls   75 Threaded sleeves   76 Locknuts   79 Lever
80 Catch   81 Locking plugs   94 Lever   95 Lever
96 First and second-speed fork shaft   97 Fork   99 Third
and fourth-speed fork shaft   100 Fork   101 Reverse shaft
102 Fork   103 Eighteen balls

the mandrel A at the same time with the tube 70. Fit the circlip 69 in the groove of the tube 70, between the distance piece 78 and the shim 77.

13 Check the tension of the locking lever spring 68, the length of which under a load of 29 ± 1.5 kg should be 52 mm.

14 Fit the spring and the cup 67 on the locking lever 66. Engage the locking lever in the support tube 70 and with the latter push out the mandrel B. Fit the circlip 65 retaining the locking lever and the sealing cap 83 with a reliable sealing compound.

15 To adjust the shafts controlling the forks, screw in the sleeves 75 of the fork shafts for a few threads, together with the locknuts 76. Then put the shaft 96 in the first-speed position. Screw up the threaded sleeve in order to bring it against the shaft, unscrew the sleeve a quarter of a turn and lock the locknut. Carry out the same operation for the second-speed position (shaft 96) and for the reverse speed shaft 101.

16 Note that in cars after February 1961, the second-speed position must be adjusted after the gearbox has been fitted on the vehicle. Also note that in cars before January 1960, the shaft 99 of the third and fourth-speed is adjusted when the cover is mounted on the gearbox. It should be ensured that the slide blocks of the third and fourth speed are in position when fitting the cover on the gearbox.

17 Ensure that the sliding gears are in neutral and then similarly place the selector forks in the neutral position.

18 Attach the gearbox cover gasket to the cover with grease, and also attach the selector slide blocks of the third and fourth-speeds with grease.

19 Locate the cover on the gearbox, ensuring that the forks engage correctly in the sliding gears and that the first gear control lever is engaged in the first and second gear selector fork shaft.

20 Secure the cover to the gearbox by means of two locating screws then by means of the other screws and studs.

21 To reconnect the gearchange control, fit a sealing ring 20 on the sheath end piece on the gearbox cover side.

22 Fit the cable guide on the cable from the front end, ensuring that the part of the tube projecting beyond the plate is at the front. Place a plain washer and a serrated washer on the threaded sleeve.

23 Place the cable and support assembly in position from the front of the car. Engage the rod of the cable 3 in the selector. Place the guide in position and tighten the fixing screw.

24 Put the speedometer cable in position in the cable guide and turn down the clips on the speedometer cable.

25 With the control tube 5 on the gearbox cover in the neutral position, place the seal 6 on the tube 5 and fit the pin coupling the shaft of the cable to the locking lever 16 (see **FIG 7:11**).

26 Bring the coupling flange 7 against the cover of the gearbox. Hold the flange 7 in position and pull on the sheath of cable 3 in order to fit the key 8 and the key retaining circlip 9.

27 Raise the suspension reservoir and put the connecting tube 1 in position. Insert the distance washers 10

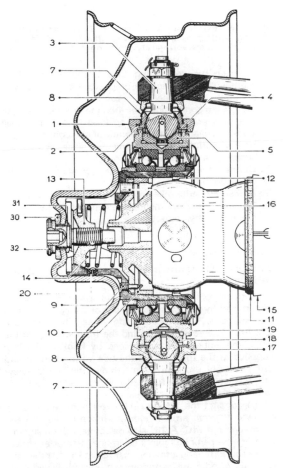

FIG 7:15   A sectional view of the front axle

Key to Fig 7:15   1 Steering lever   2 Upper pivot ball socket   3 Upper ball joint   4 Distance piece   5 Lower pivot ball socket   7 Rubber cups   8 Nylon or metal cups   9 Locking screw   10 Ring nut   11 Drive shaft dust cover   12 Seal   13 Wheel locking cone   14 Spring   15 Half shells retaining dust cover   16 Driving dogs   17 Flange   18 Socket   19 Play compensating spring   20 Wheel positioning dowel   30 Washer   31 Circlip   32 Wheel screw

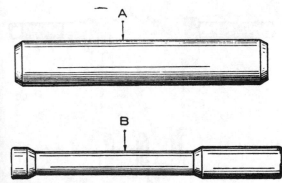

FIG 7:14   Mandrels No. 1793.T **A and B** used for adjusting lateral clearance of the levers operating the selector shafts (manual control)

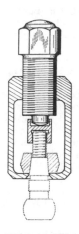
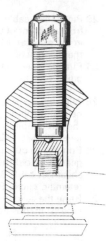

FIG 7:16 Extractor Nos. 1964.T (left) and 1864.T (right), with pressure pad No. 1968.T, used for disconnecting the steering relay rod from the steering lever

between the connecting tube 1 and the flange 7. Tighten the fixing screws on gearbox cover side with spring washers under the heads.

28 Secure the connecting tube 1 on the bracket 34 on the sidemember. The connecting tube 1 must be positioned accurately in the centre of the control tube 5 on the gearbox cover. Tighten the collars securing the suspension reservoir.

29 Connect the cable 3 to the selector lever and fit the coupling pin.

30 Adjust the front brake connecting cable (see **Chapter 10**) and refit the remaining assemblies in the reverse manner of their removal.

DS19 and ID19:

7:6 Drive shaft and pivot assemblies removal and refitting

Removal of a drive shaft and pivot assembly is undertaken by first raising the front of the car and fitting firm supports. Remove the spare wheel, the wing (see **Chapter 1, Section 1:2**) and the front wheel. For the latter, the embellisher is detached by hooking the tool supplied in the tool kit into the tyre valve aperture and using a slight pressure. Then remove the centre screw of the wheel using the long lever also provided. Referring to **FIG 7:15**, proceed as follows:

1 Disconnect the steering relay rod from the steering lever 1, using an extractor as shown in the lefthand drawing in **FIG 7:16**, also disconnect the axle arms from the pivot ball joints using an extractor as shown in the righthand drawing in **FIG 7:16**. Remove the cups 7 and 8 and withdraw the drive shaft and pivot assembly.

2 To dismantle the pivot, place the assembly in a vice support as in **FIG 7:17**. Drill through the centre punch marks and remove the locking screw 9 from the ring nut 10.

3 Take out the rivets from the half shells 15 retaining the universal joint dust cover 11 and remove the cover towards the splined drive coupling.

4 Using a screwdriver, disengage the oil seal 12 from the groove in the pivot hub.

5 To remove the drive shaft fixing ring nut 10 from the pivot nut groove, keep the drive shaft perfectly straight and fit the spanner 1920.T (see **FIG 7:17**) on the nut. Place a tubular extension on the spanner as the nut is tightened to a torque of 288 lb ft. Remove the drive shaft and nut assembly from the pivot. Remove the spring 14 and the cone 13, also the oil seal 12 from the splined end.

6 To refit the drive shaft, locate in position the wheel locking cone 13, with the dowel engaged in one of the slots of the hub, and the spring 14.

7 Insert the drive shaft in the pivot hub, with the holes of the driving plate of the drive shaft opposite the dogs 16 on the hub. The hole for the locking screw 9 should be opposite the tapped hole in the hub. Engage the driving dogs in their housings by tapping the end of the drive shaft.

8 Tighten the nut 10 (see Operation 5) to a torque of 288 lb ft. Engage the locking screw 9 and secure it with two centre punch marks.

9 Fit the seal 12. Deform the seal by squeezing it, tilt the splined end of the shaft and work the seal into position by rotating it on the shaft. Do not damage the ribbing on the seal by rubbing it against the splines. Engage the seal lip in the hub groove, using a tool with a rounded end.

10 Fit the dust cover 11 on the double universal joint and locate the retaining half shells 15. Bring the edges together and rivet them with a pair of universal pliers.

11 Locate the drive shaft and pivot assembly on the car. Clean the tapers of the ball joint and the arms. Engage the drive shaft in the splined drive coupling previously coated with graphite grease.

12 Connect the axle arms to the pivot ball joints and fit the cups 7 and 8. Tighten the nuts and fit a splitpin. Fit the dust cover on the gearbox side with its retaining clips.

13 Connect the steering lever ballpin on the pivot to the steering relay rod and fit the cups. Tighten the nut and fit a new splitpin.

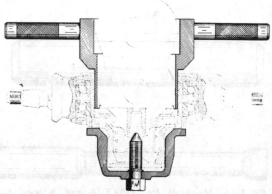

FIG 7:17 Spanner No. 1920.T and support No. 1922.T used for removing and refitting drive shaft ring nut

14 Fit the wing, the spare wheel and the road wheel. Lower the car to the ground and tighten the wheel fixing screw to a torque of 108 to 144 lb ft. Put the suspension system under pressure.

7:7 Fault diagnosis

(a) Jumping out of gear

1 Excessively worn locating slots in striking fork rods
2 Selector fork locking screws loose
3 Worn synchromesh units

(b) Noisy gearbox

1 Insufficient oil
2 Worn or damaged bearings
3 Worn or damaged gear teeth

(c) Difficulty in engaging gear

1 Clutch clearance, clutch drag, clutch engagement control or slow-running out of adjustment (DS19)
2 Incorrect setting of hydraulic gear selector and gear-lever (DS19)
3 Gearlever selector gate assembly unserviceable (DS19)
4 Operating pressures not maintained (DS19)
5 Incorrect clutch pedal adjustment (ID19)
6 Worn synchromesh cones

(d) Oil leaks

1 Worn or damaged oil seals
2 Loose or distorted front bearing caps or top cover
3 Defective joints

CHAPTER 8

THE FRONT AND REAR SUSPENSION

8:1 General description

Independent suspension of the weight of the car on each wheel is obtained by the use of separate hydro-pneumatic units of pressure spheres and cylinders as described in **Chapter 2**. The front suspension consists of two transverse arms on each side similar to a divided wishbone arrangement. At their front ends the arms are connected by ball joints (see **FIG 8:2**) to the front half-axle and pivot assembly. The rear ends are supported by taper roller bearings in an assembly attached to the chassis. The rear end of the upper arm is connected to a lever (see **FIG 8:1**) which operates the piston rod of the hydraulic cylinder, which is kept constantly supplied with fluid under pressure. The piston then moves in the cylinder according to wheel displacement and provides compensatory pneumatic damping in the pressure sphere. The lever carries two buffer arms and also another projection on which a coupling sleeve is connected and drops down to be attached to one end of the anti-roll or torsion bar.

From the centre of the anti-roll bar a rod is connected to the control valve of the height corrector shown in the righthand illustration in **FIG 8:1**. This valve, in conjunction with a similar unit on the rear suspension, adjusts the flow of hydraulic fluid into the suspension cylinders so that the static height of the car remains the same

irrespective of alterations of load at front or rear. When at rest the car is down at the rear, but when the engine is started the corrector system comes into operation and the rear of the car then rises until it reaches the normal height designed for comfortable travel. A manual control lever (see **FIG 8:3**) is linked by rods to both front and rear units. The lever 1 is normally in position 2, but if rough or rutted ground is being negotiated the ground clearance can be increased by about an inch if the lever is moved to 3. A further 2 inch of clearance is obtained by moving the lever to 4. There are also the extreme positions 5 and 6 for raising the car to change a wheel with the aid of the chassis prop provided, but these are not intended to be used in normal driving. However, 5 may be used exceptionally in extreme circumstances such as very rugged roads or snow drifts.

The rear suspension consists of a trailing arm pivoting on an articulating arm and bearings on each side and located on the rear half-axles as shown in **FIG 8:4**. Levers on the pivots of the arms are connected to the suspension cylinder pistons and an anti-roll bar is attached by coupling flanges to the two pivot bearings. From the centre of the bar a control rod runs to the height corrector, from which feed pipes are provided to each of the hydro-pneumatic units shown in detail in **FIG 2:6** in **Chapter 2**.

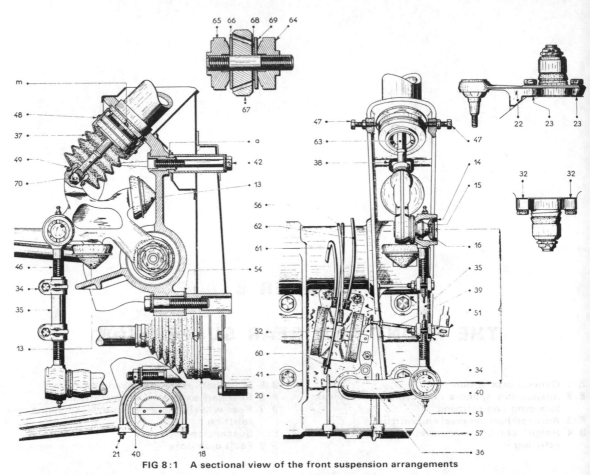

FIG 8:1   A sectional view of the front suspension arrangements

Key to Fig 8:1   13 Rubber buffer   14 Adjusting nut, ball joint on anti-roll bar connecting rod   15 Corrector control rod spherical bearing   16 Ball   18 Dust cover on flexible coupling   20 Adjusting shims   21 U-bolts   22 Steering lever
23 Adjusting washers   32 Washers   34 Collars   35 Anti-roll bar coupling sleeve   36 Anti-roll bar bearing caps   37 Cylinder dust cover   38 Connecting pin   39 Adjustable rod   40 Nut on locating stud   41 Outer screw   42 Upper screw   46 Connecting rod of suspension buffer bracket, or lever ballpin end piece   47 Cylinder fixing screw   48 Rubber band for fixing clip   49 Rubber band on dust cover   51 Connecting rod slot   52 Yoke of corrector control rod   53 Nut   54 Adjusting washers or shims
56 Overflow return pipe   57 Control lever   60 Suspension cylinder feed pipe   61 Corrector feed pipe   62 Corrector outlet pipe
63 Piston rod   64 Damper valve hexagon, sphere side   65 Damper valve hexagon   66 Valve   68 Valve   69 Valve   70 Ball
a Packing pieces fitted before October, 1956   **1** Dimension between centres of anti-roll bar ball joints and the suspension buffer bracket   **m** Engagement of point of cylinder fixing screw

8:2 Suspension spheres and cylinders removal, servicing and refitting

When work is undertaken on the hydro-pneumatic suspension units it is essential to observe extreme cleanliness. The units should be washed externally with a hose and the parts wiped dry to avoid water entering the system when dismantling. After removing the suspension sphere the damper housing in the sphere and cylinder should be cleaned with alcohol with the aid of a syringe. Use very clean plugs and close the openings.

Removal operations for a front suspension sphere and cylinder need firstly the removal of the wing, raising the front of the car, fitting firm supports and removing the wheel. Then release the pressure in the suspension system by unscrewing the pressure regulator bleed screw. Put the manual height control lever in the low position. Proceed as follows:

1 Remove the suspension sphere from the suspension cylinder for which a strap wrench 2223.T is available. On a lefthand unit make sure that a distance piece is removed from the sphere. Place a cloth under the cylinder in order to avoid spilling fluid on the side-member and the steering, and seal the openings of the cylinder and sphere.
2 Disconnect the feed pipe from the suspension cylinder and remove the side protection panel. Seal the openings.
3 Referring to **FIG 8:1,** remove the clips fixing the dust covers 37 on the cylinder and on the socket of the ball 16. Drain off any fluid released. Remove the dust cover from the piston rod bearing cup and the cylinder and leave the cover attached to the overflow return pipe. This pipe is not flexible and should not be bent.

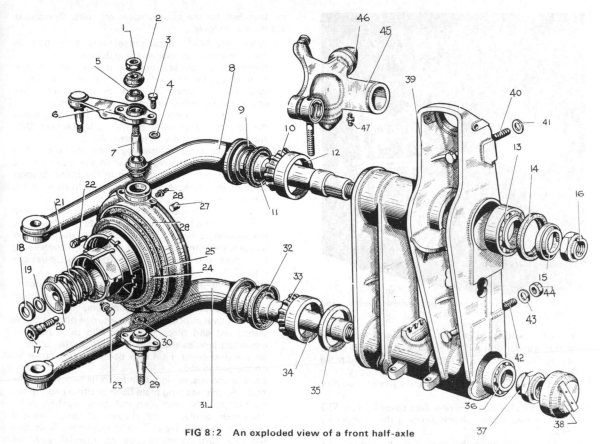

FIG 8:2   An exploded view of a front half-axle

Key to Fig 8:2   1 Nut for swivel ballpin   2 Rubber joint   3 Screw securing coupling lever and swivel flange   4 Adjusting washer   5 Articulation cup   6 Coupling lever on pivot   7 Ballpin assembly   8 Upper link arm   9 Cup for oil seal   10 Taper roller bearing cage   11 Oil seal   12 Bearing outer race   13 Bearing   14 Oil seal   15 Distance piece for suspension lever 16 Locking nut on arm   17 Wheel screw   18 Thrust washer   19 Retaining washer   20 Cone   21 Spring for cone   22 Locking screw for stub axle nut   23 Wheel positioning dowel   24 Ring seal deflector   25 Ring seal   26 Swivel and hub   27 Centring dowels for swivel   28 Grease nipple   29 Ballpin assembly   30 Spring for swivel ballpin   31 Lower link arm   32 Oil seal 33 Taper roller bearing cage   34 Bearing outer race   35 Adjusting washer for castor angle   36 Bearing   37 Locking nut on arm 38 Metal cap   39 Bracket for link arms   40 Screw retaining bracket   41 Washer   42 Screw retaining bracket   43 Washer 44 Nut   45 Suspension lever   46 Rebound rubber buffer   47 Grease nipple

4 Withdraw the connecting pin 38 from its anchor holes on the socket of the ball 16 and remove the piston rod 63 by lowering the axle arms as far as possible. The rod can only be disengaged when the holes for the connecting pin are parallel.

5 Unlock the locknut and unscrew the pointed cylinder fixing screws 47, when the cylinder can be withdrawn.

6 Referring to **FIG 8:5**, prise off the cap if unserviceable and remove the felt seal 16. Use a vice with wooden insertions in the jaws and tighten gently on the shoulder 'b' with the nut upwards.

7 Turn the cylinder over and hold the nut 17 in the vice with moderate compression. Unscrew the cylinder from the nut, using a C-spanner fitted on the boss of the feed pipe union 'c'. Remove the seal retaining washer 18 and the seal 19. Remove the piston 14. Carefully clean the parts and blow out with compressed air.

8 To reassemble, fit the felt seal-retaining cup 15 on the nut 17 with a press and using a bush. Soak the rubber

seal 19 in hydraulic fluid and assemble it in the seal thrust washer 18.

9 Note that the seal thrust washer 18 is paired with the piston 14. If either of these parts has to be renewed, the cylinder-piston assembly must be replaced or a part of the same class fitted. A number is engraved on the edge of the thrust washer and stamped on the head of the piston.

10 Immerse the felt seal 16 in hydraulic fluid and fit it in the nut. Note that it should be left to soak in hydraulic fluid for several hours. Fit the thrust washer and seal assembly on the cylinder and fit the nut 17 without tightening it.

11 Oil the piston with hydraulic fluid and insert it in the cylinder. If there is only slight scoring it is permissible to polish it lightly with abrasive paper No. 600.

12 Hold the cylinder in the vice by the nut 17, using wooden jaws, and tighten moderately. Tighten the cylinder on the nut to a torque of 14 lb ft, using a C-spanner gripping the feed union boss. This torsion

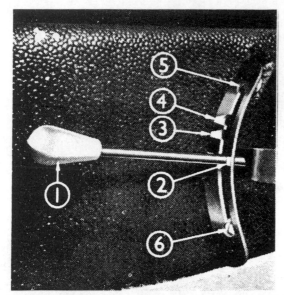

FIG 8:3 Ground clearance adjustment lever and positions

is very important, to prevent chattering of the piston in the cylinder or a serious leakage of fluid. Take care not to drop the piston during this operation and make sure that the piston slides freely. It is desirable to check the sealing of the piston and cylinder assembly by a bench test.

13 To refit the cylinder, fit a new dust cover 37 (see **FIG 8:1**) and its rubber sleeve, holding the cylinder by hand.

14 Fit the cylinder with the grooves at 'm' towards the pointed fixing screws. Position the dust cover overflow channel in relation to the nylon overflow pipe. Fit the clip on the rubber sleeve 48 and tighten the pointed screws 47 moderately in their housings. Lock the locknuts.

15 Assemble the piston rod 63 together with the connecting pin 38 in the cylinder and in the cup of the lever, by lowering the arm as far as possible. Make sure that the rubber sleeve 49 is fitted on the dust cover 37, also that the ball is in position. Engage the ends of the connecting pin in the holes of the cup.

16 Position the dust cover 37 on the cup of the ball 16, then fit the rubber sleeve and its clip.

17 Connect the feed pipe to the suspension cylinder and tighten the union.

18 Fit the suspension sphere and tighten by hand. On the lefthand side make sure that the suspension sphere is fitted with its distance piece. The front suspension spheres are marked with a number 59 stamped on the cap.

19 Start the engine. Retighten the pressure regulator bleed screw and put the suspension system under pressure. Check the unions for leakage. Refit the lateral protection panel, the wheel and the wing. Lower the car to the ground and tighten the wheel fixing screw to a torque of 108 to 144 lb ft.

The removal and refitting of a rear suspension unit is preceded by similar operations on the rear of the car

as described for the front suspension units. Operations are then as follows:

1 Referring to **FIG 8:6,** disconnect the feed pipe 52 from the suspension cylinder and plug the openings.

2 Remove the clips securing the dust cover 2 to the cylinder and to the overflow return pipe 53. If necessary, drain off any fluid from the dust cover. Disconnect the overflow return pipe from the cover.

3 Remove the connecting link 8 and the clip 9 fixing the ball joint dust cover on the buffer bracket. Disengage the dust cover 10 towards the rear.

4 Press on the arm and disengage the piston rod 7. The rod can only be disengaged when the holes for the connecting link in the rod and in the buffer bracket are parallel. If necessary, remove the front stop 14. Remove the two dust covers.

5 Remove the suspension sphere 54 using a strap wrench. Detach the retaining plate 55 from the suspension cylinder and withdraw the cylinder towards the front, turning it if necessary. Overhauling procedure is as described in the previous Operations 6 to 12.

6 When refitting, engage a new dust cover on the piston rod 7 and position the aperture of the overflow return pipe perpendicular to the connecting link pin hole. Put the cover in position on the knurled portion of the piston rod and place the fixing clip on a band of insulating tape as shown at 'f'. Fit the rubber bush 57 on the dust cover. Fit a new ball joint dust cover 10 on the piston rod.

7 Engage the suspension cylinder in its support on the body. Fit the retaining plate 55 in position and tighten the fixing screws with plain and spring washers under the heads. Screw on the suspension sphere 54 and connect the feed pipe 52 to the cylinder. Note that the rear suspension spheres are marked with the number 26 stamped on the cap.

8 To fit the piston rod, clean the extremities of the piston and the cylinder with alcohol. With the arm in its lowest position, put the piston rod 7 in the piston and then in the buffer support, with the overflow return pipe towards the top of the dust cover.

9 Before fitting the connecting link, make sure that the piston rod is in good contact with the ball, so that when raising the arm, the piston rod will not slip right off the buffer support. Fit the ball joint dust shield 10 in position so that the holes for the connecting link correspond. Fit the clip 9. Fit the connecting link with the longest leg through the buffer support and turn down the end of the connecting pin on the support as shown at 8. If it has been removed, replace the buffer 14.

10 Fit the rubber bush 58 on the overflow return pipe and fit the clip. Assemble the dust cover on the suspension cylinder together with the flexible bush 57 and tighten the clip.

11 Refit the wheel and the rear wing. Lower the car to the ground and put the systems under pressure. Check the unions for leakage.

Sectional views of the front and rear damper valves are shown in **FIGS 8:1** (items 64 to 67) and **8:6** (items 65 to 73). Their examination and servicing require very great care and precision and it is advised that a complete unit should be renewed if its operation is doubtful.

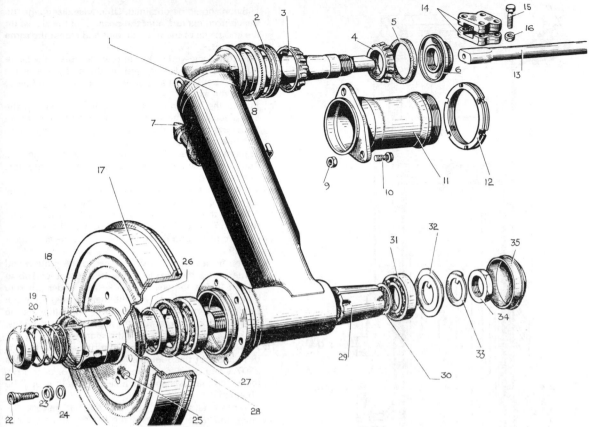

FIG 8:4   An exploded view of a rear half-axle

Key to Fig 8:4   1 Rear link arm   2 Sealing ring   3 Taper roller bearing   4 Taper roller bearing   5 Rubber sealing ring   6 Nut with cup for shaft   7 Rebound buffer   8 Cup for sealing ring   9 Nut   10 Screw securing bearing housing   11 Bearing housing   12 Ring nut securing arm   13 Torsion anti-roll bar   14 Clamp for anti-roll bar   15 Clamp screw   16 Nut   17 Brake drum   18 Stub axle   19 Spring for cone   20 Screw securing brake drum   21 Cone   22 Wheel screw   23 Washer   24 Retaining washer   25 Wheel positioning dowel   26 Spacer ring for stub axle bearing   27 Thrust bearing   28 Oil seal   29 Distance piece for stub axle bearing   30 Adjusting washer   31 Thrust bearing   32 Thrust washer   33 Lockwasher   34 Nut securing stub axle   35 Cap for stub axle bearing

8:3 Anti-roll bars removal and refitting

Initial operations for the removal of a front anti-roll bar include raising the front of the car and fitting firm supports, removing the front wheels, the spare wheel and its support and the lateral and lower protection panels. Release the pressure in the suspension system by unscrewing the pressure regulator bleed screw and put the manual height control lever in the low position. Further operations are as follows:

1 Referring to **FIG 8:1,** disconnect the corrrector feed pipe 61 at the front upper union and the return pipe 62 at the rear upper union. Disconnect the overflow return pipe 56 from the corrector and connect it to the return pipe in order to avoid draining the reservoir. Disconnect the feed pipe 60 for the suspension.

2 Unscrew the clamp fixing the corrector control rod on the anti-roll bar, also the clamps 34 in **FIG 8:1** of the anti-roll bar coupling sleeves 35. Unscrew the sleeves in order to disconnect the anti-roll bar from the front half axle.

3 Remove the corrector fixing screws and disengage the corrector, fitted with its bracket. Remove the adjustable rod 39.

4 Remove the U-bolts 21 fixing the anti-roll bar bearings, the bearing caps 36, the adjusting shims 20, the nylon bearings and the anti-rattle springs where fitted. Remove the anti-roll bar from the lefthand side of the car.

5 When refitting, smear the anti-roll bar bearings with graphite grease. The longest bearing is fitted on the lower bearing block. Locate the anti-roll bar in position, engaging it from the lefthand side of the car. Smear the bearings with graphite grease when refitting the bearing caps. With the nuts of the U-bolts tightened to a torque of 9 lb ft the anti-roll bar should turn under a load of 9 to 13 lb applied on the ball joint. If not, the thickness of the shims needs adjustment.

6 To fit the anti-roll bar to the half-axle in cars before February 1962, connect the anti-roll bar sleeve 35. Screw the sleeve on a few threads together with the

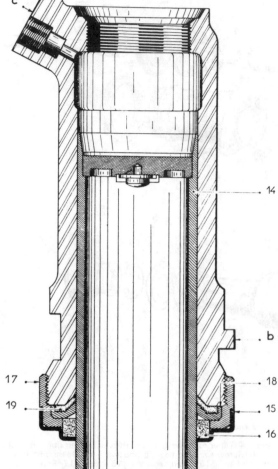

FIG 8:5 A sectional view of a suspension cylinder

Key to Fig 8:5 14 Piston 15 Retaining cup 16 Felt seal
17 Nut 18 Seal retaining washer 19 Joint **b** Shoulder
c Feed pipe union

198 mm should be obtained. Otherwise disengage the sleeve from the rod, alter the position of the sleeve on the end piece of the rod ball joint and repeat the same operations.

(c) Adjust the screwed sleeve in order to obtain the same number of threads engaged on the end piece of the anti-roll bar ballpin and on the lever ballpin end piece 46 on the axle.

(d) Locate the lefthand sleeve 35 a few threads on the end piece 46 of the suspension lever ballpin. Connect the sleeve on the anti-roll bar end piece and adjust it to obtain a dimension 'I' of 199 mm.

(e) Tighten the collars 34 of the right and lefthand sleeves. The slots in the collars should be in-line with the slots in the sleeves.

8 To fit the height corrector, engage the ball joint of the corrector control rod in the bore of the bearing cap 36. Offer up the corrector and bracket assembly. Connect the return pipe 62, the feed pipe 61, the overflow return pipe 56 and the feed pipe 60. Fit the adjustable rod 39.

9 Fit the front wheels, lower the car to the ground and tighten the wheel fixing screw to a torque of 108 to 144 lb ft. Put the suspension system under pressure and check for leakage. Put the manual height control in the normal position, opposite the white line. Fit the lateral and lower protection panels, the front wings, the spare wheel support and the spare wheel.

10 A check on the front heights after these operations is desirable, but this requires the use of special gauges 2307.T and the car positioned on a lift or over a pit, for which the assistance of a service agent should be obtained.

To remove and refit a rear anti-roll bar, release the pressure and raise the rear of the car on firm supports. Remove the corrector protection panels, then remove the clamp 1 (see **FIG 8:7**) of the rear corrector control rod 2 from the anti-roll bar. Remove the anti-roll bar coupling flanges 3 and disengage the bar.

When refitting, note that anti-roll bar and axle arm units of two different dimensions have been fitted successively and that the parts are not interchangeable. Fit the bar to give equal clearance between the bar and the articulating spindle on each side. Fit the coupling flanges 3 and tighten the nuts to a torque of 36 lb ft. Fit the control rod 2 and tighten the clamp. Refit the corrector protection panels, put the system under pressure and lower the car to the ground. Adjustment of the rear heights, if required, should be undertaken by a service agent with the necessary facilities.

8:4 Height corrector removal, dismantling and refitting

The removal and refitting of a front height corrector is described in the previous Section. For a rear height corrector, release the pressure and raise the rear of the car on firm supports. Remove the lefthand rear wing, the wheel and the lateral protection panel. Referring to **FIG 8:7**, disconnect the pipes 63, 62, 61 and 64, in that order. Connect 62 to 63 to avoid draining the fluid reservoir. Seal the openings of the pipes and the corrector and remove the corrector retaining screws, situated inside the rear boot at the front of the wheel arch.

clamps 34 on the connecting rod 46 of the suspension control lever. Connect the threaded sleeve on the anti-roll bar rod. Carry out the same operation for the other side. Simultaneously, screw the right and left sleeves in order to obtain a dimension 'I' of 198 mm on the righthand side and 199 mm on the lefthand side between the centres of the anti-roll bar joints and the suspension control lever. Tighten the clamp. The slots in the clamps should be in-line with the slot in the sleeve.

7 In cars since February 1962, a slightly different procedure is used as follows:

(a) Screw the righthand sleeve 35 on the threaded end piece of the anti-roll bar ball joint up to 5 mm before the end of the thread of the end piece. Bring the end piece 46 of the suspension lever on the axle into contact with the sleeve.

(b) Screw in the sleeve 35 one turn, then measure the distance between the centre line of the rod ballpin and the centre line of the lever ballpin. A dimension 'I' of

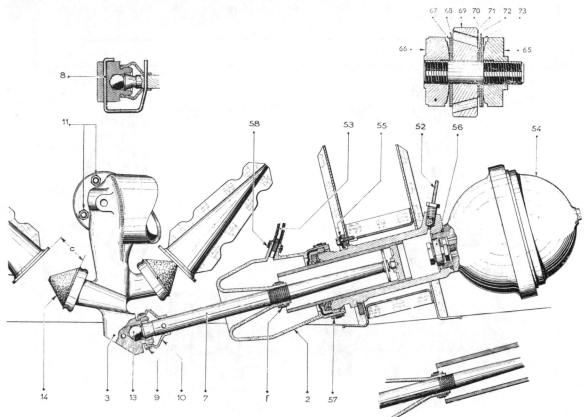

FIG 8:6   A sectional view of a rear suspension unit

Key to Fig 8:6   2 Dust cover   3 Buffer support   7 Piston rod   8 Retaining clip   9 Clip   10 Dust cover   11 Shouldered nuts fixing bearing housing on sidemember   13 Ball   14 Front rubber buffer   52 Cylinder feed pipe   53 Overflow return pipe   54 Pressure sphere   55 Retaining plate   56 Damper valve   57 Rubber bush   58 Rubber bush   65 Hexagon   66 Hexagon   67 Valve   68 Valve   69 Body   70-73 Valves   c 35 mm   f Insulating tape

The procedure for dismantling and reassembling a height corrector in cars since February 1960, is as follows:

1 Referring to **FIG 8:8**, remove the front rubber sealing caps 21. Remove the cap 22 retaining the rubber cups 23. If necessary, screw a plug D.391-63 (see **FIG 2:7** in **Chapter 2**) in the opening nearest to the cap and disengage by levering with a small screwdriver.

2 Remove the front nut 24 and disengage the steel cup 25, the rubber cup 23 and the inner steel cup 26.

3 Disengage the rubber cap 27 from the cup 28, proceeding as in Operation 1.

4 Remove the rubber cup 29 from the groove in the corrector body, also the valve and rear cup assembly.

5 Hold the control arm 30 in a vice and remove the locknut 31. Disengage from the valve 32 the control 30, the rubber cup 27, the washer 33, the steel cup 34, the rubber cup 29 and the steel cup 35.

6 Thoroughly clean the parts in alcohol and dry with compressed air. Note that the steel wire in the hole drilled in the body of the corrector, parallel to the spindle, must not be removed.

7 To reassemble, fit on the end of the valve 32 with the longer threaded portion the steel cup 35, the rubber

cap 29 (previously dipped in hydraulic fluid), the cup 34, the washer 33 and the rubber cap 27. Screw on the valve control arm 30 and tighten to a torque of 4 lb ft. Tighten the locknut 34.

8 Oil the valve with hydraulic fluid and insert it in the body of the corrector.

9 On the front end of the valve 32 fit the steel cup 26, the rubber cup 23 (previously dipped in hydraulic fluid), the steel cup 25 and tighten the nut 24 to a torque of $1\frac{3}{4}$ lb ft.

10 Immerse the corrector in hydraulic fluid and position the control arm by turning the valve and cup assembly.

11 Locate the rubber cups 23 and 29 in the grooves of the corrector body and fit caps 22 and 28 on the rubber cups 23 and 29. Fit the closing plugs in each of the corrector openings.

12 Remove the corrector from the fluid bath and fit the rubber caps 21 and 27 on the caps 22 and 28.

Operations are similar on correctors in cars before February 1960, but steel caps are fitted which are removed by blowing compressed air through the overflow return pipe. If one of the caps remains in position the plug D.391-63 is used as described in Operation 1.

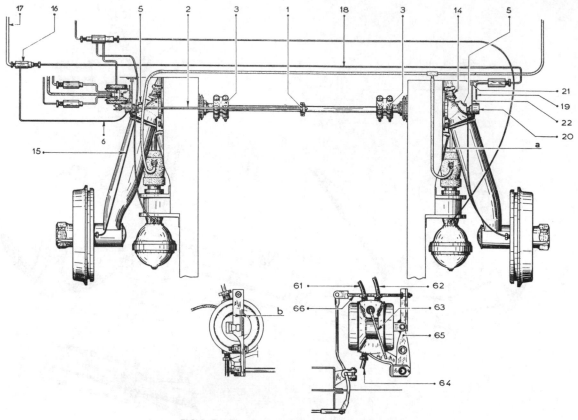

FIG 8 : 7   Rear axle and anti-roll bar assembly

Key to Fig 8 : 7   1 Corrector control rod clamp   2 Control rod   3 Anti-roll bar coupling flanges   5 Locking screw retaining articulating spindle   6 Pipe   14 Rubber buffer   15 Articulating pipe to wheel cylinder   16 Three-way union   17 Rear brake feed pipe   18 Righthand brake connecting pipe   19 Pipe   20 Articulating spindle   21 Support on sidemember   22 Retaining plate for articulating piping   61 Height corrector feed pipe   62 Overflow pipe   63 Overflow return pipe   64 Corrector pipe to suspension cylinder   65 Yoke of control rod (2)   66 Height variation control rod   **a** Minimum of .5 mm clearance   **b** 1 mm sideplay between fork base and corrector ballpin

8 : 5 Front half-axle removal and refitting

Raise the front of the car on firm supports and remove the front wheels, the spare wheel, the spare wheel support, the front wings and the side and lower protection panels. Release the pressure in the suspension system and set the height control lever in the low position. Proceed as follows:

1 Unscrew the clamp retaining the height corrector control rod to the anti-roll bar.

2 Referring to **FIG 8 : 1,** unscrew the collar 34 of the anti-roll bar coupling sleeves 35. Mark with paint the position of the coupling sleeves on the connecting rods and unscrew the sleeves to disconnect the anti-roll bar.

3 Disconnect the overflow return pipe 56 from the height corrector and disconnect the corrector pipe assembly union plate. Remove the height corrector assembly and pipes as described in **Section 8 : 3.** Remove the anti-roll bar bearing cap 36.

4 Remove the suspension cylinder as described in **Section 8 : 2.**

5 Put the manual height control in high position and disconnect the control by slackening the locknut and removing the control rod 39. In the case of cable controls before November 1957, the control should be placed in the low position to disengage the rod.

6 Disconnect the steering lever ballpin from the steering rod, for which service agents use an extractor 1964.T with pressure pad 1968.T (see **FIG 7 : 16**).

7 Disconnect the rubber dust cover 18 from the splined coupling on the gearbox.

8 Remove the screws fixing the half-axle and withdraw the latter. Do not mislay the existing adjusting washers 54 between the half-axle and the sidemember.

9 When refitting, note that on cars produced before October 1956, it is necessary to fit packing pieces 3 mm thick under the upper fixing of the half-axle at 'a'.

10 Offer up the half-axle on the car and engage the driveshaft in the splined coupling. Fit the half-axle with the nut 40 on the locating stud (plain and serrated washers), the outer screw 41 (plain and serrated washers), the inner screw and the upper screw 42

(plain and serrated washers). Tighten these screws and nuts slightly so as to seat the bosses on the half-axle on those on the sidemember. On cars produced since April 1958, fit a packing piece only between the half-axle and the body.

11 Using a set of feelers, measure the gap existing between the central fixing bosses on the side-member and the half-axle. Use two shims 54 of a thickness corresponding to the gap measured. Loosen the fixing of the assembly and locate the shims in position. Fit and tighten the screws with plain and serrated washers. Refit the rubber dust cover on the flexible coupling and attach the clip.

12 Connect the steering lever ballpin to the steering rod. Fit the steel and nylon cups on the stem of the ballpin. Tighten the nut and splitpin.

13 Adjust the fit of the anti-roll bar and connect the coupling sleeve as described in **Section 8 : 3**.

14 Refit the suspension cylinder and sphere as described in **Section 8 : 2**. Fit the lower suspension buffer 13 on its bracket if it was removed. Refit the height corrector assembly and pipes also as previously described.

15 Refit the wheel, tightening the fixing screw to a torque of 108 to 144 lb ft.

16 Fill the reservoir with fluid, start the engine, put the systems under pressure and check the unions for leakage. Lower the car to the ground and put the manual height control in the normal position.

17 Adjust the toe-in and the steering lock (see **Chapter 9**).

18 Check the level of the fluid in the reservoir with the engine running and the car in the normal position. Refit the lower and side protection panels, the front wings, the spare wheel support and the spare wheel.

8 : 6 Rear half-axle removal and refitting

Raise the rear of the car on firm supports, remove the rear wing and the wheel and release the pressure in the system. Remove the mud shield from the height corrector, the rear crossmember closing panel and the rear seat squab. Then proceed as follows:

1 Referring to **FIG 8 : 7**, disconnect the clamp 1 of the corrector control rod 2 after having marked its position on the anti-roll bar.

2 Disconnect the anti-roll bar coupling flanges 3, and disengage the anti-roll bar.

3 Referring to **FIG 8 : 9**, clear the metal from the groove in the sidemember to release the ring nut 4 and remove the nut, for which a special spanner No. 1757.T is available.

4 Remove the bleed screw and disconnect the brake feed pipe 15 (see **FIG 8 : 7**) from the wheel cylinder.

5 Remove the union locking screw 5 and disconnect the three-way union 16 from the feed pipe and the right-hand brake pipe.

6 In order to remove the righthand half-axle it is necessary to remove the rear wing, the wheel and the lefthand mud shield, also to remove the pipes from the retaining bushes in the sidemember in order to remove the pipe assembly.

7 Disconnect the piston rod 7 in **FIG 8 : 6** as described in **Section 8 : 2**.

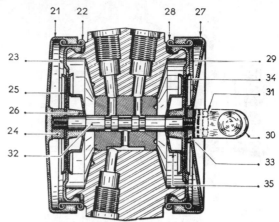

FIG 8 : 8   A sectional view of a height corrector

Key to Fig 8 : 8   21 Rubber sealing caps   22 Retaining cap   23 Rubber cups   24 Retaining nut   25 Steel cup   26 Inner steel cup   27 Rubber cap   28 Cup   29 Rubber cap   30 Control arm   31 Locknut   32 Valve   33 Washer   34 Steel cup   35 Steel cup

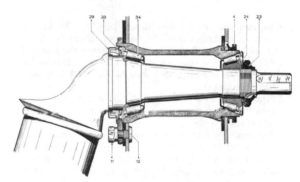

FIG 8 : 9   A sectional view of the rear articulated bearings

Key to Fig 8 : 9   4 Ring nut   11 Bearing housing nut   12 Housing fixing screws   23 Nut   24 Taper roller bearing   29 Oil retainer   33 Seal   34 Taper roller bearing

8 Remove the three nuts 11 fixing the bearing housing on the sidemember. Disengage the arm, if necessary by striking the end of the spindle with a mallet.

9 Drive out the housing fixing screws 12 (see **FIG 8 : 9**) only if they are damaged or worn and take care not to lose them inside the sidemember.

10 Clean the housing with petrol in order to remove the ball 13 (see **FIG 8 : 6**) from the buffer support 3. Remove the half-axle.

11 When refitting, if removed hammer in position the screws 12 fixing the bearing housing in the side-member.

12 Fit the arm in the sidemember and provisionally screw on the ring nut 4 (see **FIG 8 : 9**), the thin collar in contact with the sidemember.

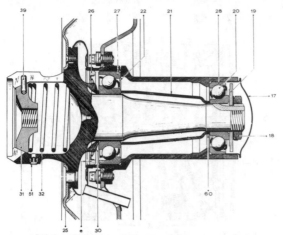

FIG 8:10   A sectional view of a stub axle

Key to Fig 8:10   17 Hub sealing cap   18 Stub axle nut
19 Bearing thrust washer   20 Inner ballbearing   21 Distance
piece   22 Outer ballbearing   25 Oil retainer   26 Seal
27 Outer race of ballbearing   28 Outer race of ballbearing
30 Bearing distance piece   31 Wheel locking cone
32 Spring   39 Dowel pin   51 Wheel positioning dowel
60 Washer   e Dimension of 4.5 mm from the hub face

13 Tighten the three shouldered nuts 11 fixing the
bearing housing. Do not fit a washer. Check that there
is not less than .5 mm clearance between the arm and
the ridge of the support at 'a' in **FIG 8:7**. Otherwise,
remove the front rubber buffer 14 (see **FIG 8:6**) and
file the support.

14 Finally tighten the ring nut 4 (see **FIG 8:9**). Knock
over the metal of the nut at one point into the grooves
in the sidemember.

15 Assemble the piston rod as described in **Section 8:2**.
Before fitting the retaining clip, make sure that the
piston rod is in good contact with the ball, so that
when raising the arm, the piston rod will not slip out
of the buffer support.

16 Fit the anti-roll bar, giving equal clearance on both
sides and so as to line up the marks made when dismantling the corrector control rod. Tighten the flange
screws to a torque of 36 lb ft.

17 Place the corrector control rod 2 on the mark made
when dismantling so as to give a side play at 'b' (see
FIG 8:7) of approximately 1 mm between the base
of the fork and the corrector ballpin. Tighten the
clamp 1.

18 If an anti-roll bar with a corrector control rod have
been replaced, the heights should be pre-adjusted
with the assistance of a service agent.

19 Fit the brake pipe by engaging the trunnion of the
union in the bore of the arm spindle. Tighten moderately the locking screw 5 and tighten the locknut.

20 Connect the pipe 15 to the wheel cylinder and fit the
bleed screw.

21 Align the pipe 6 so that the centre line of the feed pipes
in the three-way union and the centre line of the
articulating union are parallel. This operation is very
important. It is necessary that the articulating movement is not under strain, otherwise there is a risk of
seizure. Tighten the nuts on the three-way union 16.

22 Put the systems under pressure by running the engine,
refit the items removed during the preliminary
operations, fix the pipe assembly in the sidemember
by fitting the pipes in the sockets of the retaining
bushes and lower the car to the ground. Finally bleed
the brake system as described in **Chapter 10**.

8:7 Rear wheel stub axle removal, servicing and refitting

Raise the rear of the car on firm supports and remove
the wing and the wheel. To remove and refit the stub axle,
operations are as follows:

1 Referring to **FIG 8:10**, remove the hub sealing cap 17.
Lock the brake drum by tightening the brake shoe
adjusting cams. Remove the nut 18, the lockplate and
the thrust washer 19.

2 Unscrew the brake adjusting cams. Unscrew the brake
drum fixing screws and remove the drum after having
marked its position.

3 Remove the stub axle, for which service agents use an
extractor No. 2018.T.

4 Remove the ballbearing 20 and the distance piece 21.
Take care not to scatter the balls of the outer race.
Remove the oil seal 26 and remove the bearing cup 27
of the outer bearing 22 from the axle arm, for which
service agents use an extractor No. 2019.T.

5 Remove the inner race of the outer bearing from the
hub, for which an extractor No. 2020.T is available,
and remove the stop or distance piece 30.

6 Remove the wheel locking cone 31. Press the cone
into the housing of the spring 32 and pivot it through
a quarter turn round an axis passing through the centre
of the cone locking dowel 39. Remove the wheel
positioning dowel 51, using a drift.

7 Reassemble by fitting the outer race 27 of the outer
bearing 22 and fitting the inner bearing 20 in the hub
with a press. Lightly oil the outer races in order to ease
their fitting.

8 Grease the outer race 22 and put in position. Fit the
oil seal 26 at a distance 'e' of 4.5 mm from the outer
face of the axle arm.

9 Locate the spring 32 and the wheel locking cone 31
in position, after lightly oiling. Fit the wheel positioning dowel 51. Offer it up on its housing and locate it in
position with a drift. Hold the hub vertically, for which
a stand 1922.T is available, and position the distance
piece 30.

10 Fit the axle arm on the stub axle. Hold the arm by hand
and fit the bearing 22 on the journal on the stub axle,
using a press and a tube. Fill the bearing housing with
$3\frac{1}{2}$ oz. of special bearing grease.

11 Fit the distance piece 21 and the washer 60 if found
when dismantling. Fit the ball cage 20 previously
greased. Put the inner race in position with a press.

12 Fit the bearing retaining washer 19, the lockwasher
and the nut 18. Tighten the nut to a torque of 72 lb ft
with surface and threads greased. Turn over the lockwasher.

13 Fit the steel end cap filled with special bearing grease.
Fit the rubber pipe to the outlet of the oil retainer.

14 Adjust the brake shoes as described in **Chapter 10**.
Lock the nuts of the brake shoe articulating spindles
and turn over the lockwasher.

15 Fit the brake drum, noting the marks made when dismantling, and tighten the fixing screws. Fit the wheel and the wing and lower the car to the ground.

8:8 Suspension geometry

Suspension geometry applies to the camber and castor angles and also the swivel hub inclination, all of which have an important effect on the handling of the car. Camber is an outward inclination of the top of the front wheels to facilitate cornering. The castor angle, obtained by inclining the steering pivot, gives a self-centring action to the steering effort.

The inclinations employed are given in the Technical Data Section of the Appendix. Specially designed gauges are available to check the camber and castor angles for adjustment if necessary, for which the assistance of a well-equipped service agent should be obtained.

8:9 Fault diagnosis

(a) Wheel wobble

1 Worn hub bearings
2 Defective flexible couplings
3 Defective suspension units
4 Loose wheel fixings

(b) Bottoming of suspension

1 Check 3 in (a)
2 Faulty pressure system
3 Unserviceable damper valves
4 Worn suspension buffers
5 Incorrect buffer setting

(c) Heavy steering

1 Neglected lubrication of front suspension pivots
2 Incorrect suspension geometry
3 Front tyres under-inflated

(d) Rattles

1 Anti-roll bar connections loose
2 Loose pipework anchorages

CHAPTER 9

THE STEERING GEAR

9:1 Operating principles

The steering gear consists of a rack and pinion unit with two separate track rods, one for each front wheel. Under manual operation a pinion at the bottom of the steering column moves the rack from side to side. Otherwise the steering is hydraulically assisted by a booster cylinder on the end of the rack.

With hydraulic operation, fluid under pressure from the central system is applied direct to the appropriate sides of a piston in the cylinder through a rotating valve (see **FIG 9:2**) operated by the steering wheel shaft. As described in **Section 2:9, Chapter 2**, pressure is applied to one end of the cylinder and exhausted from the other according to the direction of turn. No mechanical contact exists between the steering shaft and the pinion except in case of failure of the hydraulic system, when the shaft and pinion are mechanically engaged. Otherwise the pinion merely takes up an idling position.

The steering wheel and the steering column are of integral construction, the single spoke of the wheel being formed by bending over an extension of the column into the wheel rim and thus improving safety and visibility. A turning circle of 36 feet is obtained.

9:2 Steering adjustments

Adjustments which may be made on the steering are concerned with (a) the lateral position, (b) the angular position, (c) the alignment, (d) the straight-ahead position, (e) the steering lock and (f) the cross-over pressure. For these operations, it is usually necessary to raise the front of the car, fit firm supports and remove the wing or wings, the battery, tray and support, as required for the work to be undertaken.

To adjust the lateral position, loosen the bearing cap screws and move the steering in its bearings to obtain a dimension of 122.5 ± 2.5 mm between the centre line of the lower relay lever and the centre line of the rack pressure pad (see **FIG 9:8**). Fit the bearing cap screws without tightening and adjust the angular position by fitting the fixture No. 1955.T (see **FIG 9:1**). Turn the steering assembly in its bearings in order to bring the groove 'c' in contact with the centre gauge pin 'D' of the fixture. Tighten the bearing cap screws and remove the fixture.

For the adjustment of the alignment the wheels should toe-in at the front from 1 to 3 mm. This can be

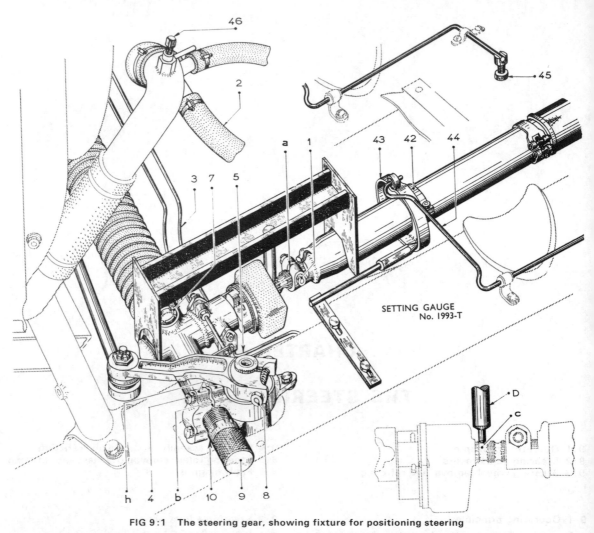

FIG 9:1 The steering gear, showing fixture for positioning steering

Key to Fig 9:1   1 Screw, steering tube to pinion   2 Hose assembly   7 Nut   8 Screws, steering levers to relay shafts   9 Cap   10 Locknut   42 Fixing collar   43 Centring cam   44 Torsion rod   45 Nut   46 Bleed screw   **a** Slot in tube   **b** Position of steering in relay bearings   **c** Groove c to be in contact with the centre gauge pin D of the fixture   3 Control pipes   4 Bearing cap fixing screws   5 Feed pipe

precisely determined by using special proprietary equipment or somewhat less accurately by ordinary measurement, when it is necessary to have the car at its normal height and on level ground with both front tyres inflated to the same pressure. With the wheels in the straight-ahead position, measure the distance between the rims at wheel centre height at the front. Mark these two points of measurement and then roll the car forward for exactly half a revolution of the wheels, so that the marks finish up at the rear. Measure again between the marked points. The difference between the measurements is the amount of toe-in. The alignment is set by altering the length of the righthand track rod. Referring to **FIG 9:2**, loosen the clamps 11 and turn the sleeve 12, on which a quarter of a turn corresponds to an alignment alteration of approximately 1 mm. Retighten the clamps to a torque of $7\frac{1}{4}$ lb ft and recheck the adjustment in the manner

described. Position the clamps so that the locking screws are opposite the slots in the sleeve (see **FIG 9:9**) and ensure that the ball joint of the track rod is not strained. Turn the steering fully each way to see that the clamp screws are clear of the front crossmember or radiator intake cowl.

Adjustment of the position of the steering in which the car runs in a straight line can only be carried out on the road. Travel on a straight flat road and hold the steering wheel to follow a straight line. Stop the car and mark the rim of the steering wheel with chalk in line with a similar mark on the dashboard. Adjust the position of the centring cam (see 43 in **FIG 9:1**) if required. Turn the steering wheel so that the marks made previously correspond. Loosen the fixing collar 42 of the cam and turn these until the roller is in the hollow of the cam. Tighten the collar to a torque of $3\frac{1}{4}$ lb ft. The roller should be parallel to the cam

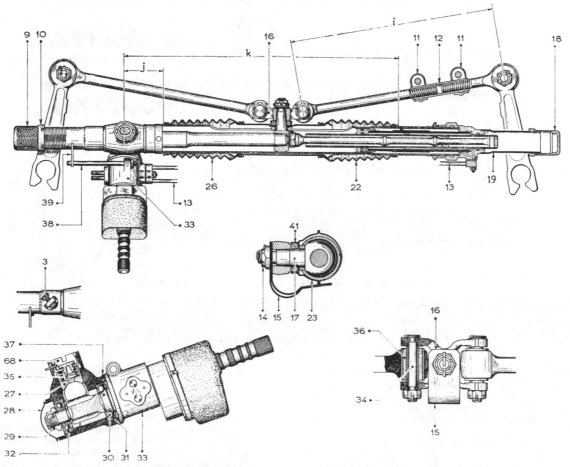

FIG 9:2 Steering linkage and pressure distributor

Key to Fig 9:2 3 Stop screw 9 Cap 10 Locknuts 11 Collars 12 Sleeve 13 Control pipe assembly
14 Nut 15 Retaining spring 16 Central shackle 17 Ballpin 18 Cap 22 Dust cover 23 Steel dust cover 26 Dust cover
27 Rack support plunger and pressure pad 28 Steel cap 29 Nut 30 Bearing balls 31 Rear upper bearing 32 Front lower
bearing 33 Rotating union 34 Pins 35 Spring 36 Silent blocks 37 Rubber sealing joint 38 Stop rod on rotating union
39 Support 41 Rubber sealing washer 68 Nut j 56 ± 2.5 mm k 574 ± 2.5 mm i 402 mm

and in the centre of it to within approximately 2 mm. Again drive along the road and check that the car runs in a straight line.

The steering lock should be set at $42 \pm {}^0_1$ deg. in order to avoid undue strain on the driveshafts. Place the steering wheel as for running in a straight line and turn the wheel exactly $1\frac{1}{2}$ turns towards the left. Adjust the cap 9 in **FIG 9:2** if necessary and tighten the locknut 10. Carry out the same operation to the right with exactly $1\frac{1}{2}$ turns of the wheel. Adjust the cap 18 and tighten the locknut. On early models, the righthand lock is set by the stop screw 3.

Adjustment of the cross-over pressure involves removing the pipe assembly and connecting it to two pressure gauges on a test bench (see **FIG 2:8, Chapter 2**) for which the assistance of a service agent should be obtained. Briefly, the operation is to turn the steering wheel to the right or left to obtain a pressure difference of

853 lb/sq in, then reversing the wheel direction and observing the pressure when the two gauges show the same reading, which should be 995 ± 150 lb/sq in. Adjustment is made on one of the adjusting screws (see 8 in **FIG 9:4**) in the pressure distributor.

The need for adjustment of the cross-over pressure may arise in the case of a knocking in the steering, if the steering flickers in the central position or if the steering is abnormally harsh in operation or stiff on the locks. In the first instance, the knocking can equally be caused by excessive clearance on the joint between the piston washers, a clearance on the shackle pin 19 (see **FIG 9:3**), an excessive clearance on the rack support plunger 27, or harsh spot on the slide valves or dashpot. In this case, it is necessary to overhaul the steering.

If the steering flickers in the central position the plug and cup assemblies 8 in **FIG 9:4** should also be checked after

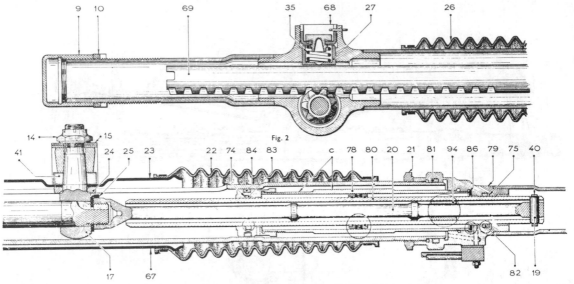

FIG 9:3   A sectional view of the hydraulic steering assembly

Key to Fig 9 : 3   9 Cap   10 Locknut   14 Nut   15 Spring   17 Ballpin   19 Connecting pin   20 Control rod   21 Locknut   22 Dust cover   23 Steel dust cover   24 Ball guide   25 Locking plate   26 Dust cover   27 Pressure pad or rack support plunger   35 Spring   40 Circlip   41 Rubber sealing washer   67 Steel dust cover   68 Nut   69 Rack   74 Rilsan washer   75 Rilsan washer   76 Teflon seal   78 Cylinder   79 Steering housing end piece   80 Piston   81 Ring seal   82 Ring seal   83 Ring seal   84 Ring seal   85 Rubber seal   86 Fibre joint   87 Shouldered washers   88 Circlip   89 Washers   94 Anti-rattle bush   c Engraving

releasing the pressure, to ensure ease of operation and absence of any burrs. Note that each cup is paired with its plug and the parts must not be mixed. For harsh operation, the alignment and the lateral and angular positions of the steering must also be checked, as already described.

If the steering shows signs of leakage it may be either a leakage causing a noise resembling an escape of gas when turning the steering a few degrees without moving the wheels or a leak causing the inflation of the rubber dust covers, leading to exterior leakage of fluid, when it is necessary to overhaul the steering assembly. In the first instance disconnect the pipe assembly controlling the rack from the steering end housing and close the openings with seal plates. If the leak persists it comes from the rotating union, which must be renewed or repaired. If the leak disappears, it came from the rack piston and cylinder assembly, which must similarly be renewed or repaired.

Note that before doing any work on the hydraulic control of the steering assembly it should be ensured that the ball joints of the steering or track rods are in good condition. Using a suitable extractor, disconnect the ball-pin on the pivot lever and ensure that the ballpins on the pivot lever and relay spindle (see **FIG 9 : 9**) move without binding and without tight spots even at the limits of their movement.

9 : 3 Steering wheel removal and refitting

In cars with power-assisted steering, mark the position of the locating cam 43 in **FIG 9 : 1** in relation to the steering column. Also mark with paint the position

of the pinion opposite the slot of the steering column at 'a'. Further operations are as follows:

1 Unscrew the collar 42 and remove the cam towards the front end of the column.

2 Remove the glove box and with a hand through the opening disengage the sealing sleeve 46 (see **FIG 9 : 5**) towards the front. Turn the steering wheel, in order to obtain access to the screw 47 of the collar 48.

3 Obtain an assistant to hold the spring 49 (service agents use the compressor No. 1991.T shown in the illustration) and unscrew the collar 48, for which the spanner No. 1994.T is used.

4 Remove the screw 1 (see **FIG 9 : 1**) coupling the steering column to the steering pinion and disengage the steering column.

5 Disengage the locating cam, the collar 48 (see **FIG 9 : 5**), the distance piece 60 (in cars since May 1958), the steel cup 50, the spring 49, the steel cup 51 and the conical cup 52.

6 To refit, offer up the steering column in its bracket on the scuttle shelf. Fit the conical cup 52, the steel cup 51, the spring 49, the steel cup 50, the distance piece 60, the collar 48, the cam 43 (see **FIG 9 : 1**) and its collar 42. Engage the steering column on the pinion, with the marks made when dismantling corresponding with the slot on the steering column. If the steering wheel has been renewed, turn the pinion in order to bring the outer bush of the flexible bearing of the lefthand steering rod to a distance 'f' of 275 mm from the centre line of the rack pressure pad (see **FIG 9 : 7**). A difference greater than 1 mm on this distance will cause excessive play on the steering wheel. Locate the steering wheel with the arm set at 30 deg. below the horizontal on the lefthand side.

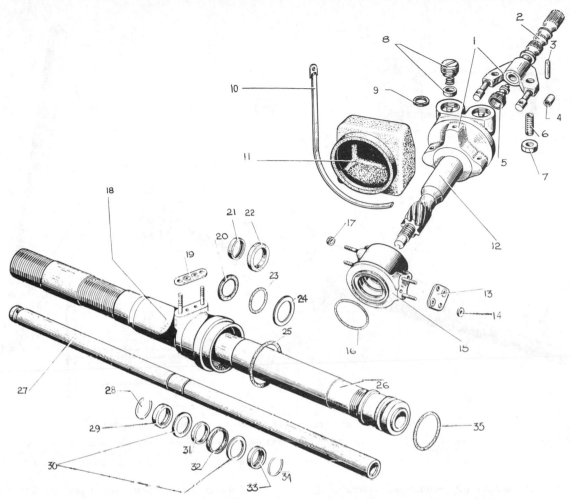

FIG 9:4   An exploded view of the steering hydraulic components

Key to Fig 9:4   1 Pinion assembly, complete with rotating union and coupling fork   2 Coupling fork for pinion   3 Needle operating slide valve   4 Rubber bush   5 Pinion spherical end piece   6 Adjusting screw for rotating union slide valve   7 Nut 8 Cap for dashpot, spring and thrust washer for valve   9 Sealing ring   10 Cover clip   11 Rubber cover   12 Pinion   13 Seal plate   14 Ring seal   15 Rotating union   16 Ring seal   17 Nut   18 Control for rack, with casing end piece, cylinder and piston 19 Seal plate   20 Washer   21 Joint for piston rod   22 Joint for piston rod   23 Ring seal   24 Sealing washer   25 Ring seal 26 Control cylinder for rack   27 Control rod for piston   28 Circlip   29 Shouldered washer   30 Washer   31 Ring seal   32 Joint 33 Shouldered washer   34 Circlip   35 Ring seal

7 Locate the coupling screw in the first groove of the pinion. Note that only the screw DM.441.100 with a smooth portion under the head should be used.

8 Place the gear selector lever in the second-speed position. Press lightly on the steering wheel and measure the distance 'm' (see **FIG 9:5**) between the knob of the gear selector lever and the edge of the steering wheel rim, which should be between 40 to 60 mm. Otherwise use another groove on the pinion. Tighten the nut of the coupling screw after making sure that it is properly in position in the groove.

9 Compress the spring 49 and when the coils are touching, tighten the screw 47 on the collar 48. Make sure that there is no play when pushing and pulling alternately on the steering wheel.

10 Refit the sealing sleeve 46 on the support tube and locate the steering locating cam on the positioning mark made when dismantling. Tighten the collar 42.

11 Refit the glove box where necessary and check the straight-ahead position of the steering as described in the preceding Section.

In cars with manual steering (see **FIG 9:6**), remove the battery and the instrument panel cover. Mark the position of the steering pinion as previously described. The retaining collar is then removed, also the screw attaching the steering column to the flexible coupling, when the steering column may be withdrawn. Refitting operations are the reverse of those used in removal, noting that the spring must be fully compressed when tightening the screw of the collar.

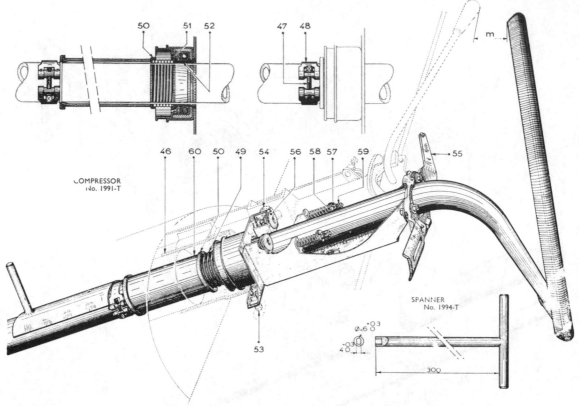

FIG 9 : 5   Details of the steering wheel assembly (power-assisted steering)

Key to Fig 9 : 5   46 Sealing sleeve   47 Screw   48 Collar   49 Steering wheel retaining spring   50 Steel cup   51 Steel cup   52 Conical cup   53 Front fixing screws, steering column bracket   54 Screw fixing gearlever assembly   55 Steering column finisher   56 Rubber washers   57 Washers   58 Springs   59 Nuts   60 Distance piece   **m** 40 to 60 mm (other dimensions in mm)

9 : 4 Steering assembly removal and refitting

To remove and refit a power-assisted steering assembly as a unit, operations are as follows:

1 Remove the spare wheel, the spare wheel support and the lefthand front wing. Release the pressure.
2 Remove the battery and tray, and either drain the hydraulic fluid from the reservoir or fit a closing plate to the flange of the steering feed pipe assembly 5 (see **FIG 9 : 1**).
3 Remove the collars fixing the reservoir. Disengage the high pressure pump feed pipe from the battery bracket and remove the bracket together with the bonnet lock control cable.
4 Remove the steering relay protection shields. Put the steering column setting gauge No. 1993.T in position and disconnect the steering column from the pinion.
5 Disconnect the pipe assembly 5 from the pinion housing. Remove the seal plates and fit a closing plate on the flange of the pipe assembly if the reservoir has not been drained.
6 Disconnect the steering levers from the relay shafts.
7 Remove the steering bearing caps.
8 Remove the steering assembly from the steering column and withdraw the assembly from the lefthand side of the car.

9 In the case of manual steering arrangements, the battery, tray and instrument panel cover are removed. Further procedure is to slacken the screw of the collar, in this instance above the spring, and disconnect the flexible coupling from the steering pinion. Then to release the steering assembly disconnect the steering levers from the relay shafts, remove the steering bearing caps and withdraw the assembly from the lefthand side of the car.
10 When refitting, set the arm of the steering wheel so that it is 30 deg. below the horizontal on the lefthand side. Turn the pinion to bring the outer bush of the lefthand steering rod silent block (see **FIG 9 : 7**) to a distance 'f' of 275 mm from the centre of the rack pressure pad. A difference of more than 1 mm in this dimension will give excessive play on the steering wheel.
11 Offer up the assembly from the lefthand side of the car and engage the pinion into the splines of the steering column. Fit the steering into its bearings. Adjust the lateral position, in order to obtain a distance 'g' of 122.5 ± 2.5 mm, between the centre line of the lower lefthand relay lever and the centre of the rack pressure pad as shown in **FIG 9 : 8**. Fit the bearing caps and the screws without tightening, inserting spring washers.

Fit the screw 1 (DM.441.100) coupling the steering column to the pinion and tighten the nut and a spring washer. Make sure that the screw is correctly positioned in the groove of the pinion. The dimensions stated in this and the preceding Operation also apply when refitting a manual steering assembly in the reverse manner of its removal as described in Operation 9.

12 Adjust the angular position of the steering (see **Section 9:2**).

13 Fit the fixture No. 1955.T, then turn the steering assembly in its bearings in order to bring the groove 'c' into contact with the gauge pin 'D' of the fixture. Tighten the fixing screws 4 of the bearing caps and remove the fixture.

14 Connect the steering levers to the relay shafts with the nuts 8 towards the outside. Tighten the nuts to 18 lb fit and remove the setting gauge No. 1993.T.

15 Connect the feed pipe assembly 5 to the pinion housing. Fit the seal plates, so that the holes for the fluid correspond to those on the union plate. Tighten the nuts and spring washers.

16 Refit the items removed when commencing operations. Refill or top up the reservoir, start the engine, put the systems under pressure and check for leaks. Adjust the alignment, the straight-ahead position and the steering lock as described in **Section 9:2**.

A rack hydraulic control can be removed without removing the steering as follows:

1 Raise the front of the car on firm supports and remove the front righthand wing and wheel. Release the pressure.

2 Disconnect the steering pipe assembly flange from the steering housing. Place a cloth under the flange to avoid spilling fluid on the brake unit. Drain the steering system by turning the steering on full lock on both sides.

3 Remove the protection shield from the righthand steering relay housing. Unscrew the locknut of the righthand steering lock cap and remove the cap.

4 Turn the steering fully to the left. Referring to **FIG 9:3**, remove the circlip 40. Remove the connecting pin holding the piston to the rack control rod, for which service agents use an extractor No. 1969.T. Remove the righthand bearing cap.

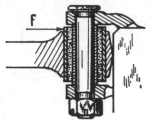

FIG 9:7   Outer bush of steering rod bearing

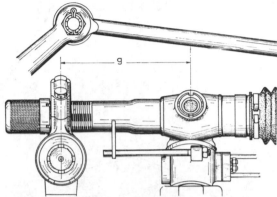

FIG 9:8   Distance between centre line of lower lefthand relay lever and the centre of the rack pressure pad

5 Unscrew the locknut 21 of the steering casing piece and hold the steering in a straight line.

6 Unscrew the rack control assembly and remove by pulling towards the front of the car within the limit permitted by the steering column.

7 When refitting, make sure that the piston-cylinder assembly and the bore of the casing are well cleaned, also that the seals 84 and 81 are in position on the cylinder end piece and in the casing end piece. Dip the parts in hydraulic fluid before assembly.

8 Engage the rack control in the steering tube by pulling the steering towards the front, within the limits permitted. Screw up the rack control assembly until the pipe assembly flange is in position, without using force. Fit the righthand bearing cap and tighten the fixing screws and spring washers.

9 Hold the steering housing end piece 79 and tighten the locknut 21. Connect the control pipe assembly flange, inserting a seal plate. Tighten the nuts and spring washers.

10 Turn the steering on the left lock, so that the hole in the control rod 20 is in line with the holes at the end of the piston 80. Align the two parts with a conical drift. Locate the connecting pin 19 in position and fit the circlip 40.

11 Refit the items removed when commencing operations, lower the car to the ground, start the engine, put the systems under pressure and check the unions for leakage.

Complete dismantling, overhaul and reassembly of the steering mechanism requires not only special tools, equipment and fixtures but also precise measurement methods and careful selection of seals and washers for correct adjustment on reassembly according to changes

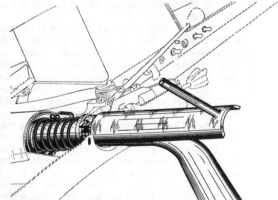

FIG 9:6   Upper connection of steering column for manual steering

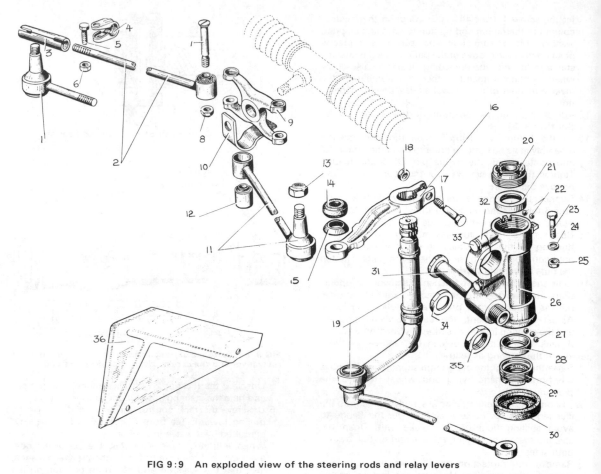

FIG 9:9   An exploded view of the steering rods and relay levers

Key to Fig 9:9   1 End piece with ballpin   2 Steering rod   3 Adjusting sleeve on steering rod   4 Clamp for adjusting sleeve
5 Screw   6 Nut   7 Bolt for steering rod shackle   8 Nut   9 Shackle for steering rods   10 Spring retaining rack ballpin
11 Steering rod and ballpin   12 Flexible bush   13 Ballpin nut   14 Rubber washer   15 Sealing cup   16 Relay upper lever
17 Screw   18 Nut   19 Relay lower lever with tie rod   20 Nut, top of relay housing   21 Outer bearing race   22 6.74 mm balls
23 Screw   24 Adjusting washer   25 Nut   26 Relay housing   27 6.74 mm balls   28 Outer bearing race   29 Nut, bottom of
relay housing   30 Rubber ring   31 Bolt securing housing   32 Cap   33 Cap screw   34 Washer   35 Nut   36 Shield
for housing

in design which have been made at different times.
Work of this nature comes within the province of an
experienced service agent with the necessary facilities.

9:5 Steering relay removal, overhaul and refitting

Preliminary operations are to raise the front of the car
on firm supports, and remove the spare wheel and its
support, the front wing and the battery and its tray. In cars
fitted with manual steering remove the instrument panel
cover and turn the steering wheel so as to unscrew the
collar mentioned in the first Operation 9 in **Section 9:4.**
For power-assisted steering, release the pressure, drain
the reservoir, remove its fixing collars and disengage the
high pressure pump feed pipe from the battery support.
Remove the support, the bonnet lock control cable and
the relay housing mud shield 36 (see **FIG 9:9**). Then
proceed as follows:

1 Disconnect the pipe assembly 5 in **FIG 9:1** from the
steering distributor and remove the seal plates.

2 Disconnect the steering lever from the spindle of the
relay under attention.

3 Mark the position of the steering in the relay bearings
with paint. Remove the bearing caps and lower the
steering assembly and column assembly slowly, in
order to avoid damage to the steering wheel assembly.

4 Disconnect the steering rod from the steering lever
on the pivot, for which service agents use an extractor
No. 1964.T with pressure pad No. 1968.T (see **FIG
7:16**). Remove the rubber seal and nylon cup.

5 Referring to **FIG 9:9,** remove the screw 23 fixing the
relay assembly on the sidemember. Remove the nut
from the relay fixing spindle 32 and disengage the
relay assembly and steering rod. Keep carefully the
relay assembly adjusting washer 24.

6 Disengage the rubber bush 30. Remove the retaining
metal to disengage the lower nut 29. Remove the
lower lever 26, the steering rod assembly and the
lower bearing race 28. Take care of the ballbearings.

7 Remove the retaining metal to disengage the upper nut 20 and remove the upper bearing race 21. Clean the parts.

8 To reassemble, refit the upper bearing race 21 and the upper nut 20 until the upper face is about 1 mm from the upper face of the relay housing. Insert about $\frac{3}{4}$ oz of EP grease into the housing.

9 Locate the 14 ballbearings in the upper bearing race 21 and secure with grease.

10 On the lower lever fit the rubber bush 30, the lower nut 29, and the lower bearing race 28.

11 Holding the lower lever 19 in a vice, fit the bearing race 28 slightly below the lower groove in the lever. Put 14 balls in the race and secure them with grease. Also use grease to hold the lower nut 29 on the the bearing race 28. Fit the race on the lever with the balls in position in their bearing groove. Turn the housing over and engage the lever 19 vertically.

12 Hold the bearing race 28 and screw up the nut 29. If necessary, use a tube to position the race in the housing. Lock the nut 29 by turning down the metal. Locate the rubber bush 30 in position.

13 Tighten the upper nut 20 to a torque of 43 lb ft, then unscrew the nut and retighten to a torque of 14 to 22 lb ft. Lock the nut by turning down the metal.

14 If the work carried out has been made necessary by seizure of a ball joint, even at the limit of its movement, the operation of the ball joints of the other relay lever and the pivot levers should be checked.

15 Refit by offering up the relay and steering rod assembly. Put the relay fixing spindle 31, fitted with its washer and previously oiled, in position. Fit the nut on the spindle without tightening. Note that since June, 1958, the fitting of the spindle is reversed, with the head of the spindle on the engine side and the nut on the outside. The spindle is fitted with a washer under the head. The new type relay spindle can be fitted in place of the early type. Note that the washer is fitted with the concave part towards the head of the spindle and the flat positioned downwards.

16 Connect the rod of the steering lever on the pivot. Insert a nylon cup and the rubber seal 14. Tighten the nut to a torque of 29 lb ft and insert a new splitpin.

17 Fit the steering in its bearings, noting the paint marks made when dismantling. Put the roller in position on the steering locating cam. Fit the bearing cap fixing screws 33. Adjust the angular position of the steering, using the fixture No. 1955.T (see **FIG 9:1**).

18 Turn the steering assembly in its bearings, so that the groove 'c' touches the centre gauge pin (D) of the fixture. Tighten the fixing screw 4 in **FIG 9:1** of the bearing caps and remove the fixture.

19 Connect the steering lever to the relay spindle with the nut on the engine side. Tighten the nut to a torque of 18 lb ft.

20 Connect the feed pipe assembly to the rotating union. Fit the seal plates with new ring seals, so that the holes for the fluid correspond to those in the union plates. Tighten the nuts and spring washers.

21 Fit the relay housing mud shields and other items removed when commencing operations.

22 Refill the reservoir, lower the car to the ground, start the engine and put the systems under pressure. Check the unions for leakage and recheck the fluid level in the reservoir. Check the alignment, the straight-ahead position and the steering lock.

9:6 Fault diagnosis

(a) Wheel wobble

1 Unbalanced wheels and tyres
2 Slack steering connections
3 Incorrect steering geometry
4 Excessive play in steering gear
5 Worn hub bearings

(b) Wander

1 Check 2, 3 and 4 in (a)
2 Uneven tyre pressures
3 Uneven tyre wear

(c) Heavy steering

1 Check 3 in (a)
2 Very low tyre pressures
3 Neglected lubrication
4 Wheels out of alignment
5 Steering shaft bent
6 Lateral or angular positions maladjusted
7 Incorrect cross-over pressure

(d) Lost motion

1 Worn pinion splines
2 Loose pinion coupling
3 Worn rack and pinion teeth (manual steering)
4 Worn ball joints

(e) Steering knocks

1 Check 7 in (c)
2 Worn shackle pin
3 Excessive clearance on rack support plunger
4 Worn pressure distributor components

(f) Flickering in central position

1 Check 7 in (c) and 4 in (e)

CHAPTER 10

THE BRAKING SYSTEM

10:1 Description of layout

Both front and rear brakes in DS19 cars are operated hydraulically from the main servo system by foot pressure on a plunger with a small circular pad. This has very limited travel, sufficient only to open two distribution valves, one each for the front and rear hydraulic circuits, and hence needs only light application. As described in **Chapter 2,** the proportion of effort applied to front and rear braking is automatically adjusted according to the loading of the car.

Disc-type front brakes are mounted on the end of each front wheel drive shaft. A moving carrier in each caliper unit compresses the pads against the disc when hydraulic pressure is applied through pistons. Air inlets from the front of the car provide for brake cooling. The rear brakes are of the expanding type, the drums incorporating leading and trailing shoes and mounted on the rear hubs.

In early DS cars fluid pressure is fed from the main accumulator to two brake pressure spheres or accumulators (see **FIG 10:1**) each connected to a distributor valve for either the front or rear brake circuits. An accelerated idling control (see **Chapter 3**) relates brake pressure to engine speed. In later cars (see **FIG 10:2**)

one front brake accumulator receives its pressure from the front suspension circuit. Pressure is bled off from the rear suspension system direct to a distributor valve for the rear brakes. A warning light on the facia comes into operation to indicate any loss of brake pressure and another warns of low fluid level in the reservoir.

In addition to the hydraulic brakes a cable operated mechanical brake is operated by a pendant pedal for emergency use on the front brakes only. It also serves as a parking brake after the pedal has been depressed and then locked down by means of a knob with a safety catch below the facia. When the knob is released the brake can be used for normal pedal application, but with no servo assistance much greater pressure has to be applied.

In ID19 cars similar hydraulically operated disc and drum brakes are used at front and rear respectively, but different methods of application are employed. Until August 1961, operation was by pendant pedal gear through a master cylinder and with a separate brake fluid reservoir. In later cars the pedal gear operates a brake control unit connected to the main servo system, with a security valve installed between the pressure regulator, the general piping and the control unit.

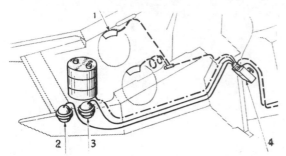

FIG 10:1 DS19 hydraulic brake system before July 1960

Key to Fig 10:1 1 Front brake cylinder   2 Rear brake accumulator   3 Front brake accumulator   4 Brake pedal assembly

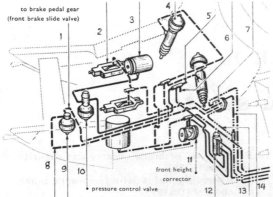

FIG 10:2 DS19 hydraulic brake system since July 1960

Key to Fig 10:2 1 To brake pedal gear, front brake slide valve 2 Front brake unit   3 High pressure pump   4 Front suspension cylinder 5 To hydraulic gear selector 6 To steering 7 Union flange to brake pedal gear   8 Front brake accumulator feed, front suspension pressure   9 Front brake accumulator 10 Pressure control valve   11 Front height corrector 12 Pressure distribution block   13 To brake pedal gear, rear brake slide valve, rear suspension pressure   14 To brake distribution cylinder

10:2 Routine maintenance, brake shoe adjustment

The gauge showing the level of the hydraulic fluid in the reservoir should be inspected at intervals of not more than 500 miles and the fluid topped up as necessary. It is essential that **only an approved fluid should be used,** as described in **Chapter 2, Section 2:1** together with the necessary attention to be given to the reservoir filter. When adding fluid according to the instructions on the outside of the reservoir **the maximum mark should not be exceeded,** otherwise excess fluid may be forced through the breather hole in the filler cap with a low suspension setting. Bleeding will be necessary after cleaning the filter. Open the bleed screw on the pressure regulator (see **FIG 2:1**) one full turn, take the cap off the reservoir and start the engine. When it is seen that the fluid entering the reservoir is free from air bubbles, tighten the bleed screw and refit the cap. In those ID cars which have a separate brake fluid reservoir, the maintenance of its fluid level should be similarly observed, adding the recommended fluid as far as the inlet to an overflow pipe connected to the main reservoir.

The disc brakes are self-adjusting. As the lining material of the brake pads becomes worn, fluid under pressure in the caliper cylinders and pipelines will compensate for wear. Adjustment of the height of the brake unit is made by adjusting the nuts of the front support rod so that the linings project slightly at the front of the disc by about 1 mm. Adjusting the position of the unit is carried out by first operating the mechanical brake control several times to take up the clearance of the pads. Then proceed as follows:

1 Slacken the screw 21 (see **FIG 10:3**) locking the spherical bush in the rear support bracket 10, so that the pin 19 will slide freely in the bush. Unscrew cautiously as otherwise the plug 22 will become displaced. Ensure that the ball slot is vertical.

2 Depress the mechanical brake pedal and lock it in the parking position. Ensure that the end of the pin is level with the inside face of the brake unit, then tighten the screw 21 to a torque of 28 lb ft to lock the pin. Finally secure this screw with wire to the screw 24 through the holes in the screw heads.

To adjust the rear brake shoes, raise the rear of the car on firm supports and remove the rear wings. Then turn the two hexagon-headed adjusting pins on the backplate of each brake, one at a time, until the shoe contacts the drum. Mark with chalk the position of the adjuster relative to the backplate. Now knock back the adjuster about one flat by tapping the spanner with the hand. To obtain the correct clearance, knock it forward again until the mark on the adjuster is just short, say $\frac{1}{8}$ inch, of the mark on the backplate. Rotate the wheel to check that no binding occurs. Repeat with the other adjuster, then carry out the same operations on the remaining wheel.

10:3 Brake pads and brake shoe linings

The front brake pads or shoe linings should be renewed when the thickness of the linings is less than .3 mm. Scoring on the linings presents no danger, but they must be dry and free from oil. In order to equalize the braking it is necessary to renew the four shoes at the same time. Operations are as follows:

1 Raise the front of the car on firm supports and remove the front wheels. When renewing the pads on the lefthand side, remove the battery and tray. On ID cars disconnect the generator support, put the generator against the water pump, drain the radiator and disconnect the flexible water pipe and the steel pipe.

2 Remove the cover 1 (see **FIG 10:3**). Unscrew the brake shoe locking spring and remove the trunnion 6 and the screw 4.

3 Referring to **FIG 10:4** locate the fork No. 2128.T in position as shown and in cars before late 1961 slowly tighten the screw so as to free the clearance adjusting ratchet. In later cars press on the ratchet lever with a long screwdriver.

4 Press down the rubber cover on the sidemember and insert the special spanner and extension No. 2129.T in the hole 'a' in the brake unit. Unscrew the unit bleed screw if necessary. Also when unscrewing the shoes make sure that they do not become wedged. The adjustable thrust sleeve now freed may engage on the mechanical brake control shaft and the brake unit must then be completely dismantled. Note that

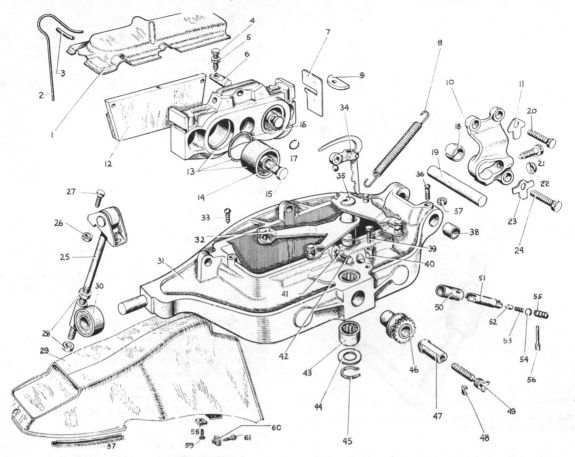

FIG 10:3   An exploded view of a front brake unit

Key to Fig 10:3   1 Cover   2 Retaining spring   3 Rubber sleeve   4 Pointed screw locking lining plate
5 Nut   6 Pin   7 Shim for adjusting moving carrier   8 Return spring for control lever   9 Guide plate for moving carrier
10 Rear support bracket   11 Lockwasher   12 Lining plate   13 Moving carrier, pistons and ring seals   14 Piston
15 Piston rod   16 Ring seal   17 Piston rod circlip   18 Spherical bush   19 Rear support pin   20 Screw securing rear support
21 Locking screw for spherical bush   22 Plug locking spherical bush   23 Lockwasher   24 Screw securing support
25 Front adjustable support   26 Nut   27 Screw   28 Nut   29 Cooling duct   30 Adjustable support, female unit
31 Cradle   32 Brake control cranked lever   33 Locking screw for guide plate   34 Pawl   35 Lever and spindle for
mechanical control   36 Screw securing control lever return spring   37 Nut   38 Cradle bush   39 Screw for eccentric bush,
control lever adjustment   40 Eccentric bush   41 Nut   42 Control lever pin   43 Needle roller bearing on cradle   44 Washer
45 Circlip on mechanical control spindle   46 Adjustment wheel   47 Adjustable pushrod, female   48 Clip retaining male plunger
49 Adjustable pushrod, male   50 Guide bush   51 Locking pin   52 Plunger   53 Spring   54 Disc   55 Locking spring
56 Spring stop pin   57 Rubber sealing joint   58 Nut   59 Screw   60 Nut clips   61 Screw

on DS cars since June 1958, the movable brake shoe return spring is discontinued. Press the movable shoe backwards with a screwdriver, so that it remains in contact with the plunger.

5 Disengage the brake shoes, for which service agents use an extractor No. 2133.T.

6 Clean the disc and ensure that it is free from grease or oil. Fit new lining units, for which it is preferable to renew the plates and linings as complete assemblies. Take care not to handle them with greasy fingers. Refit the trunnions so that the points of the screws enter the milled conical impressions in the brake shoes. Operate the mechanical brake pedal or the handbrake handle several times to take up the clearance on the shoes.

7 Level and adjust the height of the brake unit as described in the previous Section. Refit the cover, also the wheels and other items dismantled for access and lower the car to the ground.

Renewal of the rear brake shoe linings is undertaken as follows. As for the front brakes, to ensure even braking it is necessary to renew the brake linings on both rear wheels at the same time.

1 Raise the rear of the car on firm supports and remove the wings and the wheels. Mark the position of the brake drum on the stub axle, remove the fixing screws and then the drum.

2 In cars since December 1957, referring to **FIG 10:5**, unhook the brake shoe return spring 35 using spring pliers.

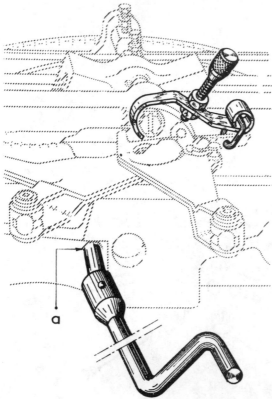

FIG 10:4 (Top) Fork No. 2128.T (Bottom) Articulating spanner No. 2129.T

3 Remove the cups 56 from the springs 57 by turning a quarter of a turn, in order to unlock them from the rods 58. Hold the rods with the spring pliers.

4 Turn down the lockwasher 41 and remove the nuts from the spindles 40 and the lockwasher. Disengage the brake shoes and remove the eccentric bushes 43.

5 Renewal of linings is preferably to be undertaken by fitting new brake shoe and lining assemblies complete. Fit the eccentric bushes on the brake shoes.

6 Fit the brake shoes on the brake backplate, the shoe with the longer lining towards the front and with the paint mark towards the operator. Assemble the lock-washer 41 and fit the nuts without tightening. Assemble the rods 58, the springs 57 and the cups 56.

7 Lock the cups 56 on the rods by turning through a quarter of a turn. Hook on the brake shoe return spring 35.

8 Adjust the brakes as described in **Section 10:2** and complete operations in the reverse order of dismantling.

9 To remove the brake shoes in cars before December 1957, after removing the return spring 35 remove the splitpins from the shoe guide pins 36 and disengage the washers 37, the springs 38 and the retaining washers 39. Remove the nuts from the anchor pins 40, the retaining washers and the distance washers 42. Withdraw the brake shoes. Refit by following the removal operations in reverse and adjust the brakes as described in **Section 10:2**.

10:4 Handbrake adjustment

The mechanical pedal-operated brake in DS cars serves also as a parking brake when the control mentioned in **Chapter 1** is locked by hand and to this extent can be termed a handbrake. In ID cars the mechanical brake is operated by pulling on a swivelling handle (see **FIG 10:6**) with a locking arrangement supplemented by a safety device. In both cases the brake acts on the front wheels.

Adjustments on the operating cables are undertaken after first removing the spare wheel and its support, the wing, the lefthand cover, the battery and battery tray. Referring to **FIG 10:7**, with the brake in the fully off position the dimension 'a' should be 60 mm. Adjust the control cable if necessary by slackening the locknut and turning the threaded sleeve. Retighten the locknut to a torque of 32 lb ft.

The connecting cable is correctly set when the lever 7 is on the point of separation from the stop 8. Adjustment if required is made by altering the positions of the nut and locknut 5 and 6 with the pedal in DS cars pressed down threequarters of its travel. After retightening release the pedal and check the positions of the levers relative to their stops, also that there is no play at 'd'. Refit the equipment removed for access.

10:5 Removing, servicing and refitting front brakes

To remove and refit a front brake unit it is necessary to drain and remove the radiator, also the front engine support crossmember and the brake cooling duct. Disconnect the connecting cable from the control levers and remove the sheath stop.

Release the pressure and remove the brake shoes as described in **Section 10:3**. Disconnect the brake feed pipe and the connecting pipe, sealing the brake unit and pipe openings. In DS cars disconnect the accelerated idling control feed pipe from the lefthand brake unit and the centrifugal regulator (where fitted) pipe from the righthand brake unit.

Remove the brake unit articulating spindle, first removing the locking wire from the screws 21 and 24 in **FIG 10:3**. The screw 21 must only be loosened, not removed. If necessary extract the spindle with the aid of a 10 mm dia. x 125 mm pitch screw. The unit may now be disengaged by tipping it towards the front.

Detach the two vertical pad locking bolts and lever out the pads by inserting a screwdriver into the holes at each end of the shoes. Lift the locking lever on top of the caliper and insert the special adjusting tool (see **FIG 10:4**) into the adjusting hole near the centre of the side of the caliper. Rack off the adjustment completely by turning the tool anticlockwise. Remove the two movable carrier securing bolts and ease the two horizontal steel keys 9 in **FIG 10:3** out of the carrier slots. Remove and keep carefully any shims 7 from between the caliper and the front and rear faces of the carrier and lift out the carrier assembly.

Place the carrier with the pistons uppermost, disengage the piston rods 15 (see also **FIG 10:8**) and remove the pistons 14. Remove the ring seals 16, using a 2 mm dia. brass wire hook with a flattened end and avoiding scratching the cylinders. If the grooves are badly pitted and corroded the carrier should be renewed. Otherwise clean all the parts thoroughly, including the pistons, with alcohol and blow with compressed air. The pistons

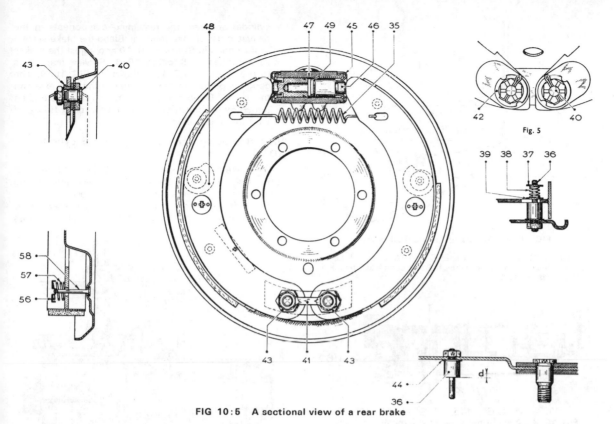

FIG 10:5 A sectional view of a rear brake

Key to Fig 10:5   35 Brake shoe return spring   36 Brake shoe guide pins   37 Washers   38 Springs   39 Brake shoe
retaining washers   40 Spindles (anchor pins)   41 Lockwasher   42 Distance washers   43 Eccentric bushes
44 Distance washers   45 Dust covers   46 Pistons   47 Circlips   48 Adjusting cams   49 Ring seals   56 Cups
57 Springs   58 Rods   **d** 3.25±.1 mm

should be renewed if showing signs of having been
knocked or scratched.

Fit new seals, moistened with hydraulic fluid and
carefully seated in their grooves. To refit the pistons it is
necessary to immerse the carrier completely in a clean
container filled with new hydraulic fluid, to ensure that the
minimum amount of air is trapped in the carrier when the
pistons are fitted. Insert the pistons in the cylinders up to
about two-thirds of their height. The part then protruding
from the movable carrier must be between 8 to 10 mm. In
each of the openings for the feed pipes or bleed screw, fit a
sealing lining and screw in the closing plug No. D.391.63
(see **FIG 2:7** in **Chapter 2**). Withdraw the carrier from
the container, dry it and clean with alcohol.

Reassembly of the carrier is in general undertaken in
the reverse manner of its removal. Shims 7 must be fitted
on either side of the carrier to give a clearance of .25 mm.
After fitting the carrier and pads, locate the caliper and
tighten the two bracket bolts. Turn the adjuster with the
special tool until the pads grip the disc, then lock the
longitudinal screw and wire together with the bolts on
the bracket to lock the setting. The adjustment is then
racked off gently until the caliper is free to swing up and
down. Check that the front support is free to turn and
reconnect. Refit the remaining components removed
when dismantling and bleed the brake system as described
in **Section 10:10**.

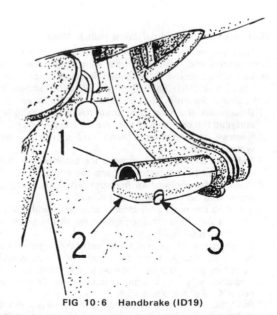

FIG 10:6 Handbrake (ID19)

Key to Fig 10:6   1 Swivelling handle   2 Locking lever
3 Locking screw

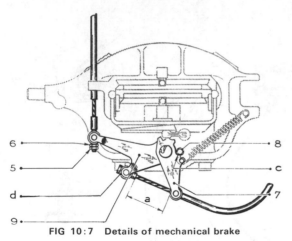

FIG 10:7 Details of mechanical brake

Key to Fig 10:7 5 Locknut 6 Nut 7 Lever
8 Stop 9 Lever a 60mm when brake is completely released
c Stop d See text

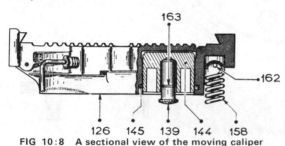

FIG 10:8 A sectional view of the moving caliper

Key to Fig 10:8 126 Brake block 139 Piston rod
144 Piston 145 Ring seal 158 Return spring
162 Spring anchor pin 163 Circlip

10:6 Removing and refitting rear brakes

Raise the rear of the car on firm supports, chock the front wheels and remove the rear wing, rear wheel and brake drum as previously described. Release the pressure in DS and later ID cars. Remove the brake shoes as instructed in **Section 10:3** and proceed as follows:

1 Disconnect the feed pipe from the wheel cylinder and plug the openings of the cylinder and feed pipe.
2 Remove the retaining screws and disengage the wheel cylinder.
3 Referring to **FIG 10:5,** remove the bleed screw, the dust cover 45, the piston 46, and the circlip 47.
4 Remove the ring seal 49 from the piston 46, using a brass wire hook flattened at the end.
5 Clean all the parts with alcohol and blow with compressed air. When reassembling, dip all the parts in new hydraulic fluid.
6 Locate the circlip 47 in position and fit the ring seals 49 on the pistons 46. Insert the pistons 46 in the wheel cylinders after having made sure that there are no scratches or burrs or signs of seizure. Refit the dust cover 45 and the bleed screw.
7 Refit the wheel cylinder on the brake backplate and tighten the fixing screws with spring washers under the heads. Connect the feed pipe to the wheel

cylinder and refit the remaining components in the reverse order of their removal. Bleed the brake system as described in **Section 10:10** and adjust the brakes as described in **Section 10:3**. Service practice is to use the gauge 2115.T shown in **FIG 10:9**. The gauge is placed on the hexagon of the stub axle and the screw **D** tightened. The brake shoes are then turned by the adjusting cams until the index **B** is level with the lining all round.

10:7 Removing and refitting master cylinder (ID19)

The brake hydraulic system in ID19 cars up to August 1961, is shown in **FIG 10:10**. The removal and refitting of the master cylinder is undertaken as follows:

1 Seal off the feed aperture in the fluid reservoir by inserting a plug with tapered end to avoid fluid loss

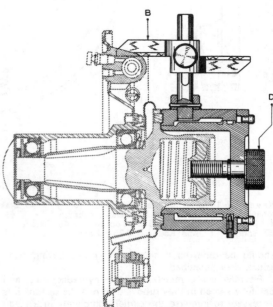

FIG 10:9 Gauge No. 2115.T for adjustment of rear brake shoes

Key to Fig 10:9 B Index finger D Tightening screw

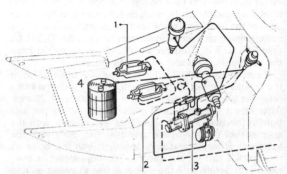

FIG 10:10 ID19 hydraulic brake system before September 1961

Key to Fig 10:10 1 Front brake cylinder 2 Four-way union
3 Master cylinder 4 Fluid reservoir

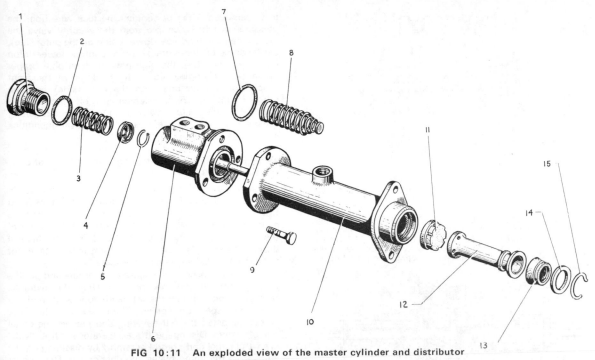

FIG 10:11   An exploded view of the master cylinder and distributor

Key to Fig 10:11   1 Distributor cap   2 Ring seal
6 Distributor body with slide valve   7 Ring seal   8 Spring
12 Piston   13 Secondary cup   14 Piston stop washer

3 Spring for slide valve   4 Cup   5 Circlip
9 Screw   10 Master cylinder body   11 Main cup
15 Circlip

when the master cylinder is removed. In cars since February 1958, release the pressure and set the height control at 'low'.

2 Disconnect the master cylinder feedpipe or pipes and the front brake connecting pipe. Slightly slacken the front union in cars before February 1958.

3 Disconnect the rear brake connecting pipe. Remove the fixing nuts and withdraw the master cylinder from its bracket.

4 Referring to **FIG 10:11,** remove the circlip 15 retaining the piston 12 and hold the latter to prevent the parts from scattering under the pressure of the spring 8.

5 Remove the stopwasher 14, the piston 12 complete with the secondary cup 13, the main cup 11, and the spring 8 together with its steel cup behind the main cup 11.

6 Disconnect the distributor body 6 from the master cylinder. Remove the seal 7 from the distributor body, also the cap 1, the spring 3, the seal 2 and the slide valve, together with the cup 4 and the circlip 5.

7 Remove the cup and the circlip from the slide valve, also the cup from the piston.

8 Clean all the parts in alcohol or clean brake fluid, but no other preparation.

9 The master cylinder and the high pressure supplementary feed control must be free from all traces of rust and wear, otherwise they must be renewed. Inspect carefully and make sure that all passages are not blocked. Before reassembly immerse all parts in clean brake fluid.

10 Reassemble by putting the circlip and the cup on the slide valve. Locate this assembly in the 'high pressure supplementary feed control' or distributor body 6. Continue operations in the reverse order of those used to dismantle the unit.

11 Note that in cars since February 1958 the distributor section of the master cylinder is discontinued and the

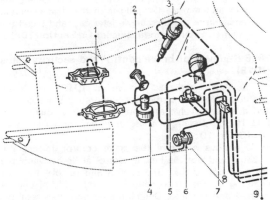

FIG   10:12   ID19   hydraulic   brake   system   since September 1961

Key to Fig 10:12   1 Front brake housing   2 High pressure pump   3 Front suspension cylinder   4 Pressure regulator   5 Brake control   6 Front height corrector 7 High pressure supply to brake control system, front brake slide valve   8 Security valve   9 To brake control, rear brake slide valve, rear suspension pressure

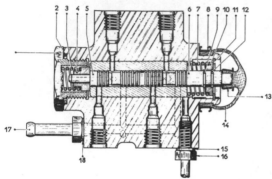

FIG 10:13 A sectional view of the hydraulic brake control (ID19)

Key to Fig 10:13   1 End cap   2 Ring seal   3 Spring
4 Thrust washer   5 Slide valve   6 Spindle   7 Spring
8 Bush   9 Circlip   10 Cup   11 Circlip   12 Circlip
13 Steel cup   14 Rubber protector   15 Copper gasket
16 Overflow return   17 Exhaust connecting tube   18 Copper
gasket

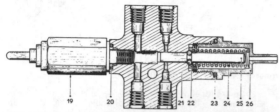

FIG 10:14 A sectional view of the security valve (ID19)

Key to Fig 10:14   19 Pressure switch   20 Ring seal
22 Thrust washer   23 Ring seal   24 Spring
25 Slide valve   26 Plug

cylinder body extended to incorporate a feedpipe union and control rod.

12 Refit the cylinder by locating it on its bracket with its retaining nuts and spring washers. Reconnect the pipes and remove the plug from the fluid reservoir. Reconstitute the pressure in later cars and bleed the system according to the instructions in **Section 10:10**.

10:8 Renewal of brake control and security valve (ID19)

The brake hydraulic system in ID19 cars since September 1961, incorporates a hydraulic brake control and a security valve as shown in the flow diagram in **FIG 10:12**. Details of these units are shown in **FIGS 10:13** and **10:14**.

To remove and refit the brake control, release the pressure and put the height control at 'low'. Uncouple the pipe unions from the control and remove the two retaining screws. Then remove the assembly of control support and pushrod. Detach the rubber tubes, seal off the openings and remove the unit. Reverse these operations to refit the unit and adjust the brake pedal by means of the adjusting screw and locknut to obtain a pushrod clearance of .05 to .50 mm.

To remove and refit the security valve with the same preliminary operations, the spare wheel, the lefthand wing and the side panel over the suspension have additionally

to be removed. Then disconnect the feed wire from the pressure switch. Uncouple from the security valve the rear suspension feedpipe (lower union on the outer side), the feedpipe of the hydraulic brake control (lower union on the engine side), the high pressure inlet pipe (upper union on the engine side), the feedpipe of the front suspension (upper union on the outer side) and the rubber return pipe to the reservoir. Seal off the tubes and the holes in the security valve, then remove the retaining screws and the valve. Refit as in the removal operations in reverse order.

10:9 Removing and refitting hydraulic brake control (DS19)

The hydraulic brake control or pressure distributor in DS19 cars automatically adjusts the braking power on front or rear brakes according to the load carried, as as described in **Chapter 2**. A typical sectional view of the unit is shown in **FIG 10:15**. Minor mechanical design changes have been made from time to time but the general principles remain the same.

To remove the control, release the pressure and put the height control in the 'low' position. Drain the hydraulic fluid reservoir, remove the lefthand front wing and the lefthand suspension sphere. Then take out the floor carpet, unfasten the felt covering and remove the panel fixing screws. Disengage the accelerator control. Withdraw the panel and control assembly by disengaging the studs from the union plates and dust covers. Disconnect the wires from the pressure switches 22 (see **FIG 10:15**) and the stoplamp switch 24.

Remove the two articulating screws and the pedal 5, then disengage the roller trolley. Lift it up to make the flats on the spindle 7 correspond with the hooks on the trolley. Do not turn the spindle on the screwed control rod 8 or the adjustment of the brake compensator will be altered. Remove the distributor or compensator plate 9 by unhooking the ends of the spring retaining plate 10 from under the plate 9. Disengage both plates.

Remove the brake pressure distributor or compensating cylinder 32. Remove the valve housing from the casing 18 and hold the housing in a vice with lead inserts. Remove the thrust cup 14 (see **FIG 10:16**), the rubber cups 15 and the distance piece 16, or the felt washers in cars since July 1960. Then remove the plugs 33 and the slide valves 36 and 37. Examine the valves carefully. If they are scratched it is preferable to renew the control unit because of possible internal leakage.

Keep all parts in strict order for refitting in the same positions as they are paired. Clean the components carefully, especially in the fluid holes, and moisten them with hydraulic fluid for reassembly. Reassemble and refit the unit in the reverse order of the removal operations. Note that the rubber distance pieces 16 should be fitted on the stems of the valves, with the slots towards the overflow return hole, even if not present when dismantling. If required, the unit may be adjusted on a test bench with the aid of a service agent. Refit the items removed for access and reconstitute the pressure.

10:10 Bleeding the brake system

Bleeding the brakes in DS19 cars is undertaken by raising the rear of the car on firm supports and releasing

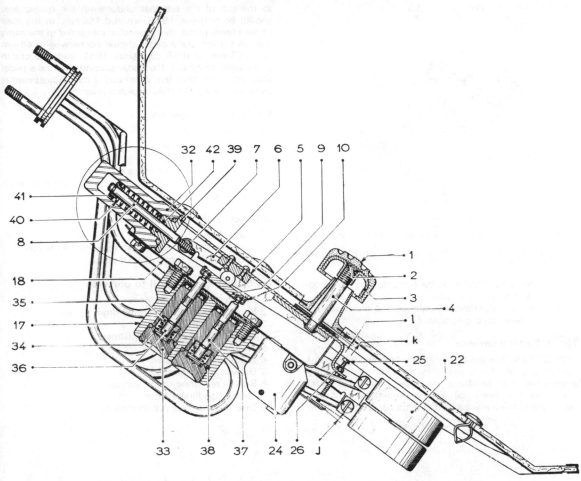

FIG 10:15 A sectional view of the hydraulic brake pressure distributor (DS19)

Key to Fig 10:15   1 Pedal rubber   2 Screw   3 Pedal knob   4 Control rod   5 Pedal   6 Roller trolley
7 Spindle   8 Screwed control rod   9 Compensator plate   10 Spring retaining plate   17 Distribution unit
18 Bracket   22 Pressure switches   24 Stop lamp switch   25 Adjusting screw   26 Locknut   32 Braking distributor
33 Plug   34 Springs   35 Spring cups   36 Valve   37 Valve   38 Joint   39 Guide cap   40 Spring
41 Cup   42 Ring seal   j Clearance .4 to .6 mm   k Measuring base   l Maximum clearance 2 mm

the pressure, keeping the height control in the normal position. Then proceed as follows:

1 Fit a flexible tube on the rear bleed screw of the centrifugal regulator and on the accelerated idling control for the front righthand and lefthand brakes respectively. Put the ends of the tubes in the reservoir. Fit another flexible tube on each rear cylinder bleed screw and insert the ends of these tubes in a transparent container half-filled with fluid.

2 Untighten the front bleed screw in cars before September 1960 and the rear bleed screw. Then tighten the pressure regulator bleed screw. Depress the brake button lightly, start the engine and allow the fluid to flow through the tubes until it is seen to be clear of air bubbles. Then tighten the bleed screws and remove the tubes. Leave the engine idling to put the systems under pressure. With the height control in

the 'low' position, top up the fluid level. Stop the engine and lower the car to the ground. Restart the engine and top up the fluid in the reservoir with the height control in the normal position.

In earlier ID19 cars fitted with a separate brake fluid reservoir and master cylinder, bleeding operations entail ensuring that the fluid level in the reservoir is kept topped up as necessary. Operations are are follows:

1 Fit the rubber tube over the front righthand brake bleed screw with the other end of the tube immersed in a container half filled with brake fluid.

2 Undo the bleed screw and obtain an assistant to operate the brake pedal. With each movement of the pedal, a certain amount of fluid will escape from the tube, bringing with it the air bubbles in the piping.

3 Continue to operate the pedal until no more air bubbles appear. Then with the pedal held down and

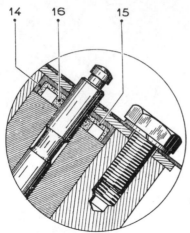

FIG 10:16   A sectional view of a control valve

Key to Fig 10:16   14 Thrust cup   15 Rubber cup
16 Distance piece

the tube still immersed in the fluid, tighten the bleed screw and remove the tube.

4 Repeat these operations in turn on the bleed screws of both rear brake cylinders.

10:11 Pedal clearance

In ID19 cars the pedal clearance is adjusted by altering the setting of the grubscrews and locknuts bearing against the stops located at the upper ends of the pedal arms. For the brake pedal, the dimension from the underside of the pedal pad with the rubber cover removed to the top of the felt mat underneath the rubber mat should be between 155.5 mm and 156 mm. In the case of the clutch pedal, the dimension measured in the same way as for the brake pedal should be between 148 mm and 153 mm. In ID19 cars since 1961, with the clutch pedal pressed against the pedal support the brake pedal play should be between .2 mm and .3 mm. Adjustment is by repositioning the clutch control lever.

10:12 Fault diagnosis

(a) 'Spongy' pedal

1 Leaks in the system (early ID)
2 Worn master cylinder (early ID)
3 Leakage in hydraulic brake controls
4 Choked orifices or unserviceable slide valves in controls
5 Air in the system

(b) Excessive pedal movement

1 Check 1 and 5 in (a)
2 Very low fluid level in brake reservoir (early ID)
3 Too much free movement of pedal

(c) Brakes grab or pull to one side

1 Rear brake backplate loose
2 Scored, cracked or distorted drum
3 High spots on drum
4 Unbalanced rear shoe adjustment
5 Wet or oily linings
6 Worn steering connections
7 Uneven tyre pressures
8 Broken rear shoe return springs
9 Seized handbrake cable
10 Disc brake caliper piston sticking

CHAPTER 11

THE ELECTRICAL EQUIPMENT

11:1 The system, exchange units, test equipment

The electrical system is of the negative earth return type, with a 6-volt circuit in cars before 1960 and a 12-volt circuit in later cars. A generator controlled by a regulator charges the battery, which in turn supplies electrical energy to operate the starter motor, the ignition (see **Chapter 4**), the lights and other accessories. Fuses are fitted as shown in the wiring diagrams in the Appendix, where details are also given of the various makes and types of generators and starter motors employed.

Major mechanical and electrical defects in the generator, starter motor and other integral features of the system are best remedied by fitting new units on an exchange basis, but instructions are given on overhaul and adjustments which can be undertaken with some basic understanding of electrical theory and practice and without elaborate equipment. The wiring diagrams will assist in tracing wiring faults. In the absence of a voltmeter a useful item of equipment is a test lamp, consisting of a small 6-volt or 12-volt bulb in a holder with two well-insulated leads ending in crocodile clips. If one lead is earthed, the bulb will light if the other lead is connected to any terminal or point in the system which is 'live'.

11:2 Battery maintenance and testing

Regular attention is necessary to keep the battery in good working order and to extend its life. The top of the battery should be kept clean and dry. Any signs of corrosion may be removed by a weak solution of ammonia and hot water. The terminals should be coated with petroleum jelly and anti-sulphuric paint may be used for adjacent parts such as battery bolts and support. If the electrolyte level is less than $\frac{1}{4}$ inch above the plates, distilled water should be added. Should leakage or spilling require the addition of dilute sulphuric acid of the correct specific gravity it can usually be obtained already diluted. But if strong sulphuric acid is used, remember when diluting **always to add acid to water** and on no account add the water to the acid.

The specific gravity of the electrolyte in each cell may be checked by using a hydrometer. Readings as follows should be obtained for an electrolyte temperature of 16°C (60°F). The readings should be corrected by adding or subtracting .002 for each 3°C (5°F) rise or fall from that temperature.

Cell fully charged	..	..	1.270 to 1.290
Cell half discharged	..	..	1.190 to 1.210
Cell fully discharged	..	..	1.110 to 1.130

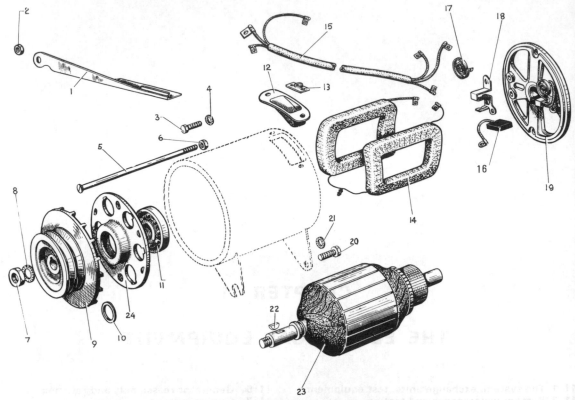

FIG 11:1   An exploded view of the generator

Key to Fig 11:1   1 Belt tensioning arm   2 Nut   3 Screw securing adjusting stay   4 Shakeproof washer
5 Assembly rod   6 Nut   7 Pulley nut   8 Shakeproof washer   9 Pulley   10 Adjusting washer   11 Bearing
12 Wiring support   13 Wiring plate   14 Field coils   15 Generator wiring   16 Brush   17 Brush spring
18 Brush holder, positive and negative   19 Commutator bracket or bearing end plate   20 Screw securing generator to
flywheel housing   21 Shakeproof washer   22 Woodruff key   23 Armature   24 Drive bracket or bearing end plate

11:3 Generator maintenance, electrical tests in situ

Maintenance requirements are limited to checking and, if necessary, adjusting the belt tension at periodic intervals, as described in **Chapter 5.** Every 1250 miles a few drops of engine oil should be inserted into the oiler for the generator spindle. Apply sparingly to avoid any oil reaching the commutator or generator brushes.

To test the output of the generator, first make sure that there is no belt slip and that the output and field terminals on the generator are correctly connected to their respective terminals on the regulator. Operations are then as follows:

1 Disconnect the wires from the output and field terminals of the generator and join the terminals together with a short piece of wire.
2 Connect a 0–30 voltmeter between this junction and earth. Run the engine at a fast idling speed when the voltage reading should rise rapidly without fluctuation. Do not increase the engine speed above a fast idle or the generator may be damaged.
3 If there is no reading, first check the generator leads, brushes and brush connections. If the reading is very low, the field or armature windings may be at fault.

4 If the generator is in good order, leave the temporary link in position between the terminals and restore the original connections correctly. Remove the output lead from the regulator and connect the voltmeter between this lead and a good earth. Run the engine as before, when the reading should be the same as that measured directly on the generator. No reading indicates a break in the cable from generator to regulator. Repeat the test on the field cable and finally remove the temporary link from the generator.

11:4 Removing and dismantling generator

The main elements of the generator are shown in **FIG 11:1,** which can be taken as typical of the various types of Ducellier and Paris-Rhone units employed. Details of assembly design and mechanical construction differ according to manufacturers' individual practices, but the general principles of removing and dismantling a generator are as follows:

1 Disconnect and remove the battery, together with the clamping rods, protection plate and battery tray.
2 Remove the generator tie rod. Slacken the retaining screws, swing the generator towards the engine and disengage the belt(s) from the pulley as described in

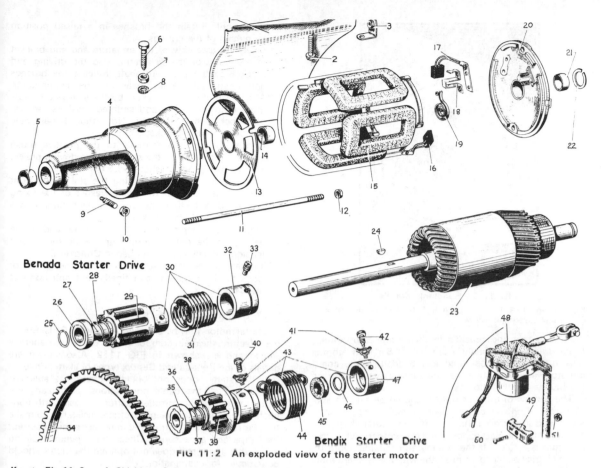

Benada Starter Drive

Bendix Starter Drive

FIG 11:2 An exploded view of the starter motor

Key to Fig 11:2 1 Shield   2 Terminal   3 Screen support   4 Bearing housing   5 Bush   6 Screw securing motor
7 Nut   8 Shakeproof washer   9 Grubscrew for starter motor reaction   10 Nut   11 Assembly rod   12 Nut
13 Intermediate bearing plate   14 Bush   15 Field coils   16 Brush   17 Brush   18 Brush holder   19 Brush spring
20 Brush gear end plate   21 Bush   22 Circlip   23 Armature   24 Key for pinion drive   25 Circlip for thrust ring
26 Pinion thrust ring   27 Threaded sleeve   28 Spring   29 Pinion   30 Starter drive complete   31 Driving spring
32 Driving sleeve   33 Grubscrew   34 Gear ring   35 Pinion spring thrust nut   36 Threaded sleeve   37 Spring
38 Distance washer   39 Pinion   40 Screw for threaded sleeve   41 Lockplate   42 Screw for driving sleeve
43 Starter drive complete   44 Driving spring   45 Rubber bush for damper   46 Washer   47 Driving sleeve
48 Solenoid   49 Clamp   50 Screw   51 Nut

Chapter 5. Remove the securing screws and detach the generator.

3 Referring to **FIG 11:1,** remove the driving pulley 9 and the Woodruff key 22. Unscrew and remove the two through-bolts 5.

4 Turn down the lockwashers if fitted and remove the retaining screws from the end brackets 19 and 24.

5 Withdraw the drive end bracket with the armature 23 from the yoke.

6 Remove the output terminal from the positive brush holder and disengage the commutator end bracket. Remove the felt washer if fitted and the brushes. If these are likely to be used again, mark them for refitting in their original positions. The brush holders are usually situated on the end brackets, but are fitted on the body in the Ducellier 7256 generator.

7 If renewal of the bearing 11 is intended, remove the bearing housing plate by grinding off the retaining rivets and press out the bearing from the end bracket.

8 Remove the bush from the commutator end bracket with the aid of a shouldered mandrel. Clean all the parts.

Removal and refitting of the field coils and their testing for continuity and earth is work which requires special equipment and which is advisable should be undertaken by a service agent.

11:5 Brush and commutator servicing

The brushes should be inspected and serviced by testing them for freedom of movement in their holders. Where the holders are incorporated in the end bracket, secure the brushes by locating the springs at the sides of the holders. Temporarily fit the commutator end bracket over the commutator, hold up each brush spring in turn and gently move the brush by pulling on the connector. If the movement is sluggish, remove the brush from its holder and ease the sides by slightly polishing them with a smooth file.

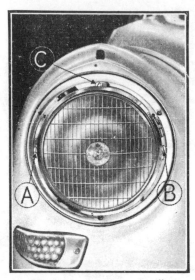

FIG 11:3 Headlamp details

Key to Fig 11:3   A/B Lateral adjustment screws
C Vertical adjustment screw

Always refit the brushes in their original positions. If the brushes are badly worn below 8 mm in length, new brushes must be fitted and bedded to the commutator. Finally remove the end bracket and reconnect the brushes to their holders.

The surface of the commutator should be smooth and free from pitting or burned spots. Clean it with a cloth moistened in petrol. If this is ineffective, carefully polish it with a strip of glasspaper, **not emerycloth,** while the armature is rotated. If the commutator is badly worn or scored it may be faced up in a lathe with a very sharp tool, but do not reduce the original diameter as given in the Technical Data Section by more than 2 mm. If necessary, undercut the insulation between the segments after rectification to a depth of $\frac{1}{32}$ inch with a hacksaw blade ground down to the thickness of the insulation. Then polish the commutator with fine glasspaper and remove all copper dust. Check the circuit to earth with a simple bulb circuit.

11:6 Generator reassembly and refitting

Following attention to the brushes and commutator assemblies as in **Section 11:5,** reassembly is undertaken as follows:

1 Locate the bush, previously oiled with engine oil, in the commutator end bracket. Refit a thrust washer or a felt washer, as provided, on the shaft adjacent to the armature. If a closing plate is fitted, knock back the metal of the bracket lightly to retain the plate. Insert a few drops of oil on the felt washer and in the oiler on the bracket.

2 Assemble the drive end bracket. Grease the bearing with high melting point grease and if it has been removed insert it into the end bracket and refit the housing plate. Replace original rivets by round-headed screws, nuts and serrated washers.

3 Fit the brushes, connect the cables and bring the brushes into contact with the armature. Make sure that the brushes are correctly positioned with free

movement. Retain the brushes in a raised position by means of the springs.

4 Insert the assembly of the armature and end bracket in the body of the generator, also the driving end bracket on the armature shaft. Release the brushes and ensure that they bear on the commutator. Attach the two end brackets by the screws and nuts fitted with insulating and serrated washers, or turn over lockwashers if fitted. Note that dowels may position the end brackets.

5 Connect the output terminal to the positive brush holder. Fit the key on the shaft and the driving pulley, with a shakeproof washer under the retaining nut.

6 Refit the generator by locating the slot in the front fixing plate between the plain washer of the fixing screw and the bellhousing. Locate the retaining screws with spring and plain washers.

7 Swing the generator towards the engine and fit the belt(s) on the pulley. Couple up the tie rod(s) and tension the belt(s) as described in **Chapter 2.**

8 Tighten the retaining screws, connect the generator leads to the regulator and finally refit and connect the battery.

11:7 Starter motor tests in situ

Starter motors may be of either Ducellier or Paris-Rhone manufacture, the main components of which are generally similar and are shown in **FIG 11:2.** Also shown are details of the Benada and Bendix types of starter drive.

If the starter does not operate, check the solenoid switch and all the cable connections, particularly the battery terminals. A corroded battery or bad earth connection may have sufficient electrical resistance to make the starter inoperative, though it may pass enough current for lamps and accessories. Check for a jammed pinion and if the starter still does not operate the motor should be removed for examination.

11:8 Removing, servicing and refitting starter

Operations to remove the starter motor are commenced by releasing the pressure and removing the sphere from the righthand suspension cylinder. Seal the cylinder and the sphere, then remove the exhaust manifold shield. Bend this if necessary to move it towards the front. Disconnect the starter feed cable and slacken the locknut and pointed screw 6 on the starter housing (see **FIG 11:2**), also the two pointed reaction screws under the clutch bellhousing. Disengage the starter from the rear, turning the body at the same time. To dismantle the starter proceed as follows:

1 Remove the circlip 22 and the distance washers, also the assembly rods 11.

2 Remove the housing 4. Disengage the armature 23 with the intermediate bearing 13 and the rear thrust washer adjacent to the armature. Remove the rear bearing plate 20, withdrawing the positive brush from its holder.

3 Remove the Bendix assembly from the armature shaft. Disengage the Woodruff key 24 and the intermediate bearing plate 13. Renewal of the field coils, if necessary, is better left to a service agent to perform.

4 The commutator should be cleaned and the starter brushes examined for wear and checked for freedom

in their holders by following the same procedures as described for the generator in **Section 11:5**.

5 The bearings may be renewed if required by driving them out with a shouldered mandrel. They are made of porouse bronze and before assembly should be soaked for 24 hours in a bath of engine oil so that the bronze becomes impregnated. No further oiling should be necessary.

6 Servicing the Benada type of pinion assembly requires the preparation of special tooling and the assistance of a service agent is advised for its overhaul if required. The Bendix drive, however, shown in **FIG 11:2**, is dismantled by removing the screws and lockwashers 40, 41 and 42, disengaging the threaded sleeve and removing the spring and other components shown at 43 to 47 inclusive.

7 Reassembly is in general undertaken in the reverse order of the removal operations. It is necessary to ensure that the lateral clearance of the intermediate bearing should be between .2 mm and 1.3 mm by modifying the number of adjusting washers if required. Refit the starter by engaging it in its housing in the crankcase, turning it with a slight push to clear the manifold. Tighten the housing screw and the reaction screws, then refit the remaining items removed for access.

11:9 Headlamp dismantling, beam setting

To adjust the beam of a headlamp, first remove the chromium plated rim by taking out the screw at the bottom and springing the ends of the rim apart. Remove the rubber ring. Referring to **FIG 11:3**, for the lateral adjustment of the beam adjust the screws shown at **A** and **B**. For the vertical adjustment of the beam, adjust the screw **C**.

Renewal of a headlamp bulb is performed by removing the chromium plated rim and rubber ring as previously described. Then turn the lamp unit anticlockwise and withdraw it from the screws **A**, **B** and **C**. Remove the bulb holder from the back of the reflector by pressing the holder and turning it anticlockwise. The bulb may then be withdrawn and a new one fitted, ensuring that the semicircular slot in the lamp flange is located over the rib in the bulb holder. Finally refit the lamp holder, the rubber ring and the plated rim.

11:10 Fault diagnosis

(a) Battery discharged

1 Terminals loose or dirty
2 Lighting circuit shorted
3 Generator not charging
4 Regulator or cut-out units not working properly
5 Battery internally defective

(b) Insufficient charging current

1 Loose or corroded battery terminals
2 Generator driving belt slipping

(c) Battery will not hold a charge

1 Low electrolyte level
2 Battery plates sulphated
3 Electrolyte leakage from cracked casing or top sealing compound
4 Plate separators ineffective

(d) Battery overcharged

1 Voltage regulator needs adjusting

(e) Generator output low or nil

1 Belt broken or slipping
2 Regulator unit out of adjustment
3 Worn bearings, loose polepieces
4 Commutator worn, burned or shorted
5 Armature shaft bent or worn
6 Insulation proud between commutator segments
7 Brushes sticking, springs weak or broken
8 Field coil wires shorted, broken or burned

(f) Starter motor lacks power or will not operate

1 Battery discharged, loose cable connections
2 Starter pinion jammed in mesh with flywheel gear
3 Starter switch faulty
4 Brushes worn or sticking, leads detached or shorting
5 Commutator dirty or worn
6 Starter shaft bent
7 Engine abnormally stiff

(g) Starter motor runs but does not turn engine

1 Pinion sticking on screwed sleeve
2 Broken teeth on pinion or flywheel gears

(h) Noisy starter pinion when engine is running

1 Restraining spring weak or broken

(j) Starter motor inoperative

1 Check 1 and 4 in (f)
2 Armature or field coils faulty

(k) Starter motor rough or noisy

1 Mounting bolts loose
2 Damaged pinion or flywheel gear teeth
3 Main pinion spring broken

(l) Lamps inoperative or erratic

1 Battery low, bulbs burned out
2 Faulty earthing of lamps or battery
3 Lighting switch faulty, loose or broken wiring connections

(m) Wiper motor sluggish, taking high current

1 Faulty armature
2 Bearings out of alignment
3 Commutator dirty or shortcircuited

(n) Wiper motor operates but does not drive arms

1 Gearbox components worn

(o) Fuel gauge does not register

1 No battery supply to gauge
2 Gauge casing not earthed
3 Cable between gauge and tank unit earthed

(p) Fuel gauge registers 'FULL'

1 Cable between gauge and tank unit broken or disconnected

CHAPTER 12

THE BODYWORK

12:1 Removing door trim

Removal of a door interior trimming panel is undertaken by first removing the window winder handle 30 in **FIG 12:1**. The handle escutcheon is pressed down strongly with a suitable forked tool, as shown in the illustration, to give access for driving out the retaining pin. Then withdraw the handle, the escutcheon, the cup and the spring.

Insert a screwdriver between the trimming panel and the steel panel and lever out the panel clips all round the panel, which is withdrawn by lifting it upwards to disengage it from the armrest support plate. Do not remove the three felt pads attached to the steel panel, but detach the vinyl sealing panels from the interior openings if access to the door mechanism is required. The same operations in reverse order are undertaken when refitting. Attach the vinyl sealing panels on the edges of the interior openings with a good adhesive and fit the trimming panel by sliding it towards the bottom of the door and anchoring it on the armrest support plate.

12:2 Servicing door locks, remote control gear

A door is opened from the interior by gripping the handle (see **FIG 12:2**) and pressing the catch 2 with the thumb. The catch moves backwards. Then push the door open. When the door is closed, lock it by moving the catch 1 forwards. To unlock it, press the button 2. The two front doors must be locked with a key and cannot be locked from the inside.

The removal and refitting of a door lock and its controls are undertaken as follows:

1 Remove the door by lifting it upwards after unscrewing the door lower pivot bracket screw. Do not unscrew the upper pivot bracket screw in order to avoid altering the adjustment of the door.
2 Remove the glass guide on the lock side, the glass and the trimming panel (see **Sections 12:1** and **12:4**).
3 Referring to **FIG 12:3**, remove the three lock fixing screws and then the lock by disconnecting the interior handle control rod 15.
4 Remove the interior handle 21. Referring to **FIG 12:1**, unscrew the handle fixing screw 17 by turning the hexagon 19 in a clockwise direction. Turn the handle a quarter of a turn to remove it from the door together with the control rod.
5 Remove the exterior door handle 14 (see **FIG 12:3**) by unscrewing the retaining screw 1 from the inside. Disengage the handle from the door by turning it a quarter of a turn.

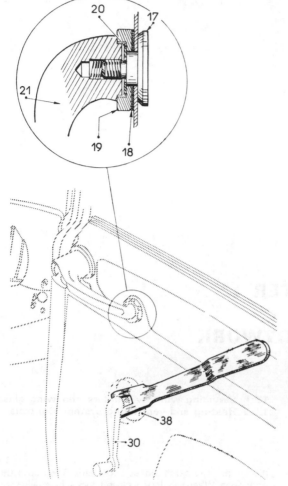

FIG 12:1   Attachment of interior door handles

Key to Fig 12:1
17 Screw securing inner door handle
18 Fibre washer   19 Locking collar   20 Washer
21 Door interior handle   30 Window handle
38 Escutcheon plate

6 To reassemble, fit the interior door handle 21 together with the shouldered rubber washer 24, the control rod 15 and the anti-rattle plate 26, introducing the rod through the hole provided in the door. Make sure that the handle screw 17 is in position on the panel. This screw passes through the hexagon 19 and is held by the split washer 18 between the hexagon and the door panel. Turn the handle a quarter of a turn to bring its end opposite the second fixing hole and secure it by turning the hexagon in an anticlockwise direction.

7 Fit the lock on the door and connect the control rod 15 on the lock catch 16. Secure the lock by the three screws 3 and check its operation.

8 Fit the exterior handle 14, also the rubber washer 7, then turn the handle a quarter of a turn.

9 Locate the fixing plate 4 on the hub of the handle from the inside of the door. Turn the plate a quarter of a turn. Fit the washer 2 between the handle and the door handle and secure by the screw 1 through the interior of the door.

10 Refit the door on the car and check the adjustment of the door as described in **Section 12:3**. Fit the glass guide and the glass (see **Section 12:4**) and fit the door panel (see **Section 12:1**).

To renew a door lock barrel, close the window and remove the window winder and door panel as previously described. Partially detach the vinyl sheet and from the inside of the door take out the retaining screw 1 (see **FIG 12:3**) and remove the door handle 14 by turning it through a quarter of a turn. Withdraw the retaining plate. Now remove the locknut 6 and the adjusting screw 5, slide out the pushbutton 11 and its return spring 13, then remove the circlip 9 and the lock barrel 10. Note the direction in which the barrel is fitted for later reassembly.

When reassembling, fit the ignition key in the lock barrel 10 and the barrel in the pushbutton 11. Press the barrel right to the bottom of the pushbutton so that it can be secured by its circlips. Fit the return spring 13 and the pushbutton in the door handle. Press down the push-button and screw together the adjusting screw 5 and the locknut 6 in the button. Fit the handle as described in the foregoing Operations 8 and 9. Refit the vinyl door lining with a good adhesive and then the trimming panel and the window winder.

12:3 Adjustment of doors

The height of the doors should be adjusted so that the front upper corner of the front door is at a distance of 577.5 mm from the top of the trimming of the side rail and the rear upper corner of the rear door 505 mm measured similarly.

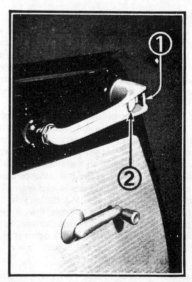

FIG 12:2   Door opening and locking mechanism

Key to Fig 12:2   1 Catch   2 Button

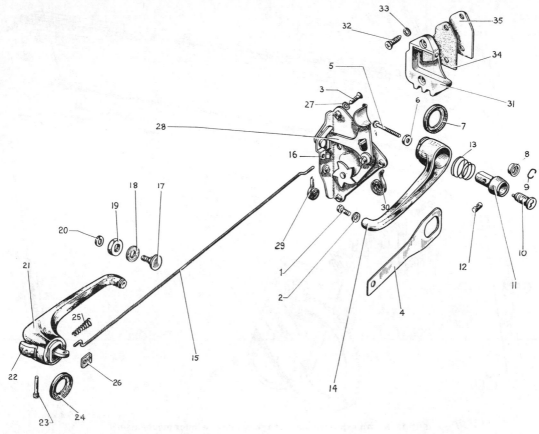

FIG 12:3   An exploded view of a door lock and remote control mechanism

Key to Fig 12:3   1 Screw, exterior door handle   2 Fibre washer   3 Screws securing lock   4 Locking plate
5 Screw for adjusting push button   6 Nut   7 Shouldered rubber washer   8 Cup retaining push button   9 Circlip
10 Lock barrel   11 Push button   12 Locking pin   13 Return spring   14 External handle   15 Remote control rod
16 Lock catch for control rod   17 Screw securing inner handle   18 Fibre washer   19 Locking collar   20 Washer
21 Interior handle   22 Tongue for safety catch   23 Pin for safety catch   24 Shouldered rubber washer   25 Return spring
26 Anti-rattle plate for control rod   27 Washer   28 Door lock   29 Spring for locking catch   30 Return spring, door lock lever
31 Striking plate   32 Screw   33 Washer   34 Plate on pillars   35 Adjusting plate

Maintaining these dimensions, the gaps between
(a) the front wing and the front door; (b) the front and
rear doors; and (c) the rear wing and rear door should
be equal at the top and the bottom, and at the same time
the gaps themselves should be equal to within about
2 mm. If necessary, alter the position of the wings. The
rear edge of the front door should stand proud of the
front edge of the rear door by 1 mm to 2 mm in order
to avoid whistling noises at high speeds.

To move the front wing forwards, insert washers as
required between the caisson front unit and the wing
fixing as at 'd' in **FIG 12:4.** The position of the rear
wings is altered towards the rear by moving the wing
fixing plate on the boot closing panel, and towards the
front by moving the positioning pins or the alignment
brackets of the wing.

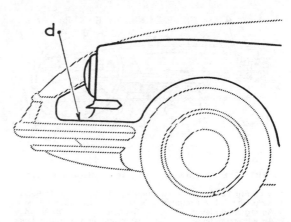

**FIG 12:4   Position of washers (d) for adjusting front
wing**

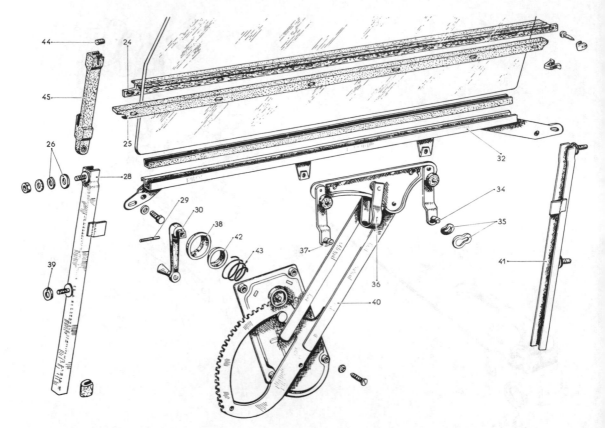

FIG 12:5   An exploded view of the window winder mechanism

Key to Fig 12:5   24 Glass sealing strip   25 Outer door sealing strip   26 Washers   28 Side runner for glass
29 Retaining pin   30 Window handle   32 Glass channel   34 Winder peg   35 Flexible washer and lockwasher
36 Felt-lined steel clamps retaining glass   37 Winder peg   38 Escutcheon   39 Nut   40 Winder mechanism
41 Side runner for glass   42 Friction cup   43 Spring   44 Rubber packing   45 Nylon glass slide

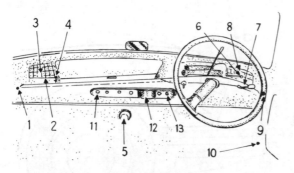

FIG 12:6   A view of the heater controls (DS19)

Key to Fig 12:6   1 Air admission lever   2 Deflector
3 Air grille   4 Air regulating lever   5 Heater control valve
6 Air regulating lever   7 Deflector   8 Air grille
9 Air admission lever   10 Warm air distribution lever
11 Interior lamps control switch   12 Ashtray   13 Fan
speed control

FIG 12:7   A view of the heater controls (ID19)

Key to Fig 12:7   A/B Grilles   6 Air deflector control
16 Air deflector control   17 Air admission levers
21 Air direction controls   22/23 Levers adjusting heating
and demisting   24 Heater control valve

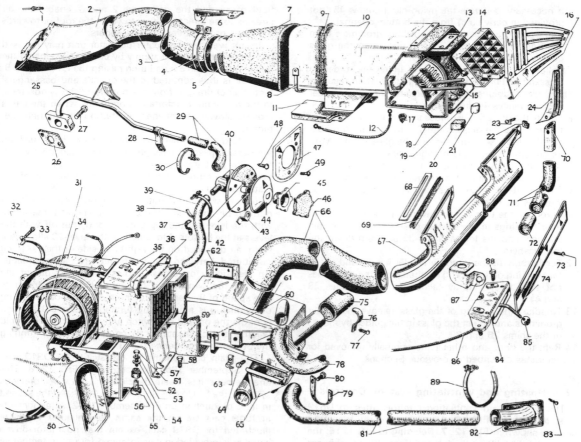

FIG 12:8 An exploded view of the heating, demisting and ventilating system (DS19)

Key to Fig 12:8
1 Rivet, air inlet duct to wing   2 Inlet duct   3 Flexible duct   4 Clip   5 Insect grille
6 Retaining plate   7 Connecting duct   8 Clip   9 Sealing strip   10 Ventilation duct   11 Shutter under duct
12 Shutter control cable   13 Upper shutter in duct   14 Grille   15 Shutter control lever   16 Dashboard grille
17 Shutter stop   18 Spring   19 Clip for lever knobs   20 Plunger locating shutters   21 Control knob   22 Clip nut
23 Screw for demister nozzle   24 Demisting nozzle   25 Heater inlet pipe   26 Joint   27 Screw   28 Support
29 Rubber pipe   30 Clip   31 Electric motor and impeller   32 Flexible pipe, water return   33 Clip
34 Half-shell motor support   35 Heater radiator   36 Securing spring   37 Clip   38 Clip, outlet and feed pipes
39 Feed pipe, shut-off valve to radiator   40 Shut-off valve   41 Rubber washer   42 Screw   43 Guide stop
44 Disc with opening mark   45 Operating knob   46 Rubber cover   47 Indicator plate   48 Screw   49 Screw
50 Turbine casing   51 Screw   52 Washer   53 Cup washer   54 Rubber bush   55 Distance piece   56 Rubber bush
57 Rear support   58 Screw   59 Flexible duct   60 Clip   61 Duct for hot air   62 Shutter   63 Clip for shutter control cable
64 Screw   65 Heater connection for rear seats   66 Flexible duct to windscreen   67 Windscreen demisting nozzles
68 Dashboard finisher   69 Sealing strip   70 Union for lateral nozzle   71 Flexible pipe for lateral demisting nozzle
72 Union   73 Screw   74 Indicator plate   75 Flexible duct for front heating   76 Clip   77 Screw
78 Flexible pipe for lateral demisting nozzle   79 Retaining clip, rear duct   80 Screw   81 Flexible duct to rear seats
82 Plate retaining duct   83 Screw   84 Control for heater shutter   85 Control lever knob   86 Shutter control cable
87 Dashboard bracket   88 Screw   89 Clip securing rear ducting

12:4 Servicing window winders, renewing glass

Operations for removing and refitting a window winder and renewing the glass are as follows. Minor modifications mentioned for early cars refer to production before May 1957.

1 Commence by removing the door, the window handle, the trimming panel and the vinyl sealing covers, as previously described.

2 Referring to **FIG 12:5**, remove the interior rubber door glass sealing strip 24 and the outer door sealing strip 25, fixed by clips or screws to the upper part of the door.

3 Bring the glass to the halfway position to obtain access to the window winder mechanism 40. Turn back the edges and remove the two window winder lockwashers 35.

4 Disengage the bottom channel 32 from the window winder. In early cars remove the two movable stops from the bottom of the channel.

5 Separate the felt lined flexible steel clamp 36 retaining the door glass, pull the glass upwards and remove it.

If necessary, separate the nylon glass guides 45 (not provided in early cars) from the bottom channel.

6 Remove the upper and lower rubber grommets from the front and rear faces of the door, also the glass guides 28 and 41.

7 Follow the removal operations in reverse order to reassemble. Fit the washers 26 and 39 when securing the glass guides 45 and ensure that the rubber packing pieces 44 are inserted.

8 Locate the glass in the guides and lower to the bottom. In early cars the glass is fitted with its glazing rubber and its rubber seal. In later cars the glass is fitted with its bottom channel and glazing rubber.

9 Raise the glass to its maximum height to engage the winder mechanism 40 in the interior of the door.

10 Fit the felt-lined flexible steel clamps 36 on the glass with the aid of pliers.

11 Introduce the two window winder pegs 37 and 34 in their housings in the bottom channel. Fit the flexible washers and the lockwashers 35 and turn down the lockwashers.

12 Temporarily fit the window winder handle and check the working of the raising mechanism. If the glass does not slide freely, lightly tallow the glass guides 28 and 41.

13 To adjust the closing of the glass, remove the rubber grommets and adjust the glass in the guides by means of the shims 26 and 39.

14 Refit the door and other parts originally removed for access as described in previous Sections.

12 : 5 Heating and ventilating system. Controls

The heating and ventilating controls fitted in DS19 cars are shown in **FIG 12 : 6** and similar controls in ID19 cars are shown in **FIG 12 : 7**. Referring to **FIG 12 : 6**, the two grilles 3 and 8 on the left and right of the dashboard admit fresh air into the car. The levers 4 and 6 regulate the flow of air and the deflectors 2 and 7 enable the air streams to be directed either towards the roof or towards the faces of the driver and passengers.

In hot weather the heater/defroster unit may be used to increase the fresh air supply by completely closing the heater control valve 5 and then raising the levers 1 and 9. Cool air is thus admitted to the driver's and passengers' feet. A cool draught from the bottom of the windscreen, to provide more comfortable conditions when the car is moving slowly, is obtained by starting up the defroster motor.

Heating arrangements are by means of fresh air from the outside passing through two special radiators which heat the air before it enters the car. For adjusting the heating, the rubber knob 5 controls the admission of hot water to the two radiators. The levers 1 and 9 allow the volume of warm air admitted by the openings at left and right to be controlled, the volume being at a maximum with the levers in the top position and shut off with the levers at the bottom. Movement of the lever 10 allows the warm air delivered on the righthand side of the car to be distributed between the front and rear compartments. An electrically driven fan blows heated air out at the base of the windscreen for defrosting and demisting. The speed of the fan controlling the degree of defrosting or demisting is adjusted by turning the knob 13 which controls the on and off switch and rheostat. In very cold weather the car heating can be augmented by running the defroster at moderate speed.

The main components of the system in DS19 cars since September 1962, are shown in **FIG 12 : 8**. This arrangement has been developed from two previous systems, the first in cars until August 1961 and the second in later production until September 1962. Arrangements in ID19 cars are on the same general lines as those illustrated for DS19 cars, except that no motor-driven impeller is provided in cars intended for use in temperate climates.

APPENDIX

TECHNICAL DATA

Engine details   Fuel system   Hydraulic system
Ignition system   Cooling system   Clutch   Gearbox
Front suspension   Rear suspension   Steering
Brakes   Electrical equipment   Tightening torques

HINTS ON MAINTENANCE AND OVERHAUL

GLOSSARY OF TERMS

INDEX

TECHNICAL DATA

ENGINE DETAILS

Type:	
DS19, ID19	4 cylinder in-line, ohv
Dimensions:	
Bore and stroke	78 x 100 mm
Capacity	1911 cc
Compression ratios:	
DS19	7.5:1 and 8.5:1
ID19	6.8:1 and 7.5:1
Brake horsepower (gross):	
DS19, 7.5:1 compression ratio	75 at 4500 rev/min
DS19, 8.5:1 compression ratio	83 at 4500 rev/min
ID19, 6.8:1 compression ratio	62 at 4000 rev/min
ID19, 7.5:1 compression ratio	69 at 4500 rev/min
Crankshaft journal diameter	54 mm
Connecting rod journal diameter	48 mm
Maximum clearances on crankshaft and connecting rod bearings—.06 mm	
Crankshaft end float—7.5:1 c.r.	.03 to .09 mm
8.5:1 c.r.	.03 to .06 mm
Engine lubrication:	
Lubrication system	Pressure feed
Oil	SAE.20 or SAE.10W.30
Oil filter	Citroen, in rocker cover
Sump capacity	7 pints (4 litres)
Difference between 'min' and 'max' on dipstick ..	1¾ pints (1 litre)
Oil pressure at 4000 rev/min, oil at 60°C to 65°C ..	54 to 58.5 lb/sq in (3.8 to 4.1 kg/sq cm)
Oil pump:	
Type	Gear
Driving pinion end float	.03 to .10 mm
Valves, springs and tappets:	
Valve type	Inclined pushrod overhead

	Inlet	Exhaust
Angle of seat (valve)	120 deg.	90 deg.
Diameter of head	42 mm	37 mm
Rockershaft diameter	18 mm	16 mm
Tappet clearances (cold)	.20 mm (.008 inch)	.25 mm (.010 inch)

Valve timing:	Before March 1961	Since March 1961
Inlet opens, before TDC ..	3° or .1 mm	0° 30' or .005 mm
Inlet closes, after TDC ..	45° or 88.7 mm	40° 30' or 83.81 mm
Exhaust opens, before TDC ..	45° or 88.7 mm	38° 30' or 87.008 mm
Exhaust closes, after TDC ..	11° or 1.2 mm	4° 30' or .226 mm

FUEL SYSTEM

Carburetters:
  Make and type—DS19 .. Weber 24/30 DCZC1 or DCLC, Zenith 20/30 EEAC, Weber 24/32 DDC
          ID19 .. Solex 34 PBIC

Component details, DS19:	Weber 24/30 DSZC1		Zenith 20/30 EEAC		Weber 24/32 DDC	
	1st Body	2nd Body	1st Body	2nd Body	1st Body	2nd Body
Venturi bore	21	26	20	26.2	21	27
Main jet	105	145	035	046	100	155
Correction jet	220	240	060	060	150	160

Component details, DS19:	Weber 24/30 DSZC1		Zenith 20/30 EEAC		Weber 24/32 DDC	
	1st Body	*2nd Body*	*1st Body*	*2nd Body*	*1st Body*	*2nd Body*
Emulsion tube	F17	F18	1	2	F16	F16
Slow-running jet ..	45	65	050	050	45	55
Air jet for emulsion tube	220	240	060	060	185	80
Starter petrol jet ..	105		—		—	
Starter air jet	450		—		—	
Pump jet (inlet)	50		40		60	
Pump outlet	.80		1.5		55	
Needle valve	1.75		2.45		1.75	
Float	18 g		13.5 g		13 g	
Float level	5 & 12		16		8 & 13.5	

Component details—ID19:	Solex 34 PBIC
Marking on starter lever	4
Venturi bore	26
Main jet	135
Compensating jet	230
Emulsion tube	28
Slow-running jet	50
Slow-running air jet	130
Starting jet	115
Starting air jet	4
Accelerator pump	72
Pump injector	High
Accelerator pump jet	50
Needle valve	2
Float	5.7 g

Slow-running adjustments—DS19:	
Normal idling	550 to 600 rev/min
Accelerated idling	900± 25 rev/min
Clutch drag	725±25 rev/min

Fuel pump:
Make and type	Guiot or AC/RH, mechanical
Fuel tank capacity	14 gallons

HYDRAULIC SYSTEM

Hydraulic fluid	BP Energol Hydraulic CF, Shell Donax D, or Castrol HF
Reservoir capacity, pints	10¼ (DS19) 9¼ (ID19)
Main accumulator initial pressure ..	925+70—210 lb/sq in (65+5—15 kg/sq cm)
Brake accumulators initial pressure ..	570±30 lb/sq in (40±2 kg/sq cm)
Front suspension spheres initial pressure	840+30—220 lb/sq in (59+2—15 kg/sq cm)
Rear suspension spheres initial pressure	370+30—150 lb/sq in (26+2—10 kg/sq cm)
Pressure regulator:	
Cutting-out	2130 to 2420 lb/sq in (150 to 170 kg/sq cm)
Cutting-in	1850 to 1990 lb/sq in (130 to 140 kg/sq cm)
High pressure pump cylinders diameter	18.5±.5 mm

IGNITION SYSTEM

Distributor:	
Type	Ducellier or SEV
Contact breaker points gap	.4 mm
Shaft end float	.4 mm maximum
Sparking plug point gap:	
Marchal 35B	.027 to .031 inch (.6 to .8 mm)
Champion H.10	.024 to .028 inch (.6 to .7 mm)

COOLING SYSTEM

Capacity, including heating system	19 pints (DS19), 18 pints (ID19)
Fan	Nylon, 8 blades
Thermostat starts to open	72°C to 76°C (162°F to 169°F)
Adjusting washer thicknesses available for pump shaft	
ballbearing	.5, 1, 1.5 and 2 mm

CLUTCH

Type	Single dry plate

Height of clutch pedal (ID19)—148 to 153 mm from underside of pedal without pad to top of felt carpet

Clearance of fork control rod from clutch housing . . . . 1 mm minimum

GEARBOX

Gear ratios (including final drive):

First	13.80:1
Second	7.35:1
Third	4.78:1
Top	3.30:1
Reverse	14.80:1

Lubrication:

Grade of lubricant	SAE.90.EP
Gearbox oil capacity, pints	4.5 (DS19), 2.8 (ID19)

FRONT SUSPENSION

Type—Hydro-pneumatic springs, half wishbones each side, anti-roll bar and height corrector

Wheel alignment:

Camber	Equal on both sides to within 1 mm
Castor angle	1° 30'
Toe-in at the front	1 to 3 mm

REAR SUSPENSION

Type—Hydro-pneumatic springs on trailing arms, anti-roll bar and height corrector

STEERING

Type	Rack and pinion
Turning circle	36 ft 1 inch
Angle of steering lock	41 to 42 deg.

Lateral positioning—122.5±2.5 mm between centre line of lower relay lever and centre line of rack plunger

Cross-over pressure . . . . 995±150 lb/sq in (70±10 kg/sq cm)

BRAKES

Type—Hydraulically operated, inboard disc-type front, outboard drum-type rear

Front brake disc diameter	11½ inch
Rear brake drum internal diameter	10 inch
Maximum disc runout	.17 mm
Lateral clearance of moving carrier	.25 mm

Pedal clearance (ID19)—155.5 to 156 mm from underside of pedal without pad to top of felt carpet

ELECTRICAL EQUIPMENT

Battery	.. ..	6-volt or 12-volt earth return, negative earth	
Generator types:		*Type*	*Commutator dia.*
DS	.. ..	Ducellier 7116A	47.0 mm
DS	.. ..	7212A	47.0 mm
ID	.. ..	7158A	47.0 mm
DS, ID	.. ..	7256G	37.0 mm
DS	.. ..	Paris-Rhone G11.R75	41.5 mm
DS	.. ..	G11.C5	40.5 mm
ID	.. ..	G11.R91	41.5 mm
DS, ID	.. ..	G10.C10	36.8 mm
Starter types:			
DS, ID	.. ..	Ducellier	6008A
DS, ID	.. ..		6087A
DS, ID	.. ..	Paris-Rhone	D11.B42
DS, ID	.. ..		D10.B38
DS, ID	.. ..		D10.B39

6-volt-regulator:

Cutting-in voltage (cold or hot)	6 to 6.7 volts
Cutting-out voltage	5.5 to 6.2 volts

Regulation at 3500 rev/min generator speed:

Voltage rise—6V ..	Ammeter reading 26 to 32 amp
6.5V	Ammeter reading 26 to 32 amp

(Progressively increase voltage to obtain reading of 0 amp. Voltage must be lower than 7.7V)

12-volt regulator:

Cutting-in voltage (cold or hot)	12 to 13.5 volt
Cutting-out voltage	11 to 12.5 volt

Regulation at 3500 rev/min generator speed:

Voltage rise—12.5V	Ammeter reading 18 to 22 amp
14.0V	Ammeter reading 18 to 22 amp
15.5V	Ammeter reading 0 to 5 amp

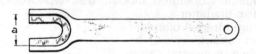

SPANNER 2219-T $a = 9 \,^{+0.2}_{0}$

SPANNER 2220-T $a = 15 \,^{+0.3}_{+0.1}$

SPANNER 2221-T $a = 10 \,^{+0.2}_{0}$

SPANNER 2222-T $a = 13 \,^{+0.3}_{+0.1}$

Spanners for unions (dimensions in mm)

TIGHTENING TORQUES (lb ft)

Clutch:
    Clutch to flywheel   ..   ..   14 to 16

Engine:
    Cylinder head 43.5
    Big-end caps   36
    Camshaft nut   110
    Crankshaft nut   145
    Crankshaft damper   ..   ..   163 to 180
    Fan   ..   ..   7.2 max.
    Main bearing caps   72
    Sump   12
    Sump drain plug   21
    Timing cover   11

Front axle:
    Clamp plate, lower swivel ball joint 35.5
    Lower arm nut (slacken 10 to 15 deg.)   64
    Upper arm nut (slacken 15 to 30 deg.)   64
    Swivel bearing   570
    Wheel nuts   ..   ..   108 to 144

Hydraulic system:
    Pressure regulator 21.75
    Sphere damper   13

Rear axle:
    Stub axle bearing..   72
    Swivel housing (slacken $\frac{1}{8}$ turn)   65
    Wheel fixing screws   ..   ..   108 to 144

Steering:
    Ball pins   28
    Casing end piece..   43
    Casing end piece locknut   72
    Centre yoke   29
    Centring cam collar 3.25
    Pinion nut   36
    Rack control rod   50
    Relay shafts to steering levers   18

Suspension:
    Anti-roll bar ball joints (slacken $\frac{1}{8}$ turn)   28
    Rear anti-roll bar flanges..   36

Transmission:
    Differential shaft nuts   72
    Drive shaft ring nut   288

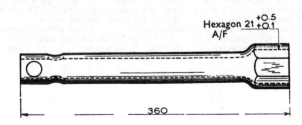

Hexagon 21 $^{+0.5}_{+0.1}$ A/F

360

Spanner No. 1603.T (dimensions in mm)

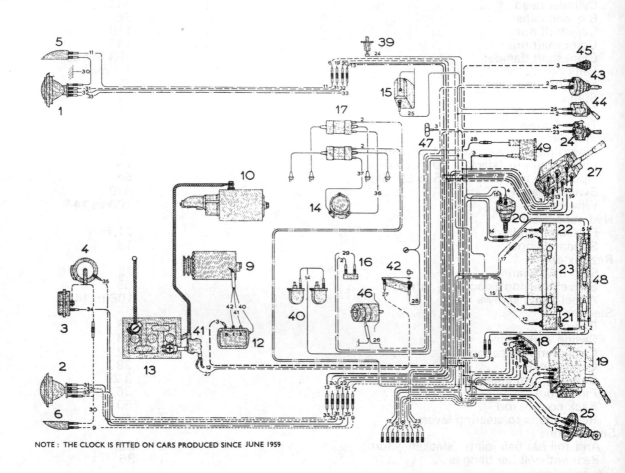

FIG 13:1 Wiring diagram, DS19 cars before 1960, front harness (6-volts)

NOTE : THE CLOCK IS FITTED ON CARS PRODUCED SINCE JUNE 1959

Key to Fig 13:1   1 Headlamp, right   2 Headlamp, left   3 Horn, low note   4 Horn, high note   5 Flashing direction indicator lamp, front right   6 Flashing direction indicator lamp, front left   9 Generator   10 Starter motor   12 Regulator   13 Battery   14 Contact breaker   15 Windscreen wiper motor   16 Stoplamp switch   17 Coils   18 Direction indicator switch   19 Flashing direction indicator, time switch   20 Rheostat for instrument panel lights   21 Ammeter   22 Petrol gauge dial   23 Dashboard lights   24 Interior light switch   25 Lighting and ignition switch   27 Lighting and horn switch   39 Switch for interior lights on front door, left   40 Pressure switches   41 Starter motor solenoid switch   42 Starter motor switch on gear selector   43 Rheostat for demister motor   44 Switch for windscreen wiper motor   45 Inspection light socket   46 Demister motor   47 Terminal for accessories   48 Warning light panel   49 Clock

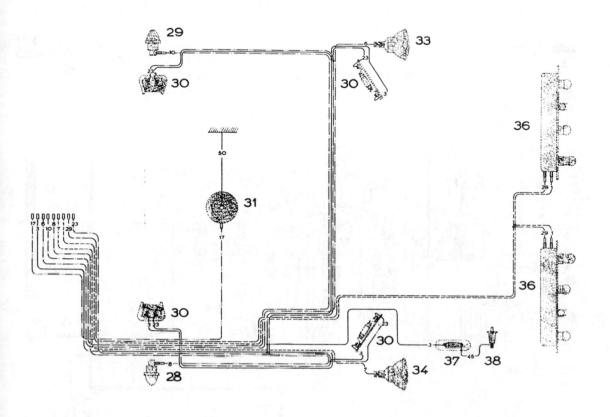

FIG 13:2   Wiring diagram, DS19 cars before 1960, rear harness (6-volts)

Key to Fig 13:2   28 Side lamp, left   29 Side lamp, right   30 Interior lamps   31 Petrol gauge tank unit
33 Flashing direction indicator lamp, rear, right   34 Flashing direction indicator lamp, rear, left   36 Rear lamps (red lights,
stoplights, number plate light)   37 Rear boot light   38 Switch for rear boot light

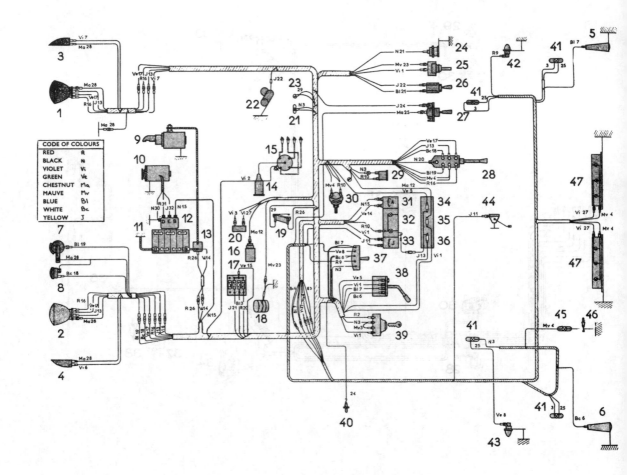

FIG 13:3   Wiring diagram, DS19 cars 1960-61 (12-volts)

Key to Fig 13:3   1 Headlamp, right   2 Headlamp, left   3 Flashing direction indicator lamp, front, right
4 Flashing direction indicator lamp, front, left   5 Flashing direction indicator lamp, rear, right   6 Flashing direction
indicator lamp, rear, left   7 Horn, high note   8 Horn, low note   9 Starter motor   10 Generator   11 Battery
12 Regulator   13 Starter solenoid   14 Coil   15 Distributor   16 Pressure switch   17 Fuses   18 Demister motor
19 Switch for starter motor on gearlever   20 Stoplamp switch   21 Terminal for accessories   22 Windscreen wiper motor
23 Earth terminal   24 Inspection light socket   25 Rheostat for demister motor   26 Switch for windscreen wiper motor
27 Interior light switch   28 Lighting and horn switch   29 Clock   30 Rheostat for instrument panel lights   31 Ammeter
32 Dashboard lights   33 Petrol gauge dial   34 Flashing indicator telltale   35 Pressure switch telltale   36 Headlamp telltale
37 Switch for parking light   38 Flashing direction indicator time switch   39 Lighting and ignition switch   40 Door switch
41 Interior lamp   42 Side lamp, right   43 Side lamp, left   44 Petrol gauge tank unit   45 Rear boot light
46 Switch for rear boot light   47 Rear lamps (red lights, stoplights, number plate light)

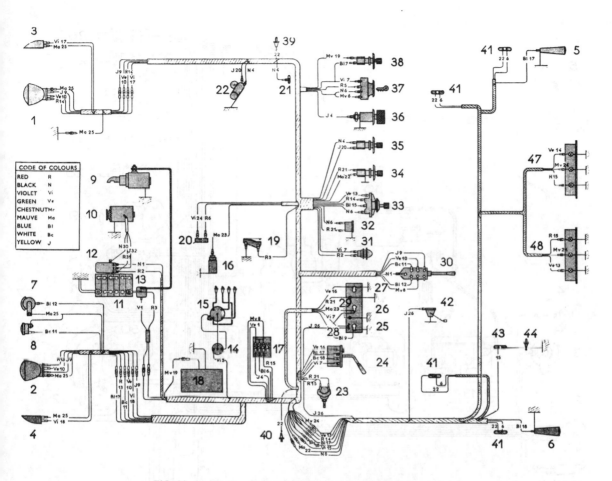

FIG 13:4   Wiring diagram, DS19 cars since 1961 (12-volts)

CODE OF COLOURS

RED	R
BLACK	N
VIOLET	Vi
GREEN	Ve
CHESTNUT	Mr
MAUVE	Ma
BLUE	Bl
WHITE	Bc
YELLOW	J

Key to Fig 13:4   1 Headlamp, right   2 Headlamp, left   3 Flashing direction indicator lamp, front, right   4 Flashing direction indicator lamp, front, left   5 Flashing direction indicator lamp, rear, right   6 Flashing direction indicator lamp, rear, left   7 Horn, high note   8 Horn, low note   9 Starter motor   10 Generator   11 Battery   12 Regulator   13 Starter motor solenoid   14 Coil   15 Distributor   16 Pressure switches   17 Fuses   18 Heater motor   19 Switch for starter motor on gear selector lever   20 Stoplamp switch   21 Terminal for accessories   22 Windscreen wiper motor   23 Rheostat for instrument panel lights   24 Flashing direction indicator time switch   25 Headlamp telltale   26 Pressure switch telltale   27 Flashing direction indicator telltale   28 Petrol gauge dial   29 Dashboard lights   30 Lighting and horn switch   31 Battery charge telltale   32 Clock   33 Parking light switch   34 Interior light switch   35 Windscreen wiper motor switch   36 Cigar lighter   37 Ignition switch   38 Heater motor switch   39 Switch for righthand door   40 Switch for lefthand door   41 Interior lamps   42 Petrol gauge tank unit   43 Rear boot light   44 Switch for rear boot light   47 Rear lamp righthand (lamp, parking, stop, number plate light)   48 Rear lamp lefthand (lamp, parking, stop, number plate light)

DS 19

151

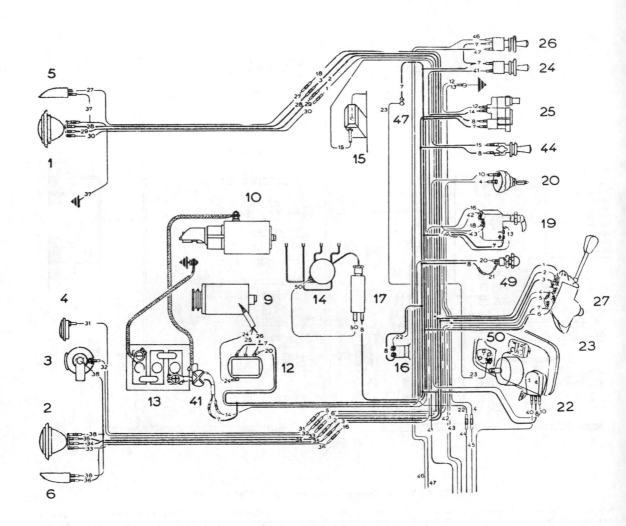

FIG 13:5 Wiring diagram, early ID19 cars, front harness (6-volts)

Key to Fig 13:5 1 Headlamp, righthand 2 Headlamp, lefthand 3 Horn, low note 4 Horn, high note
5 Flashing direction indicator lamp, front righthand 6 Flashing direction indicator lamp, front lefthand 9 Generator
12 Regulator 13 Battery 14 Distributor 15 Windscreen wiper motor 16 Stoplamp switch 17 Coil
19 Flashing lamp switch 20 Rheostat for instrument panel lights 22 Gauge dial 23 Instrument panel lights
24 Interior light switch 25 Ignition switch 27 Combined lighting and horn switch 41 Starter solenoid switch
44 Switch for windscreen wiper motor 47 Terminal for accessories 49 Warning light 50 Clock

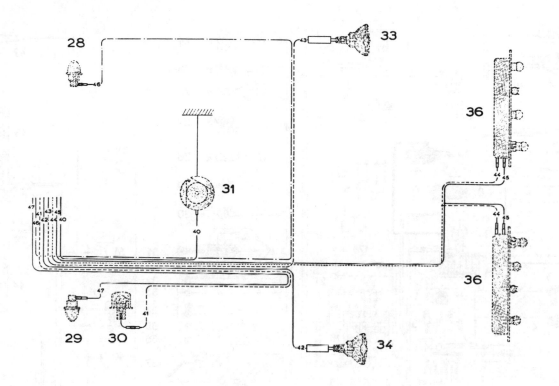

FIG 13:6   Wiring diagram, early ID19 cars, rear harness (6-volts)

Key to Fig 13:6   28 Rear parking light, righthand side   29 Rear parking light, lefthand side   30 Interior lamp
31 Petrol gauge tank unit   33 Flashing direction indicator lamp, rear righthand   34 Flashing direction indicator lamp,
rear lefthand   36 Rear lamps (red light, stoplight and number plate light)

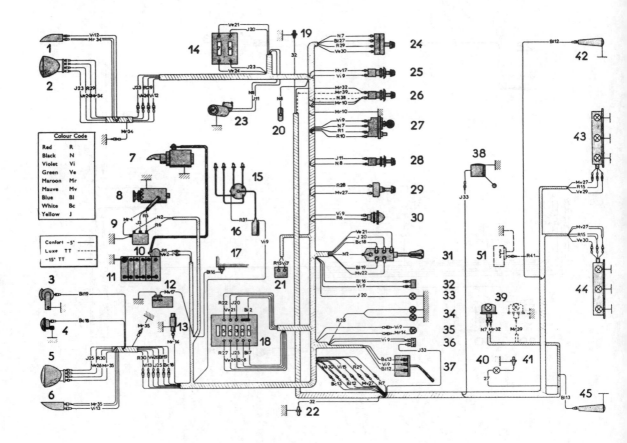

FIG 13:7   Wiring diagram, later ID19 cars (12-volts)

Key to Fig 13:7   1 Front righthand direction indicator   2 Righthand headlamp   3 Town horn   4 Country horn
5 Lefthand headlamp   6 Front lefthand direction indicator   7 Starter   8 Generator   9 Regulator   10 Contactor
11 Battery   12 Front blower-motor   13 Security valve   14 Righthand fuse box   15 Distributor   16 Ignition coil
17 Temperature detector (on cylinder head)   18 Lefthand fuse box   19 Roof light switch on right front door
20 Accessory terminal   21 Stop switch   22 Roof light switch on left front door   23 Windscreen wiper motor
24 Parking light switch   25 Front blower motor switch   26 Dashboard roof light switch   27 Ignition and starting switch
28 Windscreen wiper switch   29 Panel light dimmer   30 Charging indicator lamp   31 Lighting and horn switch
32 Temperature gauge   33 Headlamp telltale lamp   34 Panel lights   35 Brake telltale lamp   36 Petrol gauge
37 Direction indicator switch   38 Tank unit   39 Roof light   40 Boot light   41 Boot light switch
42 Rear righthand direction indicator   43 Rear righthand number plate light, tail light and stoplight   44 Rear lefthand
number plate light, tail light and stoplight   45 Rear lefthand direction indicator

Inches	Decimals	Milli-metres	Inches to Millimetres — Inches	Inches to Millimetres — mm	Millimetres to Inches — mm	Millimetres to Inches — Inches
1/64	.015625	.3969	.001	.0254	.01	.00039
1/32	.03125	.7937	.002	.0508	.02	.00079
3/64	.046875	1.1906	.003	.0762	.03	.00118
1/16	.0625	1.5875	.004	.1016	.04	.00157
5/64	.078125	1.9844	.005	.1270	.05	.00197
3/32	.09375	2.3812	.006	.1524	.06	.00236
7/64	.109375	2.7781	.007	.1778	.07	.00276
1/8	.125	3.1750	.008	.2032	.08	.00315
9/64	.140625	3.5719	.009	.2286	.09	.00354
5/32	.15625	3.9687	.01	.254	.1	.00394
11/64	.171875	4.3656	.02	.508	.2	.00787
3/16	.1875	4.7625	.03	.762	.3	.01181
13/64	.203125	5·1594	.04	1.016	.4	.01575
7/32	.21875	5.5562	.05	1.270	.5	.01969
15/64	.234375	5.9531	.06	1.524	.6	.02362
1/4	.25	6.3500	.07	1.778	.7	.02756
17/64	.265625	6.7469	.08	2.032	.8	.03150
9/32	.28125	7.1437	.09	2.286	.9	.03543
19/64	.296875	7.5406	.1	2.54	1	.03937
5/16	.3125	7.9375	.2	5.08	2	.07874
21/64	.328125	8.3344	.3	7.62	3	.11811
11/32	.34375	8.7312	.4	10.16	4	.15748
23/64	.359375	9.1281	.5	12.70	5	.19685
3/8	.375	9.5250	.6	15.24	6	.23622
25/64	.390625	9.9219	.7	17.78	7	.27559
13/32	.40625	10.3187	.8	20.32	8	.31496
27/64	.421875	10.7156	.9	22.86	9	.35433
7/16	.4375	11.1125	1	25.4	10	.39370
29/64	.453125	11.5094	2	50.8	11	.43307
15/32	.46875	11.9062	3	76.2	12	.47244
31/64	.484375	12.3031	4	101.6	13	.51181
1/2	.5	12.7000	5	127.0	14	.55118
33/64	.515625	13.0969	6	152.4	15	.59055
17/32	.53125	13.4937	7	177.8	16	.62992
35/64	.546875	13.8906	8	203.2	17	.66929
9/16	.5625	14.2875	9	228.6	18	.70866
37/64	.578125	14.6844	10	254.0	19	.74803
19/32	.59375	15.0812	11	279.4	20	.78740
39/64	.609375	15.4781	12	304.8	21	.82677
5/8	.625	15.8750	13	330.2	22	.86614
41/64	.640625	16.2719	14	355.6	23	.90551
21/32	.65625	16.6687	15	381.0	24	.94488
43/64	.671875	17.0656	16	406.4	25	.98425
11/16	.6875	17.4625	17	431.8	26	1.02362
45/64	.703125	17.8594	18	457.2	27	1.06299
23/32	.71875	18.2562	19	482.6	28	1.10236
47/64	.734375	18.6531	20	508.0	29	1.14173
3/4	.75	19.0500	21	533.4	30	1.18110
49/64	.765625	19.4469	22	558.8	31	1.22047
25/32	.78125	19.8437	23	584.2	32	1.25984
51/64	.796875	20.2406	24	609.6	33	1.29921
13/16	.8125	20.6375	25	635.0	34	1.33858
53/64	.828125	21.0344	26	660.4	35	1.37795
27/32	.84375	21.4312	27	685.8	36	1.41732
55/64	.859375	21.8281	28	711.2	37	1.4567
7/8	.875	22.2250	29	736.6	38	1.4961
57/64	.890625	22.6219	30	762.0	39	1.5354
29/32	.90625	23.0187	31	787.4	40	1.5748
59/64	.921875	23.4156	32	812.8	41	1.6142
15/16	.9375	23.8125	33	838.2	42	1.6535
61/64	.953125	24.2094	34	863.6	43	1.6929
31/32	.96875	24.6062	35	889.0	44	1.7323
63/64	.984375	25.0031	36	914.4	45	1.7717

UNITS	Pints to Litres	Gallons to Litres	Litres to Pints	Litres to Gallons	Miles to Kilometres	Kilometres to Miles	Lbs. per sq. In. to Kg. per sq. Cm.	Kg. per sq. Cm. to Lbs. per sq. In.
1	.57	4.55	1.76	.22	1.61	.62	.07	14.22
2	1.14	9.09	3.52	.44	3.22	1.24	.14	28.50
3	1.70	13.64	5.28	.66	4.83	1.86	.21	42.67
4	2.27	18.18	7.04	.88	6.44	2.49	.28	56.89
5	2.84	22.73	8.80	1.10	8.05	3.11	.35	71.12
6	3.41	27.28	10.56	1.32	9.66	3.73	.42	85.34
7	3.98	31.82	12.32	1.54	11.27	4.35	.49	99.56
8	4.55	36.37	14.08	1.76	12.88	4.97	.56	113.79
9		40.91	15.84	1.98	14.48	5.59	.63	128.00
10		45.46	17.60	2.20	16.09	6.21	.70	142.23
20				4.40	32.19	12.43	1.41	284.47
30				6.60	48.28	18.64	2.11	426.70
40				8.80	64.37	24.85		
50					80.47	31.07		
60					96.56	37.28		
70					112.65	43.50		
80					128.75	49.71		
90					144.84	55.92		
100					160.93	62.14		

UNITS	Lb ft to kgm	Kgm to lb ft	UNITS	Lb ft to kgm	Kgm to lb ft
1	.138	7.233	7	.967	50.631
2	.276	14.466	8	1.106	57.864
3	.414	21.699	9	1.244	65.097
4	.553	28.932	10	1.382	72.330
5	.691	36.165	20	2.765	144.660
6	.829	43.398	30	4.147	216.990

HINTS ON MAINTENANCE AND OVERHAUL

There are few things more rewarding than the restoration of a vehicle's original peak of efficiency and smooth performance.

The following notes are intended to help the owner to reach that state of perfection. Providing that he possesses the basic manual skills he should have no difficulty in performing most of the operations detailed in this manual. It must be stressed, however, that where recommended in the manual, highly-skilled operations ought to be entrusted to experts, who have the necessary equipment, to carry out the work satisfactorily.

Quality of workmanship:

The hazardous driving conditions on the roads to-day demand that vehicles should be as nearly perfect, mechanically, as possible. It is therefore most important that amateur work be carried out with care, bearing in mind the often inadequate working conditions, and also the inferior tools which may have to be used. It is easy to counsel perfection in all things, and we recognize that it may be setting an impossibly high standard. We do, however, suggest that every care should be taken to ensure that a vehicle is as safe to take on the road as it is humanly possible to make it.

Safe working conditions:

Even though a vehicle may be stationary, it is still potentially dangerous if certain sensible precautions are not taken when working on it while it is supported on jacks or blocks. It is indeed preferable not to use jacks alone, but to supplement them with carefully placed blocks, so that there will be plenty of support if the car rolls off the jacks during a strenuous manoeuvre. Axle stands are an excellent way of providing a rigid base which is not readily disturbed. Piles of bricks are a dangerous substitute. Be careful not to get under heavy loads on lifting tackle, the load could fall. It is preferable not to work alone when lifting an engine, or when working underneath a vehicle which is supported well off the ground. To be trapped, particularly under the vehicle, may have unpleasant results if help is not quickly forthcoming. Make some provision, however humble, to deal with fires. Always disconnect a battery if there is a likelihood of electrical shorts. These may start a fire if there is leaking fuel about. This applies particularly to leads which can carry a heavy current, like those in the starter circuit. While on the subject of electricity, we must also stress the danger of using equipment which is run off the mains and which has no earth or has faulty wiring or connections. So many workshops have damp floors, and electrical shocks are of such a nature that it is sometimes impossible to let go of a live lead or piece of equipment due to the muscular spasms which take place.

Work demanding special care:

This involves the servicing of braking, steering and suspension systems. On the road, failure of the braking system may be disastrous. Make quite sure that there can be no possibility of failure through the bursting of rusty brake pipes or rotten hoses, nor to a sudden loss of pressure due to defective seals or valves.

Problems:

The chief problems which may face an operator are:
1 External dirt.
2 Difficulty in undoing tight fixings.
3 Dismantling unfamiliar mechanisms.
4 Deciding in what respect parts are defective.
5 Confusion about the correct order for reassembly.
6 Adjusting running clearance.
7 Road testing.
8 Final tuning.

Practical suggestions to solve the problems:

1 Preliminary cleaning of large parts—engines, transmissions, steering, suspensions, etc.,—should be carried out before removal from the car. Where road dirt and mud alone are present, wash clean with a high-pressure water jet, brushing to remove stubborn adhesions, and allow to drain and dry. Where oil or grease is also present, wash down with a proprietary compound (Gunk, Teepol etc.,) applying with a stiff brush—an old paint brush is suitable—into all crevices. Cover the distributor and ignition coils with a polythene bag and then apply a strong water jet to clear the loosened deposits. Allow to drain and dry. The assemblies will then be sufficiently clean to remove and transfer to the bench for the next stage.

On the bench, further cleaning can be carried out, first wiping the parts as free as possible from grease with old newspaper. Avoid using rag or cotton waste which can leave clogging fibres behind. Any remaining grease can be removed with a brush dipped in paraffin. If necessary, traces of paraffin can be removed by carbon tetrachloride. Avoid using paraffin or petrol in large quantities for cleaning in enclosed areas, such as garages, on account of the high fire risk.

When all exteriors have been cleaned, and not before, dismantling can be commenced. This ensures that dirt will not enter into interiors and orifices revealed by dismantling. In the next phases, where components have to be cleaned, use carbon tetrachloride in preference to petrol and keep the containers covered except when in use. After the components have been cleaned, plug small holes with tapered hard wood plugs cut to size and blank off larger orifices with grease-proof paper and masking tape. Do not use soft wood plugs or matchsticks as they may break.

2 It is not advisable to hammer on the end of a screw thread, but if it must be done, first screw on a nut to protect the thread, and use a lead hammer. This applies particularly to the removal of tapered cotters. Nuts and bolts seem to 'grow' together, especially in exhaust systems. If penetrating oil does not work, try the judicious application of heat, but be careful of starting a fire. Asbestos sheet or cloth is useful to isolate heat.

Tight bushes or pieces of tail-pipe rusted into a silencer can be removed by splitting them with an open-ended hacksaw. Tight screws can sometimes be started by a tap from a hammer on the end of a suitable screwdriver. Many tight fittings will yield to the judicious use of a hammer, but it must be a soft-faced hammer if damage is to be avoided, use a heavy block on the opposite side to absorb shock. Any parts of the steering system which have been damaged should be renewed, as attempts to repair them may lead to cracking and subsequent failure, and steering ball joints should be disconnected using a recommended tool to prevent damage.

3   It often happens that an owner is baffled when trying to dismantle an unfamiliar piece of equipment. So many modern devices are pressed together or assembled by spinning-over flanges, that they must be sawn apart. The intention is that the whole assembly must be renewed. However, parts which appear to be in one piece to the naked eye, may reveal close-fitting joint lines when inspected with a magnifying glass, and, this may provide the necessary clue to dismantling. Left-handed screw threads are used where rotational forces would tend to unscrew a right-handed screw thread.

Be very careful when dismantling mechanisms which may come apart suddenly. Work in an enclosed space where the parts will be contained, and drape a piece of cloth over the device if springs are likely to fly in all directions. Mark everything which might be reassembled in the wrong position, scratched symbols may be used on unstressed parts, or a sequence of tiny dots from a centre punch can be useful. Stressed parts should never be scratched or centre-popped as this may lead to cracking under working conditions. Store parts which look alike in the correct order for reassembly. Never rely upon memory to assist in the assembly of complicated mechanisms, especially when they will be dismantled for a long time, but make notes, and drawings to supplement the diagrams in the manual, and put labels on detached wires. Rust stains may indicate unlubricated wear. This can sometimes be seen round the outside edge of a bearing cup in a universal joint. Look for bright rubbing marks on parts which normally should not make heavy contact. These might prove that something is bent or running out of truth. For example, there might be bright marks on one side of a piston, at the top near the ring grooves, and others at the bottom of the skirt on the other side. This could well be the clue to a bent connecting rod. Suspected cracks can be proved by heating the component in a light oil to approximately 100°C, removing, drying off, and dusting with french chalk, if a crack is present the oil retained in the crack will stain the french chalk.

4   In determining wear, and the degree, against the permissible limits set in the manual, accurate measurement can only be achieved by the use of a micrometer. In many cases, the wear is given to the fourth place of decimals; that is in ten-thousandths of an inch. This can be read by the vernier scale on the barrel of a good micrometer. Bore diameters are more difficult to determine. If, however, the matching shaft is accurately measured, the degree of play in the bore can be felt as a guide to its suitability. In other cases, the shank of a twist drill of known diameter is a handy check.

Many methods have been devised for determining the clearance between bearing surfaces. To-day the best and simplest is by the use of Plastigage, obtainable from most garages. A thin plastic thread is laid between the two surfaces and the bearing is tightened, flattening the thread. On removal, the width of the thread is compared with a scale supplied with the thread and the clearance is read off directly. Sometimes joint faces leak persistently, even after gasket renewal. The fault will then be traceable to distortion, dirt or burrs. Studs which are screwed into soft metal frequently raise burrs at the point of entry. A quick cure for this is to chamfer the edge of the hole in the part which fits over the stud.

5   **Always check a replacement part with the original one before it is fitted.**

If parts are not marked, and the order for reassembly is not known, a little detective work will help. Look for marks which are due to wear to see if they can be mated. Joint faces may not be identical due to manufacturing errors, and parts which overlap may be stained, giving a clue to the correct position. Most fixings leave identifying marks especially if they were painted over on assembly. It is then easier to decide whether a nut, for instance, has a plain, a spring, or a shakeproof washer under it. All running surfaces become 'bedded' together after long spells of work and tiny imperfections on one part will be found to have left corresponding marks on the other. This is particularly true of shafts and bearings and even a score on a cylinder wall will show on the piston.

6   Checking end float or rocker clearances by feeler gauge may not always give accurate results because of wear. For instance, the rocker tip which bears on a valve stem may be deeply pitted, in which case the feeler will simply be bridging a depression. Thrust washers may also wear depressions in opposing faces to make accurate measurement difficult. End float is then easier to check by using a dial gauge. It is common practice to adjust end play in bearing assemblies, like front hubs with taper rollers, by doing up the axle nut until the hub becomes stiff to turn and then backing it off a little. Do not use this method with ballbearing hubs as the assembly is often preloaded by tightening the axle nut to its fullest extent. If the splitpin hole will not line up, file the base of the nut a little.

Steering assemblies often wear in the straight-ahead position. If any part is adjusted, make sure that it remains free when moved from lock to lock. Do not be surprised if an assembly like a steering gearbox, which is known to be carefully adjusted outside the car, becomes stiff when it is bolted in place. This will be due to distortion of the case by the pull of the mounting bolts, particularly if the mounting points are not all touching together. This problem may be met in other equipment and is cured by careful attention to the alignment of mounting points.

When a spanner is stamped with a size and A/F it means that the dimension is the width between the jaws and has no connection with ANF, which is the designation for the American National Fine thread. Coarse threads like Whitworth are rarely used on cars to-day except for studs which screw into soft aluminium or cast iron. For this reason it might be found that the top end of a cylinder head stud has a fine thread and the lower end a coarse thread to screw into the cylinder block. If the car has mainly UNF threads then it is likely that any coarse threads will be UNC, which are not the same as Whitworth. Small sizes have the same number of threads in Whitworth and UNC, but in the $\frac{1}{2}$ inch size for example, there are twelve threads to the inch in the former and thirteen in the latter.

7 After a major overhaul, particularly if a great deal of work has been done on the braking, steering and suspension systems, it is advisable to approach the problem of testing with care. If the braking system has been overhauled, apply heavy pressure to the brake pedal and get a second operator to check every possible source of leakage. The brakes may work extremely well, but a leak could cause complete failure after a few miles.

Do not fit the hub caps until every wheel nut has been checked for tightness, and make sure the tyre pressures are correct. Check the levels of coolant, lubricants and hydraulic fluids. Being satisfied that all is well, take the car on the road and test the brakes at once. Check the steering and the action of the handbrake. Do all this at moderate speeds on quiet roads, and make sure there is no other vehicle behind you when you try a rapid stop.

Finally, remember that many parts settle down after a time, so check for tightness of all fixings after the car has been on the road for a hundred miles or so.

8 It is useless to tune an engine which has not reached its normal running temperature. In the same way, the tune of an engine which is stiff after a rebore will be different when the engine is again running free. Remember too, that rocker clearances on pushrod operated valve gear will change when the cylinder head nuts are tightened after an initial period of running with a new head gasket.

Trouble may not always be due to what seems the obvious cause. Ignition, carburation and mechanical condition are interdependent and spitting back through the carburetter, which might be attributed to a weak mixture, can be caused by a sticking inlet valve.

For one final hint on tuning, never adjust more than one thing at a time or it will be impossible to tell which adjustment produced the desired result.

GLOSSARY OF TERMS

Allen key   Cranked hexagonal bar for turning socket head screws.

Alternator   Rotary machine for generating alternating current electricity. Car alternators embody silicon diodes to rectify the AC output to DC for energizing the field and supplying the load.

Ambient temperature   Surrounding atmospheric temperature.

Annulus   A ring-shaped element. The outer gear of an epicyclic train.

Armature   The rotating member, comprising shaft, windings and commutator, of a generator or motor. The moving element of a relay or solenoid.

Axial   In line with, or pertaining to, an axis.

Backlash   Play between meshing gears.

Balance lever   Lever in which the force applied at the centre is divided equally between connections to the ends.

Bendix pinion   Self-meshing and disengaging pinion on the shaft of an inertia type starter motor.

Bevel pinion   Conical shaped gearwheel designed to mesh with a similar gear whose axis usually is at 90 deg. to its own.

bhp   Brake horse power, as measured on a dynamometer.

bmep   Brake mean effective pressure. The average pressure exerted on a piston during the working stroke.

Brake cylinder   Cylinder with hydraulically operated piston(s) acting on brake shoes or pads.

Brake regulator   Control valve fitted to some hydraulic braking systems to limit pressure applied to rear brakes to prevent the rear wheels locking when heavily braking.

Camber   Angle at which a front wheel is tilted from the vertical.

Capacitor   Modern term for condenser. Used across ignition make-and-break to produce a hot spark at the plug.

Castellated   Top face of a nut, slotted across the flats to take a locking pin.

Castor   Angle at which the kingpin or swivel pin is tilted from the vertical when viewed from one side.

cc   Cubic centimetres. In engine capacity, the area of the bore in sq cm multiplied by the stroke in cm and the number of cylinders.

Clevis   Forked connector with pin. Commonly used in handbrake and similar connections.

Collet   Ring or collar, usually split, to encircle a groove in a stem or shaft where it is retained by an outer ring or seating. Used to secure the springs to the valves in the cylinder head of a car.

Commutator   A segmented collar or faceplate on the armature of a generator or motor through which current is conveyed from or to the windings via the brushes. A current reversing device.

Compression ratio   Ratio of total volume (piston at bottom of stroke) to unswept volume (piston at top of stroke) in an engine cylinder.

Condenser   See 'Capacitor'.

Core plug   Plug for blanking off a core or 'fettling' hole on an iron casting. A 'Welch' plug.

Crown wheel   Large ring bevel gear, secured to differential housing in rear axle, transmitting drive from the bevel pinion on the propeller shaft to the rear wheel axles.

C spanner   Spanner shaped like a letter C with a handle. Used on screw collars with slots instead of flats for turning.

Damper   Modern term for shock absorber.

Depression   Lowering of atmospheric pressure as, for example, in the inlet manifold or carburetter.

Dowel   Close fitting pin, peg, tube or bolt for locating mating parts accurately.

Drive shaft   Output shaft of gearbox transmitting torque to the propeller shaft. Sometimes 'third motion shaft'.

Dry liner   Thin walled tube pressed into bored-out engine cylinder.

Dry sump   Sump from which all oil collected is immediately scavenged and returned to a separate tank.

Dynamo   See 'Generator'.

Electrode   Terminal part of an electrical component such as the centre element of a sparking plug.

Electrolyte   In car batteries, sulphuric acid diluted with distilled water.

End float   Play or movement on a shaft in an axial direction; end play.

EP   (Extreme pressure). As applied to lubricants, indicates special grades for heavily loaded bearing surfaces such as gear teeth in a gearbox or crown-wheel and pinion in a rear axle assembly.

Field coils   Windings on polepieces of motors and generators.

Fullflow filter   Filter in which all the oil pumped around the engine passes for filtering. If the filter element becomes clogged, a bypass valve opens to circulate unfiltered oil.

Gear pump   Pump in which oil is circulated by two meshing gears in a close fitting casing. Oil is carried from one side around the outer periphery of both gears in the spaces between the teeth to the outlet at the other, the meshing teeth in the centre preventing passage back to the inlet.

Gearshaft   Shaft transmitting drive from clutch to layshaft in the gearbox. 'First motion' shaft.

Generator   A machine for generating direct current and incorporating a commutator and brushes. A dynamo.

Grommet   Close fitting ring of rubber or plastic around pipes or cables to protect them from abrasion in passage through bulkheads and to seal the opening against entry of dirt and water.

Grubscrew   Setscrew without a head, threaded full length, with slot for turning, usually for securing a pulley or collar to a shaft.

Gudgeon pin   Shaft connecting piston to the connecting rod; a 'wrist-pin' or 'piston-pin'.

Halfshaft   One of a pair transmitting drive from the differential gearing to the wheel hubs.

Helical   In spiral form. The teeth of helical gears are cut in a spiral at an angle to the side faces of the gearwheel.

Hot spot   Heated area assisting vapourization of fuel on its way to the cylinders. Usually provided by a close contact area between inlet and exhaust manifolds.

HT   High tension. The high voltage output produced by the ignition coil for the sparking plugs.

Hydrometer   Device for checking the specific gravity of battery electrolyte.

Hypoid gear   Form of bevel gear used in rear axle crown and bevel combinations in which the bevel pinion meshes with the crownwheel below its centre line, giving a lower propeller shaft line.

Idler   Device for passing on movement, e.g. a free-running gear between driving and driven gears; a lever transmitting track rod movement to a side rod in a steering gear.

Impeller   Rotating element of a water pump to produce flow.

Intermediate gear   In a gearbox, an idler gear introduced between layshaft and drive shaft to reverse motion.

Journals   Parts of a shaft in intimate contact with bearings.

Kingpin   Main vertical pin around which the front stub axle is turned to provide steering.

Layshaft   In a gearbox, the intermediate shaft, carrying the laygear, transmitting the drive from the gearshaft, or first motion shaft, to the drive shaft, or third motion shaft. The second motion shaft.

lb ft   Pound-feet, a measure of twist or torque; the product of radius and load. A pull of 10 lb at a radius of 1 ft is a torque of 10 lb ft.

Little-end   The small, or piston, end of a connecting rod.

l.s.   The leading shoe in a brake drum, has a tendency to wedge into the drum when applied, so increasing the braking effect.

LT   Low tension. The electrical output from the battery and generator.

Mandrel   Accurately machined bar or rod used for test or centring purposes.

Manifold   Pipe or duct with several branches. In car engines the duct between the cylinder ports and the carburetter or exhaust pipe.

Needle rollers   Bearing rollers whose length is many times their diameter.

Oil bath   Reservoir for lubricating parts by immersion. In air filters a separate oil supply for wetting a wire mesh element to hold the dust.

Overlap   Period during which inlet and exhaust valves are open together.

Pawl   Pivoted catch engaging the teeth of a ratchet to permit rotation in one direction only.

Peg spanner   Spanner with pegs or pins for insertion in holes or slots in a collar or cap for turning.

Pinion   The smaller of a pair of gears; a spur gear.

Piston type damper   Shock absorber in which damping is controlled by a piston working in a closed, oil-filled cylinder.

Preloading   Preset static pressure on ball or roller bearings not due to working loads.

Radial   Radiating from a centre, like the spokes of a wheel.

Radius rod   Pivoted arm confining movement to an arc of fixed radius.

Ratchet	Toothed wheel or rack capable of movement in one direction only. Movement in the other is prevented by a pawl.
Ring gear	Large diameter toothed ring secured to the outer periphery of a flywheel for engagement with the pinion of the starter motor.
Runout	Amount by which a rotating part is out of truth.
Semi-floating axle	Outer end of rear axle halfshaft carried on bearing inside the axle casing. Wheel hub is secured to the end of the halfshaft.
Servo	Hydraulic or pneumatic device for assisting or augmenting a force applied manually.
Setscrew	A screw threaded for the full length of the shank.
Shackle	Coupling link in the form of two parallel pins connected by side plates. Used to anchor one end of a leaf spring to take up length variation on deflection.
Shell bearing	Thin walled, steel shell lined with anti-friction metal. Usually semi-circular and used in pairs for main and big-end bearings.
Shock absorber	Device linked to front and rear suspensions to damp out vertical oscillation due to uneven road surfaces; a damper.
Socket head screw	Screw with hexagonal socket in head for an Allen key.
Solenoid	Coil of wire creating a magnetic field when electric current passes through it. Commonly applied to coil, complete with armature or core, for operating a mechanical device or contacts.
Spur gear	Gear with teeth cut axially across the periphery.
Stub axle	Short axle mounted at one end only.
Steering box	Gearbox at lower end of steering column, containing gearing for translating rotational steering wheel motion into lateral movement for swivelling the front wheels.
Sway bar	Bar connected between a fixed point on the chassis or body and an axle to limit sideways movement of the axle.
Tachometer	Instrument for the accurate measurement of rotational speed. Usually indicates revolutions per minute.

TDC	Top dead centre. The point of highest travel of a piston in its cylinder.
Thermostat	Device for regulating temperature. In cars, used to restrict the circulation of cooling water through the radiator until engine temperature has risen.
Threequarter floating axle	Outer end of rear axle halfshaft flanged and bolted to wheel hub which runs in bearing mounted on outside of axle casing. The axle shaft does not bear the vehicle weight.
Thrust bearing	—or washer. Bearings or washers for reducing friction through axial loading on rotating shafts or components.
Torque	Turning or twisting effort.
Track rod	Bar across the front underside of the vehicle coupling the steering arms and maintaining the front wheels in proper alignment.
Transducer	Electrical device for converting mechanical or thermal stress into an electrical signal for operating a warning lamp or indicator.
Transmitter	Electrical device for transmitting the state of a measuring device, such as a fuel gauge, to a suitably scaled indicator.
t.s.	Trailing shoe in a brake drum, has a tendency to break away from the drum when applied, so reducing the braking effect.
UJ	Universal joint. Coupling between shafts not in alignment permitting stress-free torque transmission.
UNF	Unified national fine screw thread.
Vacuum servo	Servo device, usually for brake operation, utilising the difference in pressure between atmospheric and that in the inlet manifold to augment the manually applied braking effort.
Venturi	Restriction or 'choke' in a tube, as in a carburetter, to produce a change in velocity and pressure.
Vernier	A pair of adjacent scales for determining very small measurements.
Welch plug	See 'Core plug'.
Wet liner	Removable cylinder barrel, sealed at both ends against surrounding coolant in a cylinder block but with coolant circulating around the centre section.
Wet sump	Detachable lower half of a crankcase in which the lubricant is allowed to drain and remain until re-circulated.

164

INDEX

THE AUTOBOOK SERIES OF WORKSHOP MANUALS

Make				Author	Title
Make				*Author*	*Title*

ALFA ROMEO

1600 Giulia TI 1962–67	..	..	..	Ball	Alfa Romeo Giulia 1962–70 Autobook
1600 Giulia Sprint 1962–68	..	..	..	Ball	Alfa Romeo Giulia 1962–70 Autobook
1600 Giulia Spider 1962–68	..	..	..	Ball	Alfa Romeo Giulia 1962–70 Autobook
1600 Giulia Super 1965–70	..	..	..	Ball	Alfa Romeo Giulia 1962–70 Autobook

ASTON MARTIN

All models 1921–58	..	..	..	Coram	Aston Martin 1921–58 Autobook

AUSTIN

A30 1951–56 ..	..	..	..	Ball	Austin A30, A35, A40 Autobook
A35 1956–62 ..	..	..	..	Ball	Austin A30, A35, A40 Autobook
A40 Farina 1957–67	..		..	Ball	Austin A30, A35, A40 Autobook
A40 Cambridge 1954–57		..	..	Ball	BMC Autobook Three
A50 Cambridge 1954–57	..		..	Ball	BMC Autobook Three
A55 Cambridge Mk 1 1957–58		..	..	Ball	BMC Autobook Three
A55 Cambridge Mk 2 1958–61		..	..	Smith	BMC Autobook One
A60 Cambridge 1961–69	..	..	..	Smith	BMC Autobook One
A99 1959–61 ..	..	..	..	Ball	BMC Autobook Four
A110 1961–68	..	..	..	Ball	BMC Autobook Four
Mini 1959–70 ..	..	..	..	Ball	Mini 1959–70 Autobook
Mini Clubman 1969–70	..	..	..	Ball	Mini 1959–70 Autobook
Mini Cooper 1961–70 ..	..	..	..	Ball	Mini Cooper 1961–70 Autobook
Mini Cooper S 1963–70	..	..	..	Ball	Mini Cooper 1961–70 Autobook
1100 Mk 1 1963–67 ..	..	..	..	Ball	1100 Mk 1 1962–67 Autobook
1100 Mk 2 1968–70 ..	..	..	..	Ball	1100 Mk 2, 1300 Mk 1, 2, America 1968–70 Autobook
1300 Mk 1, 2 1968–70	..	..	..	Ball	1100 Mk 2, 1300 Mk 1, 2, America 1968–70 Autobook
America 1968–70	..	..	..	Ball	1100 Mk 2, 1300 Mk 1, 2, America 1968–70 Autobook
1800 Mk 1, 2 1964–70	..	..	..	Ball	1800 1964–70 Autobook
1800S 1969–70	..	..	..	Ball	1800 1964–70 Autobook
Maxi 1969	..	..	..	Ball	Austin Maxi 1969 Autobook

AUSTIN HEALEY

100/6 1956–59	..	..	..	Ball	Austin Healey 100/6, 3000 1956–68 Autobook
Sprite 1958–70	..	..	..	Ball	Sprite, Midget 1958–70 Autobook
3000 Mk 1, 2, 3 1959–68	..	..	..	Ball	Austin Healey 100/6, 3000 1956–68 Autobook

BEDFORD

CA Mk 1 and 2 1961–69	..	..	..	Ball	Vauxhall Victor 1, 2 FB 1957–64 Autobook
Beagle HA 1964–66 ..	..	..	..	Ball	Vauxhall Viva HA 1964–66 Autobook

BMW

1600 1966–70	..	..	..	Ball	BMW 1600 1966–70 Autobook
1600–2 1966–70	..	..	..	Ball	BMW 1600 1966–70 Autobook
1600TI 1966–70	..	..	..	Ball	BMW 1600 1966–70 Autobook
1800 1964–70	..	..	..	Ball	BMW 1800 1964–70 Autobook
1800TI 1964–67	..	..	..	Ball	BMW 1800 1964–70 Autobook
2000 1966–70	..	..	..	Ball	BMW 2000, 2002 1966–70 Autobook
2000A 1966–70	..	..	..	Ball	BMW 2000, 2002 1966–70 Autobook
2000TI 1966–70	..	..	..	Ball	BMW 2000, 2002 1966–70 Autobook
2000CS 1967–70	..	..	..	Ball	BMW 2000, 2002 1966–70 Autobook
2000CA 1967–70	..	..	..	Ball	BMW 2000, 2002 1966–70 Autobook
2002 1968–70	..	..	..	Ball	BMW 2000, 2002 1966–70 Autobook

CITROEN

DS19 1955–65	..	..	..	Ball	Citroen DS19, ID19 1955–66 Autobook
ID19 1956–66 ..	..	..	..	Ball	Citroen DS19, ID19 1955–66 Autobook

Make				Author	Title

COMMER

Cob Series 1, 2, 3 1960–65	..	..	..	Ball	Hillman Minx 1 to 5 1956–65 Autobook
Imp Vans 1963–68	..	..	..	Smith	Hillman Imp 1963–68 Autobook
Imp Vans 1969–71	..	..	..	Ball	Hillman Imp 1969–71 Autobook

DE DION BOUTON

One-cylinder 1899–1907	..	..	..	Mercredy	De Dion Bouton Autobook One
Two-cylinder 1903–1907	..	..	..	Mercredy	De Dion Bouton Autobook One
Four-cylinder 1905–1907	..	..	..	Mercredy	De Dion Bouton Autobook One

DATSUN

1300 1968–70	..	..	..	Ball	Datsun 1300, 1600 1968–70 Autobook
1600 1968–70	..	..	..	Ball	Datsun 1300, 1600 1968–70 Autobook

FIAT

500 1957–61	..	..	..	Ball	Fiat 500 1957–69 Autobook
500D 1960–65	..	..	..	Ball	Fiat 500 1957–69 Autobook
500F 1965–69	..	..	..	Ball	Fiat 500 1957–69 Autobook
500L 1968–69	..	..	..	Ball	Fiat 500 1957–69 Autobook
600 633cc 1955–61	..	..	..	Ball	Fiat 600, 600D 1955–69 Autobook
600D, 767cc 1960–69	..	..	..	Ball	Fiat 600, 600D 1955–69 Autobook
850 Sedan 1964–70	..	..	..	Ball	Fiat 850 1964–70 Autobook
850 Coupé 1965–70	..	..	..	Ball	Fiat 850 1964–70 Autobook
850 Roadster 1965–70	..	..	..	Ball	Fiat 850 1964–70 Autobook
850 Family 1965–70	..	..	..	Ball	Fiat 850 1964–70 Autobook
850 Sport 1968–70	..	..	..	Ball	Fiat 850 1964–70 Autobook
124 Saloon 1966–70	..	..	..	Ball	Fiat 124 1966–70 Autobook
124S 1968–70	..	..	..	Ball	Fiat 124 1966–70 Autobook

FORD

Anglia 100E 1953–59	..	..	..	Ball	Ford Anglia Prefect 100E Autobook
Anglia 105E 1959–67	..	..	..	Smith	Ford Anglia 105E, Prefect 107E 1959–67 Autobook
Anglia Super 123E 1962–67	..	..	..	Smith	Ford Anglia 105E, Prefect 107E 1959–67 Autobook
Capri 109E 1962	..	..	..	Smith	Ford Classic, Capri 1961–64 Autobook
Capri 116E 1962–64	..	..	..	Smith	Ford Classic, Capri 1961–64 Autobook
Capri 1300, 1300GT 1968–69	..	..	Ball	Ford Capri 1968–69 Autobook
Capri 1600, 1600GT 1968–69	..	..	Ball	Ford Capri 1968–69 Autobook
Classic 109E 1961–62	..	..	..	Smith	Ford Classic, Capri 1961–64 Autobook
Classic 116E 1962–63	..	..	..	Smith	Ford Classic, Capri 1961–64 Autobook
Consul Mk 1 1950–56	..	..	..	Ball	Ford Consul Zephyr, Zodiac 1, 2 1950–62 Autobook
Consul Mk 2 1956–62	..	..	..	Ball	Ford Consul, Zephyr, Zodiac 1, 2 1950–62 Autobook
Corsair V4 3004E 1965–68	..	..	Smith	Ford Corsair V4 1965–68 Autobook
Corsair V4 GT 1965–66	..	..	..	Smith	Ford Corsair V4 1965–68 Autobook
Corsair V4 1663cc 1969–70	..	..	Ball	Ford Corsair V4 1969–70 Autobook
Corsair 2000, 2000E 1966–68	..	..	Smith	Ford Corsair V4 1965–68 Autobook
Corsair 2000, 2000E 1969–70	..	..	Ball	Ford Corsair V4 1969–70 Autobook
Cortina 113E 1962–66	..	..	..	Smith	Ford Cortina 1962–66 Autobook
Cortina Super 118E 1963–66	..	..	Smith	Ford Cortina 1962–66 Autobook
Cortina Lotus 125E 1963–66	..	..	Smith	Ford Cortina 1962–66 Autobook
Cortina GT 118E 1963–66	..	..	Smith	Ford Cortina 1962–66 Autobook
Cortina 1300 1967–68	..	..	..	Smith	Ford Cortina 1967–68 Autobook
Cortina 1300 1969–70	..	..	..	Ball	Ford Cortina 1969–70 Autobook
Cortina 1500 1967–68	..	..	..	Smith	Ford Cortina 1967–68 Autobook
Cortina 1600 (including Lotus) 1967–68	..	Smith	Ford Cortina 1967–68 Autobook
Cortina 1600 1969–70	..	..	..	Ball	Ford Cortina 1969–70 Autobook
Escort 100E 1955–59	..	..	..	Ball	Ford Anglia Prefect 100E Autobook
Escort 1100 1967–70	..	..	..	Ball	Ford Escort 1967–70 Autobook
Escort 1300 1967–70	..	..	..	Ball	Ford Escort 1967–70 Autobook
Prefect 100E 1954–59	..	..	..	Ball	Ford Anglia Prefect 100E Autobook
Prefect 107E 1959–61	..	..	..	Smith	Ford Anglia 105E, Prefect 107E 1959–67 Autobook
Popular 100E 1959–62	..	..	..	Ball	Ford Anglia Prefect 100E Autobook

Make					Author	Title
Squire 100E 1955–59	..	..	..	..	Ball	Ford Anglia Prefect 100E Autobook
Zephyr Mk 1 1950–56		..	..	..	Ball	Ford Consul, Zephyr, Zodiac 1, 2 1950–62 Autobook
Zephyr Mk 2 1956–62		..	..	..	Ball	Ford Consul, Zephyr, Zodiac 1, 2 1950–62 Autobook
Zephyr 4 Mk 3 1962–66			..	..	Ball	Ford Zephyr, Zodiac Mk 3 1962–66 Autobook
Zephyr 6 Mk 3 1962–66			..	..	Ball	Ford Zephyr, Zodiac Mk 3 1962–66 Autobook
Zodiac Mk 3 1962–66	..	..	..	..	Ball	Ford Zephyr, Zodiac Mk 3 1962–66 Autobook
Zodiac Mk 1 1953–56	..	..	..	..	Ball	Ford Consul, Zephyr, Zodiac 1, 2 1950–62 Autobook
Zodiac Mk 2 1956–62	..	..	..	..	Ball	Ford Consul, Zephyr, Zodiac 1, 2 1950–62 Autobook
Zephyr V4 2 litre 1966–69		..	..	..	Ball	Ford Zephyr V4, V6, Zodiac 1966–69 Autobook
Zephyr V6 2.5 litre 1966–69		..	..	..	Ball	Ford Zephyr V4, V6, Zodiac 1966–69 Autobook
Zodiac V6 3 litre 1966–69		..	..	..	Ball	Ford Zephyr V4, V6, Zodiac 1966–69 Autobook

HILLMAN

Make					Author	Title
Hunter GT 1966–70	..	..	..	..	Ball	Hillman Hunter 1966–70 Autobook
Minx series 1, 2, 3 1956–59	..		..	..	Ball	Hillman Minx 1 to 5 1956–65 Autobook
Minx series 3A, 3B, 3C 1959–63		..	..	..	Ball	Hillman Minx 1 to 5 1956–65 Autobook
Minx series 5 1963–65		..	..	..	Ball	Hillman Minx 1 to 5 1956–65 Autobook
Minx series 6 1965–67		..	..	..	Ball	Hillman Minx 1965–67 Autobook
New Minx 1500, 1725 1966–70		..	..		Ball	Hillman Minx 1966–70 Autobook
Imp 1963–68	..	..	..	..	Smith	Hillman Imp 1963–68 Autobook
Imp 1969–71	..	..	..	..	Ball	Hillman Imp 1969–71 Autobook
Husky series 1, 2, 3 1958–65	..		..	..	Ball	Hillman Minx 1 to 5 1956–65 Autobook
Husky Estate 1969–71		..	..	..	Ball	Hillman Imp 1969–71 Autobook
Super Minx Mk 1, 2, 3 1961–65		..	..	..	Ball	Hillman Super Minx 1, 2, 3 1961–65 Autobook
Super Minx Mk 4 1965–67		..	..	..	Ball	Hillman Minx 1965–67 Autobook

HUMBER

Make					Author	Title
Sceptre Mk 2 1965–67		..	..	..	Ball	Hillman Minx 1965–67 Autobook
Sceptre 1967–70	..	..	..	..	Ball	Hillman Hunter 1966–70 Autobook

JAGUAR

Make					Author	Title
XK 120 1948–54		..	..	..	Ball	Jaguar XK120, 140, 150 Mk 7, 8, 9 1948–61 Autobook
XK 140 1954–57		..	..	..	Ball	Jaguar XK 120, 140, 150 Mk 7, 8, 9 1948–61 Autobook
XK 150 1957–61		..	..	..	Ball	Jaguar XK 120, 140, 150 Mk 7, 8, 9 1948–61 Autobook
XK 150S 1959–61		..	..	..	Ball	Jaguar XK 120, 140, 150 Mk 7, 8, 9 1948–61 Autobook
Mk 7, 7M, 8, 9 1950–61		..	..	..	Ball	Jaguar XK 120, 140, 150 Mk 7, 8, 9 1948–61 Autobook
2.4 Mk 1, 2 1955–67	..	..	..	..	Ball	Jaguar 2.4, 3.4, 3.8 Mk 1, 2 1955–69 Autobook
3.4 Mk 1, 2 1957–67	..	..	..	..	Ball	Jaguar 2.4, 3.4, 3.8 Mk 1, 2 1955–69 Autobook
3.8 Mk 2 1959–67		..	..	..	Ball	Jaguar 2.4, 3.4, 3.8 Mk 1, 2 1955–69 Autobook
240 1967–69	..	..	..	..	Ball	Jaguar 2.4, 3.4, 3.8 Mk 1, 2 1955–69 Autobook
340 1967–69		..	..	..	Ball	Jaguar 2.4, 3.4, 3.8 Mk 1, 2 1955–69 Autobook
E Type 3.8 1961–65	..	..	..	..	Ball	Jaguar E Type 1961–70 Autobook
E Type 4.2 1964–69	..	..	..	..	Ball	Jaguar E Type 1961–70 Autobook
E Type 4.2 2+2 1966–70	..	..	..	..	Ball	Jaguar E Type 1961–70 Autobook
E Type 4.2 Series 2 1969–70	..		..	..	Ball	Jaguar E Type 1961–70 Autobook
S Type 3.4 1963–68	..	..	..	..	Ball	Jaguar S Type and 420 1963–68 Autobook
S Type 3.8 1963–68	..	..	..	..	Ball	Jaguar S Type and 420 1963–68 Autobook
420 1963–68	..	..	..	..	Ball	Jaguar S Type and 420 1963–68 Autobook
XJ6 2.8 litre 1968–70	..		..	..	Ball	Jaguar XJ6 1968–70 Autobook
XJ6 4.2 litre 1968–70	..		..	..	Ball	Jaguar XJ6 1968–70 Autobook

JOWETT

Make					Author	Title
Javelin PA 1947–49	..	..	..	..	Mitchell	Jowett Javelin Jupiter 1947–53 Autobook
Javelin PB 1949–50	..	..	..	..	Mitchell	Jowett Javelin Jupiter 1947–53 Autobook
Javelin PC 1950–51	..	..	..	..	Mitchell	Jowett Javelin Jupiter 1947–53 Autobook
Javelin PD 1951–52	..	..	..	..	Mitchell	Jowett Javelin Jupiter 1947–53 Autobook
Javelin PE 1952–53	..	..	..	..	Mitchell	Jowett Javelin Jupiter 1947–53 Autobook
Jupiter Mk 1 SA 1949–52	..	..	..	..	Mitchell	Jowett Javelin Jupiter 1947–53 Autobook
Jupiter Mk 1A SC 1952–53	..	..	..	..	Mitchell	Jowett Javelin Jupiter 1947–53 Autobook

Make					Author	Title
LANDROVER						
Series 1 1948–58	..	..	..	..	Ball	Landrover 1, 2 1948–61 Autobook
Series 2 1997cc 1959–61	..	..	..		Ball	Landrover 1, 2 1948–61 Autobook
Series 2 2052cc 1959–61	..	..	..		Ball	Landrover 1, 2 1948–61 Autobook
Series 2 2286cc 1959–70	..	..	..		Ball	Landrover 2, 2A 1959–70 Autobook
Series 2A 2286cc 1959–70	..	..	..		Ball	Landrover 2, 2A 1959–70 Autobook
Series 2A 2625cc 1959–70	..	..	..		Ball	Landrover 2, 2A 1959–70 Autobook
MG						
TA 1936–39	..	..	..	..	Ball	MG TA to TF 1936–55 Autobook
TB 1939	..	..	..	..	Ball	MG TA to TF 1936–55 Autobook
TC 1945–49	..	..	..	..	Ball	MG TA to TF 1936–55 Autobook
TD 1950–53	..	..	..	..	Ball	MG TA to TF 1936–55 Autobook
TF 1953–54	..	..	..	..	Ball	MG TA to TF 1936–55 Autobook
TF 1500 1954–55	..	..	..	..	Ball	MG TA to TF 1936–55 Autobook
Midget 1961–70	..	..	..		Ball	Sprite, Midget 1958–70 Autobook
Magnette ZA, ZB 1955–59	..	..	..		Ball	BMC Autobook Three
Magnette 3, 4 1959–68	..	..	..		Smith	BMC Autobook One
MGA 1500, 1600 1955–62	..	..	..		Ball	MGA, MGB 1955–68 Autobook
MGA Twin Cam 1958–60	..	..	..		Ball	MGA, MGB 1955–68 Autobook
MGB 1962–68	..	..	..	..	Ball	MGA, MGB 1955–68 Autobook
MGB 1969–70	..	..	..		Ball	MG MGB 1969–70 Autobook
1100 Mk 1 1962–67	..	..	..		Ball	1100 Mk 1 1962–67 Autobook
1100 Mk 2 1968	..	..	..		Ball	1100 Mk 2, 1300 Mk 1, 2, America Autobook
1300 Mk 1, 2 1968–70	..	..	..		Ball	1100 Mk 2, 1300 Mk 1, 2, America 1968–70 Autobook
MERCEDES BENZ						
190B 1959–61	..	..	..	..	Ball	Mercedes-Benz 190B, C, 200 1959–68 Autobook
190C 1961–65	..	..	..	..	Ball	Mercedes-Benz 190B, C, 200 1959–68 Autobook
200 1965–68	..	..	..	..	Ball	Mercedes-Benz 190B, C, 200 1959–68 Autobook
220B 1959–65	..	..	..	..	Ball	Mercedes-Benz 220 1959–65 Autobook
220SB 1959–65	..	..	..	..	Ball	Mercedes-Benz 220 1959–65 Autobook
220SEB 1959–65	..	..	..	..	Ball	Mercedes-Benz 220 1959–65 Autobook
220SEBC 1961–65	..	..	..	..	Ball	Mercedes-Benz 220 1959–65 Autobook
MORGAN						
Four wheelers 1936–69	..	..	..		Clarke	Morgan 1936–69 Autobook
MORRIS						
Oxford 2, 3 1956–59	..	..	..	..	Ball	BMC Autobook Three
Oxford 5, 6 1959–69	..	..	..	..	Smith	BMC Autobook One
Minor series 2 1952–56	..	..	..		Ball	Morris Minor 1952–70 Autobook
Minor 1000 1957–70	..	..	..		Ball	Morris Minor 1952–70 Autobook
Mini 1959–70	..	..	..	..	Ball	Mini 1959–70 Autobook
Mini Clubman 1969–70	..	..	..		Ball	Mini 1959–70 Autobook
Mini Cooper 1961–70	..	..	..		Ball	Mini Cooper 1961–70 Autobook
Mini Cooper S 1963–70	..	..	..		Ball	Mini Cooper 1961–70 Autobook
1100 Mk 1 1962–67	..	..	..		Ball	1100 Mk 1 1962–67 Autobook
1100 Mk 2 1968–70	..	..	..		Ball	1100 Mk 2, 1300 Mk 1, 2, America 1968–70 Autobook
1300 Mk 1, 2 1968–70	..	..	..		Ball	1100 Mk 2, 1300 Mk 1, 2, America 1968–70 Autobook
1800 Mk 1, 2 1966–70	..	..	..		Ball	1800 1964–70 Autobook
1800S 1968–70	..	..	..	..	Ball	1800 1964–70 Autobook
OPEL						
Kadett 993cc 1962–65	..	..	..	..	Ball	Opel Kadett 1962–70 Autobook
Kadett 'B' 1965–70	..	..	..	..	Ball	Opel Kadett 1962–70 Autobook
PEUGEOT						
404 1960–69	..	..	..	..	Ball	Peugeot 404 1960–69 Autobook

PORSCHE

	Author	Title
356A 1957–59	Ball	Porsche 356A, 356B, 356C 1957–65 Autobook
356B 1959 63	Ball	Porsche 356A, 356B, 356C 1957–65 Autobook
356C 1963–65	Ball	Porsche 356A, 356B, 356C 1957–65 Autobook
911 1964–67	Ball	Porsche 911 1964–69 Autobook
911L 1967–68	Ball	Porsche 911 1964–69 Autobook
911S 1966–69	Ball	Porsche 911 1964–69 Autobook
911T 1967–69	Ball	Porsche 911 1964–69 Autobook
911E 1968–69	Ball	Porsche 911 1964–69 Autobook

RENAULT

	Author	Title
R4L 748cc, 845cc 1961–65	Ball	Renault R4, R4L, 4 1961–70 Autobook
R4 845cc 1962–66	Ball	Renault R4, R4L, 4 1961–70 Autobook
4 845cc 1966–70	Ball	Renault R4, R4L, 4 1961–70 Autobook
6 1968–70	Ball	Renault 6 1968–70 Autobook
R8 956cc 1962–65	Ball	Renault 8, 10, 1100 1962–70 Autobook
8 956cc, 1108cc 1965–70	Ball	Renault 8, 10, 1100 1962–70 Autobook
8S 1108cc 1968–70	Ball	Renault 8, 10, 1100 1962–70 Autobook
1100, 1108cc 1964–69	Ball	Renault 8, 10, 1100 1962–70 Autobook
R10 1108cc 1967–69	Ball	Renault 8, 10, 1100 1962–70 Autobook
10 1289cc 1969–70	Ball	Renault 8, 10, 1100 1962–70 Autobook
16 1470cc 1965–70	Ball	Renault R16 1965–70 Autobook
16TS 1565cc 1968–70	Ball	Renault R16 1965–70 Autobook

RILEY

	Author	Title
1.5 1957–65	Ball	BMC Autobook Three
4/68 1959–61	Smith	BMC Autobook One
4/72 1961–69	Smith	BMC Autobook One
Elf Mk 1, 2, 3 1961–70	Ball	Mini 1959–70 Autobook
1100 Mk 1 1965–67	Ball	1100 Mk 1 1962–67 Autobook
1100 Mk 2 1968	Ball	1100 Mk 2, 1300 Mk 1, 2, America 1968–70 Autobook
1300 Mk 1, 2 1968–70	Ball	1100 Mk 2, 1300 Mk 1, 2, America 1968–70 Autobook

ROVER

	Author	Title
60 1953–59	Ball	Rover 60–110 1953–64 Autobook
75 1954–59	Ball	Rover 60–110 1953–64 Autobook
80 1959–62	Ball	Rover 60–110 1953–64 Autobook
90 1954–59	Ball	Rover 60–110 1953–64 Autobook
95 1962–64	Ball	Rover 60–110 1953–64 Autobook
100 1959–62	Ball	Rover 60–110 1953–64 Autobook
105R 1957–58	Ball	Rover 60–110 1953–64 Autobook
105S 1957–59	Ball	Rover 60–110 1953–64 Autobook
110 1962–64	Ball	Rover 60–110 1953–64 Autobook
2000 SC 1963–69	Ball	Rover 2000 1963–69 Autobook
2000 TC 1963–69	Ball	Rover 2000 1963–69 Autobook
3 litre Saloon Mk 1, 1A 1958–62	Ball	Rover 3 litre 1958–67 Autobook
3 litre Saloon Mk 2, 3 1962–67	Ball	Rover 3 litre 1958–67 Autobook
3 litre Coupé 1965–67	Ball	Rover 3 litre 1958–67 Autobook
3500, 3500S 1968–70	Ball	Rover 3500, 3500S 1968–70 Autobook

SIMCA

	Author	Title
1000 1961–68	Ball	Simca 1000 1961–70 Autobook
1000 GL 1963–70	Ball	Simca 1000 1961–70 Autobook
1000 GLS 1964–70	Ball	Simca 1000 1961–70 Autobook
1000 GLA 1966–70	Ball	Simca 1000 1961–70 Autobook
1100 LS 1967–70	Ball	Simca 1100 1967–70 Autobook
1100 GL, GLS 1967–70	Ball	Simca 1100 1967–70 Autobook
1200 1970	Ball	Simca 1100 1967–70 Autobook

DS 19

Make					Author	Title

SINGER

					Author	Title
Chamois 1964–68	..	..	..	..	Smith	Hillman Imp 1963–68 Autobook
Chamois 1969–70	..	..	..	..	Ball	Hillman Imp 1969–71 Autobook
Chamois Sport 1964–68	..	..	..	..	Smith	Hillman Imp 1963–68 Autobook
Chamois Sport 1969–70	..	..	..	..	Ball	Hillman Imp 1969–71 Autobook
Gazelle series 2A 1958	..	..	..	..	Ball	Hillman Minx 1 to 5 1956–65 Autobook
Gazelle 3, 3A, 3B, 3C 1958–63	..	..	..	..	Ball	Hillman Minx 1 to 5 1956–65 Autobook
Gazelle series 5 1963–65	..	..	..	..	Ball	Hillman Minx 1 to 5 1956–65 Autobook
Gazelle series 6 1965–67	..	..	..	..	Ball	Hillman Minx 1965–67 Autobook
New Gazelle 1500, 1725 1966–70	..	..	..	..	Ball	Hillman Minx 1966–70 Autobook
Vogue series 4 1965–67	..	..	..	..	Ball	Hillman Minx 1965–67 Autobook
New Vogue 1966–70	..	..	..	..	Ball	Hillman Hunter 1966–70 Autobook

SKODA

				Author	Title
440, 445, 450 1957–69	..	..	..	Skoda	Skoda Autobook One

SUNBEAM

					Author	Title
Alpine series 1, 2, 3, 4 1959–65	..	..	..	Ball	Sunbeam Rapier Alpine 1955–65 Autobook
Alpine series 5 1965–67	..	..	..	Ball	Hillman Minx 1965–67 Autobook
Alpine 1969–70	..	..	..	Ball	Hillman Hunter 1966–70 Autobook
Rapier series 1, 2, 3, 3A, 4 1955–65	..	..	Ball	Sunbeam Rapier Alpine 1955–65 Autobook
Rapier series 5 1965–67	..	..	..	Ball	Hillman Minx 1965–67 Autobook
Rapier H.120 1967–70	..	..	..	Ball	Hillman Hunter 1966–70 Autobook
Imp Sport 1963–68	..	..	..	Smith	Hillman Imp 1963–68 Autobook
Imp Sport 1969–71	..	..	..	Ball	Hillman Imp 1969–71 Autobook
Stilletto 1967–68	..	..	..	Smith	Hillman Imp 1963–68 Autobook
Stilletto 1969–71	..	..	..	Ball	Hillman Imp 1969–71 Autobook

TOYOTA

					Author	Title
Corona 1500 Mk 1 1965–70	..	..	..	Ball	Toyota Corona 1500 Mk 1 1965–70 Autobook
Corona 1900 Mk 2 1969–70	..	..	..	Ball	Toyota Corona 1900 Mk 2 1969–70 Autobook

TRIUMPH

					Author	Title
TR2 1952–55	..	..	..	..	Ball	Triumph TR2, TR3, TR3A 1952–62 Autobook
TR3, TR3A 1955–62	..	..	..	..	Ball	Triumph TR2, TR3, TR3A 1952–62 Autobook
TR4, TR4A 1961–67	..	..	..	..	Ball	Triumph TR4, TR4A 1961–67 Autobook
TR5 1967–69	..	..	..	..	Ball	Triumph TR5, TR250, TR6 1967–70 Autobook
TR6 1969–70	..	..	..	..	Ball	Triumph TR5, TR250, TR6 1967–70 Autobook
TR250 1967–69	..	..	..	..	Ball	Triumph TR5, TR250, TR6 1967–70 Autobook
1300 1965–70	..	..	..	..	Ball	Triumph 1300 1965–70 Autobook
1300TC 1967–70	..	..	..	..	Ball	Triumph 1300 1965–70 Autobook
2000 1963–69	..	..	..	..	Ball	Triumph 2000 1963–69 Autobook
Herald 948 1959–64	..	..	..	..	Smith	Triumph Herald 1959–68 Autobook
Herald 1200 1961–68	..	..	..	..	Smith	Triumph Herald 1959–68 Autobook
Herald 1200 1969–70	..	..	..	..	Ball	Triumph Herald 1969–70 Autobook
Herald 12/50 1963–67	..	..	..	..	Smith	Triumph Herald 1959–68 Autobook
Herald 13/60 1967–68	..	..	..	..	Smith	Triumph Herald 1959–68 Autobook
Herald 13/60 1969–70	..	..	..	..	Ball	Triumph Herald 1969–70 Autobook
Spitfire 1962–68	..	..	..	..	Smith	Triumph Spitfire Vitessse 1962–68 Autobook
Spitfire Mk 3 1969–70	..	..	..	..	Ball	Triumph Spitfire Mk 3 1969–70 Autobook
Vitesse 1600 and 2 litre 1962–68	..	..	Smith	Triumph Spitfire Vitesse 1962–68 Autobook
Vitesse 2 litre 1969–70	..	..	..	..	Ball	Triumph GT6, Vitesse 2 litre 1969–70 Autobook
GT Six 2 litre 1966–68	..	..	..	..	Smith	Triumph Spitfire Vitesse 1962–68 Autobook
GT Six 1969–70	..	..	..	..	Ball	Triumph GT6, Vitesse 2 litre 1969–70 Autobook

VANDEN PLAS

					Author	Title
3 litre 1959–64	..	..	..	..	Ball	BMC Autobook Four
1100 Mk 1 1963–67	..	..	..	..	Ball	1100 Mk 1 1962–67 Autobook
1100 Mk 2 1968	..	..	..	..	Ball	1100 Mk 2, 1300 Mk 1, 2, America 1968–70 Autobook
1300 Mk 1, 2, 1968–70	..	..	..	..	Ball	1100 Mk 2, 1300 Mk 1, 2, America 1968–70 Autobook

Make					Author	Title
VAUXHALL						
Victor 1 1957–59	..	..	..	..	Ball	Vauxhall Victor 1, 2 FB 1957–64 Autobook
Victor 2 1959–61	..		..	..	Ball	Vauxhall Victor 1, 2 FB 1957–64 Autobook
Victor FB 1961–64	..			..	Ball	Vauxhall Victor 1, 2 FB 1957–64 Autobook
VX4/90 FBH 1961–64				..	Ball	Vauxhall Victor 1, 2 FB 1957–64 Autobook
Victor FC 101 1964–67		..	..		Ball	Vauxhall Victor 101 1964–67 Autobook
VX 4/90 FCH 1964–67			..		Ball	Vauxhall Victor 101 1964–67 Autobook
Victor FD 1599cc 1967–69	..		..	..	Ball	Vauxhall Victor FD 1600, 2000 1967–69 Autobook
Victor FD 1975cc 1967–69	..		..	..	Ball	Vauxhall Victor FD 1600, 2000 1967–69 Autobook
Velox, Cresta PA 1957–62	..		..		Ball	Vauxhall Velox Cresta 1957–70 Autobook
Velox, Cresta PB 1962–65	..		..		Ball	Vauxhall Velox Cresta 1957–70 Autobook
Cresta PC 1965–70	..		..	..	Ball	Vauxhall Velox Cresta 1957–70 Autobook
Viscount 1966–70	..	..	..	..	Ball	Vauxhall Velox Cresta 1957–70 Autobook
Viva HA (including 90) 1964–66		..		..	Ball	Vauxhall Viva HA 1964–66 Autobook
VIva HB (including 90 and SL90) 1966–69		..			Ball	Vauxhall Viva HB 1966–69 Autobook
VOLKSWAGEN						
1200 Beetle 1954–67	..		..	..	Ball	Volkswagen Beetle 1954–67 Autobook
1200 Beetle 1968–70	..		..	..	Ball	Volkswagen Beetle 1968–70 Autobook
1200 Karmann Ghia 1955–65	..		..	..	Ball	Volkswagen Beetle 1954–67 Autobook
1200 Transporter 1954–64		..		..	Ball	Volkswagen Transporter 1954–67 Autobook
1300 Beetle 1965–67	..		..	..	Ball	Volkswagen Beetle 1954–67 Autobook
1300 Beetle 1968–70		..		..	Bell	Volkswagen Beetle 1968–70 Autobook
1300 Karmann Ghia 1965–66	..		..	..	Ball	Volkswagen Beetle 1954–67 Autobook
1500 Beetle 1966–67	..		..	..	Ball	Volkswagen Beetle 1954–67 Autobook
1500 Beetle 1968–70	..		..	..	Ball	Volkswagen Beetle 1968–70 Autobook
1500 1961–65	..	..	..	..	Ball	Volkswagen 1500 1961–66 Autobook
1500N 1963–65	..	..	..	..	Ball	Volkswagen 1500 1961–66 Autobook
1500S 1963–65	..	..	..	..	Ball	Volkswagen 1500 1961–66 Autobook
1500A 1965–66	..	..	..	..	Ball	Volkswagen 1500 1961–66 Autobook
1500 Karmann Ghia 1966–67	..		..	..	Ball	Volkswagen Beetle 1954–67 Autobook
1500 Transporter 1963–67	..		..	..	Ball	Volkswagen Transporter 1954–67 Autobook
1500 Karmann Ghia 1968–70	..		..	..	Ball	Volkswagen Beetle 1968–70 Autobook
VOLVO						
121, 131, 221 1962–68		..	..	..	Ball	Volvo P120 1961–68 Autobook
122, 132, 222 1961–68		..	..	..	Ball	Volvo P120 1961–68 Autobook
123 GT 1967–68	..	..	..	..	Ball	Volvo P120 1961–68 Autobook
WOLSELEY						
1500 1959–65	..	..	..	..	Ball	BMC Autobook Three
15/50 1956–58	..	..	..	..	Ball	BMC Autobook Three
15/60 1958–61	..	..	..	..	Smith	BMA Autobook One
16/60 1961–69	..	..	..	..	Smith	BMC Autobook One
6/99 1959–61	..	..	..	..	Ball	BMC Autobook Four
6/110 1961–68	..	..	..	..	Ball	BMC Autobook Four
Hornet Mk 1, 2, 3 1961–70	..		..	..	Ball	Mini 1959–70 Autobook
1100 Mk 1 1965–67	..	..	..	..	Ball	1100 Mk 1 1962–67 Autobook
1100 Mk 2 1968	..	..	..	..	Ball	1100 Mk 2, 1300 Mk 1, 2, America 1968–70 Autobook
1300 Mk 1, 2 1968–70	..	..	..		Ball	1100 Mk 2, 1300 Mk 1, 2, America 1968–70 Autobook
18/85 Mk 1, 2 1967–70	..	..	..	..	Ball	1800 1964–70 Autobook
18/85S 1969–70	..	..	..	..	Ball	1800 1964–70 Autobook